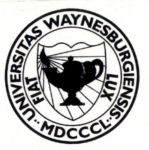

The
Humble
Approach

The
Humble
Approach

Scientists Discover God

JOHN M. TEMPLETON

THE SEABURY PRESS · NEW YORK

1981
The Seabury Press
815 Second Avenue
New York, N.Y. 10017

Printed in the United States of America

Library of Congress Cataloging in Publication Data

Templeton, John M
  The humble approach.

  Bibliography: p.
  Includes index.
  1. Religion and science—1946- I. Title.
BL240.2.T45   210   80-25106
ISBN 0-8164-0481-X

TABLE OF CONTENTS

I   An Introduction

We are perched on the frontiers of future knowledge. Even though we stand upon the enormous mountain of information collected over the last five centuries of scientific progress, we have only fleeting glimpses of the future. To a large extent, the future lies before us like a vast wilderness of unexplored reality. The God who created and sustained His evolving universe through eons of progress and development has not placed our generation at the tag end of the creative process. He has placed us at a new beginning. We are here for the future.

Our role is crucial. As human beings we are endowed with mind and spirit. We can think, imagine, and dream. We can search for future trends through the rich diversity of human thought. God permits us in some ways to be co-creators with Him in His continuing act of creation.

There is, however, a stumbling block: egotism. The closed-minded attitude of those who think they know it all inhibits future progress. Natural scientists, by and large, have overcome this hurdle. They are more open-minded. They research the natural wonders of the universe, devising new hypotheses, testing them, challenging old assumptions, competing with each other in professional rivalry. The physical future of human civilization is in their professional hands, guided by relatively tolerant and open minds.

This is not equally true concerning our spiritual future.

Some theologians, religious leaders, and lay people are frequently blind to the obstacles they themselves erect. Many are not even aware that the spiritual future could, or should, be different from anything that has ever been before. Many do not realize that spiritual reality can be researched in ways similar to those used by natural scientists. Some do not want even to consider the possibility of a future of progressively unfolding spiritual discoveries.

Why not? Many devoutly religious people are not devoutly humble. They do not admit their worldview is limited. They are not open to suggestions that their personal theology might be incomplete. They do not entertain the notion that other religious have valuable insights to contribute to an understanding of God and His creation. When people take a more humble attitude, they welcome new ideas about the spirit just as they welcome new scientific ideas about how to cure headaches, how to heat and cool their homes, or how to develop natural resources.

The humble approach to human knowledge is meant to help as a corrective to the parochialism that blocks further development in religious studies. Taking this humble approach reminds us that each person's concept of God, the universe, even his or her own self is too limited. To some extent, we are all too self-centered. We overestimate the small amount of knowledge we possess. To be humble means to admit the infinity of creation and to search one's place in God's infinite plan for creation. This approach asks each of us, whether we are students of the natural or the supernatural, to witness to the intimate relationship of physical and spiritual reality in our own lives. In a humble manner we can use our talents to explore the universe to discover future trends. There is abundant evidence that by grace God gives us talents and intelligence with which to participate in His vast creative process.

Until the emergence of human beings on the face of the earth, evolution proceeded routinely, unfolding the rich complexity of mineral, vegetable, and animal life. Now with human intelligence capable of studying the Creator and His creation, evolution no longer travels only on its own path. Possibly it was

God's plan that one day His children could serve as useful tools for His creative purposes.

At this present moment, the human race, even after thousands of years of historical development, is still at the dawn of a new creation. This is a tremendous, awe-inspiring responsibility. It should humble us.

In fact, humility is the key to progress. Without it we will be too self-satisfied with past glories to launch boldly into the challenges ahead. Without humility we will not be wide-eyed and open-minded enough to discover new areas for research. If we are not as humble as children, we may be unable to admit mistakes, seek advice, and try again. The humble approach is for all of us who are concerned about the future of our civilization and the role we are to play in it. It is an approach for all of us who are not satisfied to let things drift and who want to channel our creative restlessness toward helping to build the kingdom of God.

Every person's concept of God is too small. Through humility we can begin to get into true perspective the infinity of God. This is the humble approach.

It is also in humility that we learn from each other, for it makes us open to each other and ready to see things from the other's point of view and share ours with him freely. It is by humility that we avoid the sins of pride and intolerance and avoid all religious strife. Humility opens the door to the realms of the spirit, and to research and progress in religion.

Twenty-five centuries ago Xenophanes and twelve centuries ago Shankara taught that nothing exists independently of God and that God is immeasurably greater than all time and space, let alone the visible earth. But only in the last century have modern sciences come to realize how very tiny the earth is compared to the billions of galaxies and how very brief human history is in the ongoing creation of the universe. Only now is man beginning to find evidence of hitherto undreamed-of forces and even dimensions of reality which transcend the invisible space-time field which holds together within its astonishing configuration all that man can observe in space and time. There are vast realms reaching out beyond the known, inspiring wonder and inviting inquiry, but it is humility that opens the way forward.

It is to be hoped that this book will reach many people who are ready to benefit from this kind of experience at the frontiers of knowledge where their minds may be stretched far beyond the range of their grasp hitherto. Perhaps people will be uplifted and inspired by catching glimpses of unexpected aspects of reality that beckon their inquiry with exciting promises of still further manifestations of truth beyond anything they could anticipate. Perhaps the advance into the realms of spiritual reality and progress in religion will be as outstanding and rapid as the astonishing advances in physics, astronomy, and genetics. Church denominations may then be inspired to devote the manpower and find the funds needed for the promotion of research. Young people may be attracted to a religion that is genuinely dynamic and rapidly progressing. The visions and the teachings of the great prophets of the past need not be discarded or disputed. Rather they should be studied again and used as springboards to new and greater understanding and love of God. This book explores the possibility that humility in man's understanding of God may be more fruitful than the formal systems of thought which we have inherited, whether they be theistic, pantheistic, or panentheistic. Gradually we may learn to love every one of God's children and be grateful for an increasingly rich diversity of thought emanating from research and worship in every land. One of the purposes of this book is to examine and foster the idea that through a humble approach in knowledge in which we are open-minded and willing to experiment, theology may produce positive results even more amazing than the discoveries of scientists which have electrified the world in this last century.

Why do millions of people think theology has become obsolete, when no one thinks physics or astronomy can become obsolete? That is the subject of this book, *The Humble Approach*. Theology was called the queen of the sciences in ages gone by and can deserve that title again when it adopts the humble approach.

Several bibliographies on the subject of science and religion are included to encourage others to read and write more extensively in this important and developing field. The bibliographies include articles and books for beginners as well as for advanced thinkers, whether they are scientists or theologians. By reading and writing in this theological field, scientists and other laymen may not only enhance their own spiritual growth but also stimulate progress and expand the whole field of theology in ways that may benefit all. Let us hope that already a spiritual and religious renaissance may have started, and that a great new day may be dawning.

II   The Blossoming Time of Man

We should be overwhelmingly grateful to have been born in this century. The slow progress of prehistoric ages is over, and centuries of human enterprise are now miraculously bursting into flower. The evolution of human knowledge is accelerating, and we are reaping the fruits of generations of scientific thought: More than half of the scientists who ever lived are alive today. More than half of the discoveries in the natural sciences have been made in this century. More than half of the goods produced since the earth was born have been produced in the twentieth century. Over half the books ever written were written in the last half-century. More new books are published each month than were written in the entire historical period before the birth of Columbus.

Many astronomers believe the universe began with a "Big Bang" about eighteen billion years ago. This vast figure is about the same as the number of minutes which have elapsed since Moses was born. But not until five billion years ago did our galaxy, the Milky Way, containing over one hundred billion stars, look as it does now. At about that time, our star, the sun, was formed. About five billion minutes ago, William the Conqueror was born in Normandy. Thus seventy-two percent of the history of the universe occurred while, to quote from

Genesis, "The earth was without form and void and darkness was on the face of the deep; and the Spirit of God moved upon the face of the waters."

According to most astronomers, the earth was formed about four and one-half billion years ago. Dr. Elso Barghoorn, a paleontologist at Harvard, believes he has found evidence in Swaziland that the first living things appeared on earth three and two-fifth billion years ago. These were single-cell plants resembling algae. Three and two-fifth billion minutes ago, the year was 1330. The scourge of the Black Death had begun to spread throughout Europe and ultimately killed a fourth of the total population of the continent. It is interesting to note that while single-cell creatures first appeared on earth over three million years ago, it has taken eighty percent of the total period of evolution since that time to evolve a creature with *more* than one cell. Then microbes slowly evolved into worms, fishes, reptiles, and mammals. Humans did not appear until forty million years ago. For comparison, forty million minutes is equivalent to only seventy-six years.

It has been only six thousand years since man invented any form of writing. Thus, only the last one-seventeenth of one percent of man's existence has been within the age of written communication; and it has only been this age that has allowed the full flowering of the human intellect. For comparison, six thousand minutes is only four days.

Even then, progress continued to be slow. Ninety-seven percent of recorded history passed by before man began his rapid discovery of the secrets of nature. Two hundred years ago, there was no faster transportation than the horse on land and sailing ships on the seas. Communications two hundred years ago were scarcely faster than they had been in the days of Moses. Energy still came mostly from muscle power. Electricity was a laboratory curiosity. Germs were unknown. Photography was unheard of. Less than a million people on earth could read or write. Ninety-five percent of the workers in the world had jobs in agriculture and fishing, compared with only six percent in the United States today.

It was only about a century ago that James Clerk Maxwell

proved that light, electricity, and magnetism are all part of one continuous spectrum of wave lengths. Then followed the great discoveries of radio waves, X rays, microwaves, infrared and ultraviolet light, and with them the invention of radar, radio astronomy, television, and lasers. All of this had to do with particles of electromagnetic energy traveling at the speed of light.

After Maxwell's theory, three other major developments in physics occurred in this century: first Einstein's theory of relativity; then quantum mechanics; and, finally, antimatter. The great science of nuclear physics is less than a century old. The electron was discovered in 1914 by Ernest Rutherford, and the neutron in 1932 by James Chadwick. Less than fifty years ago physicists thought there were only three kinds of subatomic particles: electrons, protons, and neutrons. Today so many new particles are being discovered through sophisticated technology that Lawrence Berkeley Laboratory issues a new list of subatomic particles twice yearly.

Less than a century ago the only cosmic forces known were those of gravity and electromagnetism. Then the Strong Force and the Weak Force were discovered. The Strong Force binds protons and neutrons together in the nuclei of atoms. It is 10^{40} times stronger than gravity but operates only over the tiny distances inside the nucleus. The Weak Force operates in some processes where atomic particles are transformed. Since 1970 physicists have found two more cosmic forces, the Color Force and Weak Force Mark II.

Astronomy, the oldest science, has been revolutionized in the last fifty years. Edwin Powell Hubble and others proved for the first time in the 1920s that there are other galaxies far beyond our Milky Way. Today we believe there are over one hundred billion such galaxies. Sir Bernard Lovell helped initiate the science of radio astronomy in 1943. More recent is the science of X-ray astronomy. Quite recently astronomers have discovered variable stars, pulsars, and quasars. Since 1960 when Allan Sandage and others collected evidence about quasars, astronomers have estimated that there are over fifteen million quasars in the universe, the nearest being over a billion light years away, and others as far distant as six billion light years. It was not until 1968 that pulsars were discovered, and now astronomers think there may be over one hundred thousand of them in our Milky Way galaxy alone. In the past it appeared that the black distance between stars and galaxies was empty, but evidence now indicates that over half the matter in the universe is in those seemingly empty spaces. Some astronomers think there are also millions of black holes whose gravity is so great that no light can escape from them.

In 1911 Victor Hess proved that we are bombarded constantly from all directions by cosmic rays, rays which are electrically charged atomic nuclei that may have originated in the millions of supernovas that have exploded in our galaxy since it began. In 1931 Karl Jansky, a radio engineer, discovered that microwaves from the sky continuously surround and penetrate us. Microwaves travel in straight lines unaffected by magnetic fields. They are the shortest of the radio waves, but a million times as long as light waves. Only since 1950 have scientists been able to detect, with particle accelerators, the neutrinos produced when protons turn into neutrons through the nuclear reactions in the sun's core. Unnoticed by us, these unseen particles rain down on us by day; and even at night, when the earth is between us and the sun, neutrinos pass through the earth in quantities not measurably diminished. Until recently we would have denied the existence of all these unseen forces.

Things are not what they seem. Sometimes phenomena which appear real to us are actually hoaxes perpetrated by our lack of knowledge and limited senses. For example, until five hundred years ago it was assumed that lying in bed was a relatively motionless experience. This seemed an obvious fact to anyone who had ever done it. But Copernicus' discovery that the earth and the planets move around the sun implied that because the earth rotates, a person sleeping in bed moves eastward at one thousand miles an hour. The sleeper also flies one thousand and eighty miles a minute in another direction due to the earth's revolution around the sun. Just a few years ago the rotation of the Milky Way was measured, indicating that our solar system is moving at one hundred and sixty-two miles per second in yet a third direction. Also, in 1977, Ames Research

Center in California computed that our galaxy is speeding away from the original point of the big bang at four hundred miles per second toward a spot in the sky near the Constellation Hydra. So a sleeper may *seem* to be motionless, but in reality he or she has traveled a distance greater than that to the farthest point on earth, in more than four directions at once, and in less time than it took to read this page.

In humility we should admit that other universes may exist unknown to us, and not only in three dimensions but maybe in four, five, or six dimensions. Nigel Calder has argued that other universes are unobservable because, if we *could* observe them, they would be part of our own universe. But if we do not define "exist" too strictly, we may posit the existence of other universes of space and time. He suggested that, "There have been serious speculations about a co-existent anti-universe, or other realms beyond the horizon where the laws of nature were not the same. Is our universe a black hole in somebody else's universe?" [1]

Sir Bernard Lovell wrote that we have "never obtained scientific answers to the problem of whether the universe is finite or infinite, or how it began, and how it will end. Nevertheless, the perspective of these questions and the nature of the possible scientific answers have constantly changed since ancient times." [2]

This should be enough to cause all men and women to pause humbly before the majesty and infinity of what Jefferson called, "nature and nature's God." Discovery and invention have not stopped or even slowed down. Who can imagine what will be discovered if this acceleration continues? Now even the acceleration of discovery seems to be accelerating. The more we learn about the universe the more humble we should be, realizing how ignorant we have been in the past and how much more there is still to discover.

This is the Humble Approach: to assume a realistic attitude before the Creator and admit that we are not the center of the universe. The sun does not revolve around us. Our five human senses are able to comprehend only a small portion of the mysteries, forces, and spiritual realities surrounding us.

Egotism has been a major cause of many mistaken notions in the past. Egotism caused men to think that the stars and the sun revolved around them. Egotism caused men to think that mankind was as old as the universe. Egotism is still our worst enemy. In fact, things are still not what they seem. Only by becoming humble can we learn more. Forces still undreamed of are probably present around us and in us. And more revelations about God's universe will probably be discovered in the next century than in all the millenniums before. Those who believe only what they see are hopelessly self-centered and lacking in humility.

A classic example of how self-centered egotism can block scientific progress is the case of the heliocentric concept of the universe. As Lovell explains, the concept that the sun was the center of the universe afforded "centuries of a comforting philosophical stability in which the Universe was envisaged as made for many by God, who had in the beginning endowed the particles of the Universe with such properties as were necessary for the appropriate inertial motions and gravitational forces." It would not have taken two centuries to challenge this notion, he believes, were it not for the "egocentric conviction that man must be near the center of the universe. Indeed, a retrospective judgment is that the abandonment of the idea of the Sun-centered universe would not have been delayed until the twentieth century but for this egoism of man." In this case, the scientific problem of measuring the distance between stars was overcome more easily than the psychological and spiritual problem of human self-centeredness.

Humility is the gateway of knowledge. To learn more, we must first realize how little we already know. The unknown before us may be a million times greater than what we now know, despite the myriad discoveries made in recent years. Even scientists on the cutting edge of new theories about the universe admit this. Ultimate reality is vastly greater than the sum of phenomena already observed. More and more, the immensity of the physical universe points to a nonphysical Creator who is infinite. The president of a science association said recently that if a fair sample of natural scientists had been asked fifty years ago whether they believed in God, possibly twenty percent would have said yes, whereas today that figure might be as high as eighty percent. The scientists of the 1980s, in other words, believe in the unseen to a far greater extent than did scientists of the 1880s. The modern scientist is more humble than his predecessors.

By taking the humble approach, scientists are acknowledging that in spite of tremendous scientific breakthroughs in recent times, there is still an infinite amount of knowledge to be learned. Many accept an infinite God as the originator of this infinite body of knowledge. In the words of Thomas Carlyle a century ago, they might say:

All visible things are emblems. What thou seest is not there on its own account; strictly speaking it is not there at all. Matter exists only spiritually, and to represent some idea and body it forth.[3]

The question before us is whether theologians and religious scholars, clergy and laity, are also taking the humble approach. Are they affirming the infinite which surrounds us? If they accept the inexhaustibility of God's revelation in terms of science, as do many scientists, they ought to admit that God's revelations in terms of the spirit are also inexhaustible, vastly exceeding our capacities to grasp them. The greater part of divine revelation, both scientific and spiritual, may still be ahead of us, not behind us.

III The Vast Unseen

Sir James Jeans, looking at the millions of other galaxies, said:

Do their colossal incomprehending masses come nearer to representing the main ultimate reality of the universe, or do we? Are we merely part of the same picture as they or is it possible that we are part of the artist? Are they perchance only a dream, while we are brain cells in the mind of the dreamer?

Each year more leading scientists express their belief in God. Some say that nothing exists except God. Dr. Allan Sandage, director of Mount Wilson Observatory, explains:

The world is incredible—just the fact that you and I are here, that the atoms of our bodies were once part of stars. They said I am on some kind of religious quest, looking for God, but God is the way it's put together. God is Newton's and Einstein's Laws.

Sandage is not alone in his quest for God. Other scientists accompany him.

In his highly acclaimed introduction to Einstein, Lincoln Barnett wrote in 1957:

In the evolution of scientific thought, one fact has become impressively clear: there is no mystery of the physical world which does not point to a mystery beyond itself . . . . Man's inescapable impasse is that he himself is part of the world he seeks to

explore; his body and proud brain are mosaics of the same ele-
mental particles that compose the dark drifting clouds of inter-
stellar space; he is, in the final analysis, merely an ephemeral
conformation of the primordial space-time field. Standing mid-
way between macrocosm and microcosm, he finds barriers on
every side and can perhaps but marvel, as St. Paul did nineteen
hundred years ago, that the world was created by the word of
God so that what is seen was made out of things which do not
appear.[4]

The famous Cambridge astronomer, Sir Arthur Eddington,
tried to unite quantum physics and relativity with what he
called his own "mysticism," his conviction that the universe
worth studying is the one within us. He suggested that man
should use "the higher faculties of his nature, so that they are
no longer blind alleys but open out into a spiritual world—a
world partly of illusion, no doubt, but in which he lives no less
in the world, also of illusion, revealed by the senses."

Eddington wrote a parable about the small-minded egotism
of a marine biologist who cast his net into the sea to accumulate
a mass of evidence on what dwells in the deep. From the fish in
his net, he arrived at two conclusions. First, no creature is less
than two inches long; and second, all sea creatures have gills. A
critic objected that the sea contained many creatures less than
two inches long, but the scientist would have to use a finer net
if he wished to catch them. The scornful biologist replied,
"Anything uncatchable in my net is by that very fact outside the
scope of fish science. What my net can't catch isn't a fish!"

Robert Boyd, a professor of physics at London University,
has said,

I think it is quite as common to find Christians among scientists
as in any other profession. In fact, I would say that, if anything,
it is a little more common to find Christians among physicists
than it is in some other branches of science.

In other words, astronomers at work discovering the vast com-
plexities of the macrocosm, and nuclear physicists investigating
the awesome variety of the microcosm, are now concluding that
the universe could not have happened by chance. The famous

physicist Sir James Jeans (1877–1946) said that the universe is beginning to look not like a great machine but like a great thought.

In their own ways, many scientists are reaffirming St. Paul's view that, "Our eyes are fixed not on things that are seen but on the things that are unseen; for what is seen passes away: what is unseen is eternal." (II Corinthians 4:18 NEB). Or as Henry Drummond wrote:

The physical properties of spiritual matter form the alphabet which is put into our hands by God, the study of which, if properly conducted, will enable us more perfectly to read that great book which we call the Universe . . . . Law is great not because the phenomenal world is great, but because these vanishing lines are the avenues into the Eternal Order.[5]

St. Paul would have concurred with Drummond that, "The visible is the ladder up to the invisible; the temporal is but the scaffolding of the eternal."

Ralph Waldo Trine wrote:

Everything exists in the unseen before it is manifested or realised in the seen, and in this sense it is true that the unseen things are the real, while the things that are seen are the unreal. The unseen things are cause; the seen things are the effect. The unseen things are the eternal and the seen things are the changing, the transient.[6]

On a cloudy day there appears to be no sun; but we have faith that it is only hidden. However, if we had lived on Venus which is always totally covered by thick clouds (rather than on earth), agnostics might never have believed that there is really a sun and stars and galaxies.

Lowell Fillmore wrote in 1963, "Until we tune in our mind to perceive God's kingdom, we judge the world by appearances only, and therefore behold only the dark things in the world."

Material things which appear, appear only because God has given us five senses with which to perceive a few traits of a few of the myriad notes in the giant creative symphony of life which surrounds us. The unknown is found to extend vastly beyond the area of the known, even after scientists have multiplied the known a hundredfold as they have in this century alone. Maybe there are many other forms of life unseen by us? There may be other beings occupying the same time and location who have five other senses able to perceive different configurations. In that case, they would not be able to see us anymore than we can see them.

No one yet knows what gravity is. But astronomers calculate that the gravity in the universe is 100 times greater than can be accounted for by visible stars and galaxies. Some guess the vast discrepancy is caused by black holes and others guess thin gas between galaxies. Maybe even other universes inconceivable to us are present in our visible universe.

Within the human body there are as many unseen activities as there are in the world of a beehive. Hundreds of bees die and are replaced by others, but the beehive lives on. Billions of cells work together to produce a human body. Millions die daily and are replaced. Each cell, although invisible to the naked eye, is composed of millions of atoms which in turn are formed by myriad particles and waves.

The physical body has no substance or permanence. It may be only a colony of cells in which a soul may dwell temporarily and develop for a divine purpose, for contact with an external world detected through a complex of sensory nerve endings. It would be appallingly narrow and egotistical to think that nothing exists in the universe except what these "cell colonies" called humans have learned to touch or see. This would be like a worm denying the existence of a butterfly because of its feeble eyesight, or a stone denying its dimensions and weight because it cannot comprehend arithmetic.

Taking the humble approach, one considers our bodies and minds to be simply ever-changing configurations of waves and particles designed by God as temporary habitations for souls in their earthbound years. Our bodies may look opaque to our eyes, but they are as transparent as jellyfish to neutrinos passing through by the millions.

The wind is just as real as flesh and just as temporary. God's chosen way of multiplying flesh is by tiny patterns which fit atoms into molecules (called genes and chromosomes) and molecules into cells. If our body were as dense as some stars, all its subatomic particles would not fill the space of a pin head. Maybe he who thinks of his body and mind as more real than his soul proves he is a pin head! Men are like clouds—formed by the moving spirit, visible only to nerves tuned to certain wavelengths, and temporary.

A tree is a manifestation of God. In a greater sense, man is a manifestation. Likewise, the sense evidence (with which we have to do in observational science) may be also a manifestation of the spiritual world, but only a small part. The seen and the unseen both exist together; but the seen is limited and temporary.

Emanuel Swedenborg wrote that nothing exists separate from God. If God is infinite, then nothing can be separate from Him. In Him we live and move and have our being. God, he claimed, is all of you and you are a little part of God. Swedenborg taught that man is not in heaven until heaven is in man. It is on this material earth that we begin to receive the life and spirit of heaven within us. We are citizens of the spiritual world, and we are spirits from the day of our conception. Love, loyalty, patience, and mercy are more real than are tangible objects, and God seeks to instill these spiritual realities into our own lives here and now. Taking the humble approach one also believes in this natural world as an incubator, provided by God, in which our spirits can develop and seek their ultimate expression in a realm outside and beyond these earthly confines.

To demonstrate the limited ability of the human mind to comprehend the entire reality around us, in England in 1882, a headmaster named Edwin A. Abbott wrote a delightful and humorous fantasy called *Flatland*. His purpose was to help us understand that our minds are very limited so that reality may be incomprehensible to us. The people of Flatland lived in only two dimensions. They denied the possiblity of any being of three dimensions. Yet objects of three dimensions produced miraculous and mysterious phenomena by moving into or out of Flatland. The hero of the story, Mr. Squire, visited the land of no dimension (Spotland) and the land of one dimension (Lineland) whose inhabitants refused to believe in the existence of any creature of two dimensions. After returning from his later visit to the wondrous land of three dimensions (Spaceland) his Flatland rulers put him in prison for life lest he should stir up trouble among Flatlanders by talk of realms which transcend two dimensions. Finally, Mr. Squire says, "I will endure this and worse, if by any means I may arouse in the interiors of Planes and Solid Humanity a spirit of rebellion against the conceit which would limit our dimensions to two or three or any number short of infinity." Mr. Squire begs his readers not to suppose that every minute detail in the daily life of Flatland must correspond to some other detail in Spaceland; and yet he hopes that, taken as a whole, his work may prove suggestive as well as amusing to those Spacelanders of moderate and modest minds who—speaking of that which is of the highest importance, but lies beyond experience—decline to say on the one hand, "This can never be," and on the other hand, "It must needs be precisely thus, and we know all about it."

Like the inhabitants of Flatland, people collect their evidence to prove or disprove the existence of God. Some people have argued that God is our "ultimate end" or the "ground of being" or "original cause" or the "power" that maintains our existence. Philosophers and theologians, living in what we might call "Logicland," have been convinced for centuries that if their understanding of God is grounded in logic, it must be sound. But in humility should we not admit that human logic is much too inadequate to comprehend fully the infinite Creator? Proving that God exists or does not exist might be an endeavor destined to elude the capacities of the human mind no matter how rational it is. We are often like characters in a play trying to prove the existence of the playwright and then guessing his or her name. Or we are like cells in your toe, trying to prove your intelligence.

Some people think supernatural events, such as miracles, are needed to prove God's existence. But natural processes and the laws of nature may be merely methods designed by God for His continuing creative purposes. When new laws are discovered by human scientists, do they not merely discover a little more of God?

Each of us every day is swimming in an ocean of unseen miracles. For example, each living cell is a miracle; and the human body is a vast colony of over a hundred billion cells. The miracle of this body includes both our ability to recognize it as well as our inability ever to exhaust the true significance of it. As Albert Einstein said, "The most incomprehensible thing about the universe is that it is comprehensible."[7] That the universe exhibits order, not chaos, suggests the futility of trying to fathom the nature of matter without investigating the unseen spirit behind it. Each time new laws are discovered by scientists, however, we learn a little more about God and the ways He continually maintains and is building His creation.

It is reported that William Jennings Bryan squelched the famous atheist Ralph Ingersoll on this very point of recognizing the unseen in the seen. One day, Ingersoll saw an attractive globe of the earth in Bryan's office and asked, "Who made it?" Bryan replied, "No one. It just made itself." Similarly, those who argue that the universe is governed only by chance would do well to investigate the scientific studies of purposeful activity from the most simple one-cell organism responding to external stimuli and trying to maintain homeostasis, to the human animal who plans long-range goals and contemplates life's ultimate purpose. Would it not be strange if a universe without purpose accidentally created humans who are so obsessed with purpose?

A mythical observer from another universe, who might have witnessed the spectacular "Big Bang" when our universe was created about eighteen billion years ago, would have seen after the first year only a vast blackness with thin clouds of stars and other fragments flying apart. But we, who observe from the surface of our small planet Earth, see a totally different picture. We see a drama of evolution and progress on the surface of our earth which is truly amazing and miraculous. And this progress is speeding up faster and faster and faster. By an unbelievable miracle, billions of humans, each of whom is a colony of billions of atoms, have suddenly covered the face of the earth. Most amazing of all is the fact that the unseen minds of these humans are accumulating knowledge in explosive proportions—knowledge of themselves, of the universe, of their Creator. Could we ever make that observer from another universe believe this unseen explosion of human knowledge really exists? Would he believe that these new invisible minds are themselves participating creators in the ongoing drama of evolutionary creation? Or would he say that spaceships now traveling from earth just happened by chance?

The extent to which spirit and matter, the unseen and the seen, are related has been hotly debated over the centuries by theists, atheists, agnostics, pantheists, and others. The fact that these arguments continue suggests that this is still a lively question among thinking people. The vast unseen has not lost its power to tantalize our imaginations.

Traditionally, theologians have conceived God as the transcendent Lord, utterly differentiated from His creations, and sometimes as quite detached from them, but how can He be the infinite Creator and yet be detached from His creations, for He is the continuous source of their existence? Does not belief in God as Creator mean that He does not exist for Himself alone but for all that He has made and continues to support in being, through the embrace of His presence and love and power?

For centuries philosophers have debated the concept of pantheism, which means that God is everything and everything is God, and that his Spirit is present in every creature and thing. Primitive pantheists held the animistic belief that there were spirits in plants, animals, landscapes, and idols. Pantheism conceives of the Spirit dwelling in a creature as an emanation of God's being. Some modern thinkers along this line reject the idea that two separate realities dwell together in one creature but rather that nothing exists in separation from God. Paul Tillich, a Christian theologian, sometimes referred to God as the ground of being. But Mary Baker Eddy, Charles Fillmore, and Ernest Holmes went further to suggest that matter may be only an outward manifestation of divine thought, and that the creative spirit called God is the only reality.

The concept that each thing or being has its reality in God, however, contrasts sharply with the idea that material things are mere illusions not worth studying, or the pantheist notion that God is identical with nature and restricted to visible, material things. Both concepts contrast sharply with the humble approach where one takes the position that God is infinite, whereas created objects are contingent and finite. Even the vast universe falls infinitely short of what God is. God is continually creating each object and person just as he is creating his universe. For thousands of years men and women were so shortsighted and self-centered that they thought the universe was not much larger than the earth. With more humility and knowledge, we now think the universe is a billion, billion, billion times more massive. Thus, we realize that the infinite God is even "more infinite" (if we may coin a phrase) than we had supposed.

If God is infinite, then it follows that all other reality is dependent on Him and cannot exist apart from Him. Matter and energy may be only contingent manifestations of God. Space and time may be only manifestations of God. We should not think of matter and energy as created by God but as now utterly independent of God. That would mean that God is not "all in all" the creative Ground and Sustainer of all that is. Matter and energy may be only creaturely manifestations of the universal Creator. While God does not need the universe to be God, the universe needs to be unceasingly supported and enfolded in His presence and power to be what it is. It can only exist in and through God.

The excitement and importance of scientific study of nature and the cosmos are enhanced (not reduced) if we conceive of each discovery as a new revelation of a reality deriving from and grounded in God.

When new discoveries point more to the nonexistence of matter, it becomes easier to think of matter and spirit as a unity. Einstein's theory of relativity makes it easier to understand that space and time may not be exactly what they appear to be. New discoveries cause us to be increasingly humble about saying that what we see is real and what we do not see is illusion or myth. Lowell Fillmore said, "Remember that although God's principles are spirit and cannot be seen, they are more real than tangible things. God's principles are fundamental, and infinitely more far-reaching than the principles of mathematics. His invisible principles uphold that which is visible to us." Or, as it is stated in the letter to the Hebrews, "By faith we understand that the world was created by the word of God, so that what is seen is made out of things which do not appear." (Hebrews 11 : 3 RSV.)

Traditional pantheism serves a good purpose in suggesting the close intimacy of spirit and matter and the personal relationship between the Creator and creation. But it is not compatible with the Christian concept of a personal God who loves all of us, and numbers the hairs of our heads. The profound mutual indwelling between man and God is better stated by the Unity School of Christianity, "God is all of me: and I am a little part of him." Such a notion implies an interdependent relationship between God and us. As even "a little part of him," we realize the mutual unity of God and his creation. We realize that our own divinity arises from something more profound than merely being "God's children" or being "made in his image."

To the atheist, the tiny fraction of creation that can be seen and analyzed is the only reality. The confirmed atheist does not believe in either a God who permeates this creation or in one who is transcendent and totally separate from created matter. The humble men and women, however, acknowledge that we know very little about the myriad forces and beings around us and that what both the ignorant and wise call facts may be no more than optical illusions. Those choosing the humble approach shun the colossal conceit of the atheist who believes that the material world is the only reality and that it is totally explicable without a creator.

Like Thoreau, humble people hope that some ponds will always be thought of as bottomless so that the concepts of the infinite and the unseen and the unfathomable will be part of our daily experience. Would Karl Marx, Thoreau's contemporary, have dismissed as superstition the idea that his room was full of invisible cosmic rays because the scientific knowledge and technology of his day could not detect or explain them? As an atheist, he should have believed only in the material world he could perceive. How unfortunate to have been an atheist living before the invention of technology that could appreciably extend the information acquired by man's five limited senses. Who today does not have faith in cosmic rays and radio waves, even though they are invisible? As a child of the nineteenth century, Marx believed that his kitchen table was composed of solid matter. Now even scientists living in Marxist nations believe a table is, to a large degree, space or nonmatter. Its solid appearance comes only from responses by man's senses to billions of invisible electrons and wavelike particles vibrating at the speed of light in various patterns.

In 1848 when Marx was denying that people had immortal souls, psychosomatic medicine was considered superstition. Today it is widely believed that health can be restored to the body not only by chemicals but by mind and spirit as well. Recent studies around the world reveal the close interaction of body and mind, the mortal and the immortal, in the healing process. More and more doctors are now talking about "healing the patient" in addition to "curing the disease." The latter may be achieved by chemistry and physical therapy. The former, however, requires psychic and spiritual remedies not always available to the health care delivery team. Total health is not reducible to material explanations alone.

Agnostics sometimes claim that atheists who soundly deny God are small-minded, but they themselves are open-minded in affirming their uncertainty in saying they do not know. But many have erected an impenetrable barrier of doubt around their minds. This type of agnostic is like a blind man who will not admit that a rainbow is beautiful or that others enjoy it because he cannot see it personally. The more committed agnostics are to their doubt, the less humble or open-minded they are. Only that doubt which is truly humble, sincerely open-minded, should be labeled "agnostic." Only the man or woman who admits the possibility of being wrong is a humble agnostic.

Those taking the humble approach admit that the whole universe and all the creatures within it, both visible and invisible, may come from the eternal God and are manifestations of His infinite creative power. All of nature reveals something of the

Creator. And God is revealing Himself more and more to human inquiry, not always through prophetic visions or scriptures, but through the diligent research of modern scientists into observable phenomena and forces. The "golden age" of creation is being reached as God reveals Himself to human minds. As St. Paul said:

For what can be known about God is plain to them, because God has shown it to them. Ever since the creation of the world, His invisible nature, namely His eternal power and deity, has been clearly perceived in the things that have been made. (Romans 1:19–20 RSV.)

In the seventeenth century, the poet John Milton phrased it, "What if earth be but the shadow of heaven, and things therein each to other like more than on earth is thought?" Still another paraphrase in the language of modern science might be, "God is Creator of the universe of time and of men. Creation proceeds from idea to word to sensory data. The invisible Creator is the universal spirit, the causative idea which sustains and dwells in all He created and is still creating. The orderliness and lawfulness of nature and of the spirit reveal God to man."

God creates in many ways, not the least of which is through human endeavor. Like a pioneer in the wilderness, man must build the physical space in which he will live. As co-creator with God, he not only builds a material structure called "house" but imbues it with the spiritual dimension called "home." In one creative act, a log cabin, an Apollo spacecraft, or a cathedral contains both material and spiritual significance. The idea becomes a material fact; the idea, previously unseen, known only to God or to man, is now visible. The more we create, the more in some ways we are like God, especially if, like God, we create out of love.

IV   The New World of Time

Most religions agree that God created the earth at the beginning of time. But now geologists, paleontologists, and astronomers assert that creation is a continuous process and might be still in its infancy. In other words, *this* is the beginning of time. If such is the case, theologians need to keep pace with scientists and revise the old notion that God created everything once and for all. As explained by N. M. Wildiers in *An Introduction to Teilhard de Chardin:*

Over a long period—up to a century ago, one might almost say—exploration of the universe invariably had the appearance of a venture into space . . . . Very gradually we have come to realize that the picture thus formed in our imagination had only a fleeting moment, a mere fraction of a long succession of changing circumstances. As has so often been said, the major discovery of modern science has really been the discovery of time—of time as a constituent of everything.[8]

We are different from our ancestors because of our modern concept of time.

But time is still a mystery. No one knows the nature of time or what it is. It could speed up or slow down without our being aware of it. Most theologians think that God is not subject to time, that He created or is creating it. Others speak of time as an aspect of the life of God. Certainly, God does not measure time by the rotations of one little planet called Earth in one little galaxy. Progress measured against time now appears to be accelerating; but remember the observation would be similar if instead time were slowing down.

In 1895, H. G. Wells wrote *The Time Machine*. This novel deals with a theme that explorers have dreamed about for centuries—the ability to travel backward and forward in time as though it were like travel over the face of the earth. Until only a thousand years ago, the only way to travel backward in time was imaginatively through history, which led one back only six thousand years. Then backward travel was extended by archaeology, paleontology, and geology to about six hundred million years. Recently, astronomers realized they could look backward into time through light signals traveling towards us from the past at only a hundred and eighty-six thousand miles per second. Quasars, some of which are estimated at twelve billion light-years distant, look as they did when the universe was young, because their light we see left them that long ago.

Time travel into the future is still not easy! Recently astronomers have developed theories about the birth and death of stars. Thus, by observing other stars earlier or later in their life cycles, we gain a mental picture of what our own sun may have looked like in its youth and will look like in its old age. The most frequent method of imaginary time travel is to observe a trend and then extrapolate that trend forward or backward into times unknown. This simple extrapolation is now producing weird and wonderful theories about the nature of the universe eighteen billion years in the past or in the future. This is a new kind of eschatology that would have astounded biblical writers.

Now that man has landed on the moon, it is natural to speculate about visiting or at least contacting civilizations far more advanced than ours on some planets of older stars. The Milky Way Galaxy consists of more than a hundred billion stars. There may be over a hundred billion other galaxies in the universe. If only one star in a thousand has planets and if only one in a thousand of these has a planet resembling the earth, the arithmetic still indicates the possibility of ten million billion other earths in the universe. In a statement made at the 1979 meeting of the American Association for the Advancement of Science, it was estimated that in our galaxy alone there may be millions of civilizations. Whatever we may say to that, most scientists agree that *Homo sapiens,* modern man, is not likely to be the end of evolution. If God's creative process is more advanced on some other planet, man may gain awesome and amazing revelations about his own future.

It would take us too far afield to describe here the various notions that men have formed through the ages regarding the universe as existing in time. It took us a very long time from the days when the earth was thought to be a huge disc floating upon the waters and covered over by a vaulted ceiling of stars, to reach the point where we could form a more accurate idea of its dimensions as well as its relationship to other planets in our galaxy and to all the other galaxies in the universe. Then, only by extensive and painstaking investigation and research was our modern conception of the universe existing in time finally achieved.

The old world views, however much they differed from one another, had certain things in common. Typical were their constricted dimensions, mechanistic structure, and static character.

Their constricted dimensions—the Ptolemaic picture of things—continued in vogue for more than a thousand years, up to the time of the Renaissance. In this generally accepted way of envisaging the cosmos, the earth was seen as a globe encompassed by hugh cystalline spheres. It was not until modern times that man became aware of the gigantic dimensions and enormous structure of the universe.

And, the old picture was explained by a mechanistic model of the universe. This meant that men saw the world as a combination of separate, heterogeneous elements "put together" extraneously with only a mechanical relationship to one another. A view of this sort made no proper allowance for the reciprocal cohesion of all entities. Just as a machine is made up of a number of previously prepared components, so the world was imagined to be composed of preconstituted and mutually independent entities that had been conjoined artificially. The earth, the vault of heaven, the plants, animals, and men were thus pictured as so many diverse "creatures" subsisting independently of each other and only making up a whole rather like, for example, pieces of furniture make up a living room.

In the modern-world picture there is a complete reversal of these conditions. Science has gradually made it more and more clear that all entities are continuously and intrinsically interconnected, so that we can now see the world as a mighty, organic whole in which every single thing is related to everything else. The world in which we live presents itself to us not as a machine, artificially contrived, but as an organism building itself up from within, an organism whose every part has appeared through a stage-by-stage process of growth.

Finally, in the old world picture, the universe was conceived of as a fundamentally changeless and static whole. Of course, men were not blind to the mutations and motions occurring in the world; but as they saw them, these changes were always on the surface of things and did not affect their essential nature. From its moment of origin, everything assumed a form and aspect that were definitive and unchanging, constant and unalterable. The machine was activated; it ran; but the machine itself never changed.

Along with the mechanistic view of the world, the old conception of it as static is now outmoded. Nowadays we see the universe as an enormous historical process, an evolution which has been going on for thousands of millions of years and is moving on into an incalculable future. The reason why the idea of evolution is of such great importance is that it points us to the fundamental and dynamic unity, or oneness of the world. Our world view, once static, has now become entirely dynamic.

Thus, there are three principle characteristics of the modern view: we live in a universe gigantic in its dimensions, building itself up organically as a cohesive whole, and impelled by an inner dynamic and energy toward its completion. The old idea of things has gone beyond recall, and now the world is revealed to us in a totally new guise. Only in the last generation have we begun to come to terms with the revolution that this has brought about in human consciousness.

Naturally, this new picture of the world did not spring up overnight, nor has it been the outcome of one particular branch of science. Small "pockets" of insight regarding the dynamic structure of things appeared here and there. Biology and its kindred life sciences have contributed even more than astronomy to forming this world view, for it is from the study of forms of life that the idea of evolution, of a process of progressive growth, is most clearly evident. From the life sciences the concept of evolution spread gradually to the other sciences, and in some degree influences our entire way of imagining the world.

The great pioneer in this field, of course, was Darwin, whose importance goes beyond his strictly scientific theories. It was Darwin who put the idea of evolution on the intellectual map once and for all. Since his time, it has been a constantly inspiring source of insight in all of human thought. The publication of *The Origin of Species* in 1859 will always remain one of the great turning points in the history of thought, cosmology, and eschatology.

In the wake of biology, the rest of the sciences has made the concept of evolution an integral element in their outlook and approach. In physics as well as in the sciences of the mind, we have come to see that we connot ultimately understand any phenomenon unless our investigation takes into account the way in which it has come to be what it is. We now know that even the atoms have their histories; that the stars have their birth, their prime, and their decay; that the languages have had their stages of development; that cultures come and go. The historical dimension of everything has become evident to us with unprecedented force, so that from now on, the categories of historicity extend over the totality of the universe.

All this suggests that the term "evolution" can be understood in two differing ways. By "evolution" we may mean the mutations that in the course of time have taken place in the various species of life (biological evolution). Or we may mean that the cosmos as a whole is subject to the law of evolution and that everything comes to be by a process of growth (cosmic evolution). We might say that biological evolution is only a segment of a far more comprehensive phenomenon: the evolution of the universe through time.

But, as advocates of the humble approach, we should pause to consider Sir Bernard Lovell's warning in 1978:

The complex processes leading to our present understanding of the universe have led to a modern view of the cosmos which we believe to be substantially correct, but it will be a remarkable and indeed unique feature of human thought if this really is the case.[9]

Nevertheless, at this moment in time, scientists, theologians, laity, all of us must utilize this current world view in our continuing participation in creation. Admitting we might be proven wrong, we launch boldly into new discoveries. And what new discoveries are to be made? Evolution may be not ending with man on earth but only beginning. To think that man on this planet is the end of evolution would be egotistical and anthropocentric indeed. It has always been difficult to imagine what comes next; but the multitude of discoveries in this century of things previously unseen points towards the likelihood of even more amazing discoveries hereafter.

How astounding it is that after ninety-nine percent of the evolution of the earth had taken place, a new creation, a new kind of evolution, could suddenly burst forth! The dramatic change was the appearance of man, a creature with free will, the first creature on earth to be allowed to participate in the creative process. Until then, evolution followed a course fixed by the laws of nature. But now suddenly the inconceivable has happened: self-evolution, intentional evolution has begun. The earth is filled with creations of a new kind—logic, love, mathematics, worship, purpose, inventions, and multitudes of other creations never seen on earth before. In reality after four billion years of earthly evolution, a new world was born, a world of mind.

According to the Jesuit paleontologist and mystic Teilhard de Chardin, in the long story of creation there came first the sphere of mineral evolution, the geosphere; then the sphere of living things, the biosphere; and lastly the sphere of the human mind, the noosphere. This unexpected new world of the human mind is so potent and so novel that no one knows what may happen next. Evolution is accelerating. The evolution of ideas is even faster than the evolution of new materials. There is no reason to think that this new world of mind and free will is the end of evolution. After the noosphere, there may be no "Omega Point" but a new sphere. What equally unexpected new world will emerge next? Will it be a new world of soul or spirit? Are we about to witness a new dawn?

Human ingenuity has caused revolutions in the geosphere and biosphere. Synthetic materials replace natural ones. In some parts of the world, we are rapidly stripping the land of resources in order to create standards of living never dreamed of by people a century ago. Luther Burbank began a revolution in the evolution of vegetables and flowers. Thousands of varieties which never existed before were invented by man to suit his needs and whims. Animals can now be bred with almost any desired trait. Some scientists think that by genetic engineering we can even produce animals with superior brains. More than ever men and women are participating in the creation of a new world.

Theologians need to grapple with some very hard questions. For example, the various methods of birth control can reduce the miseries caused by overpopulation, but we differ over the ethical issues involved in applying these new discoveries. Even more puzzling theological questions arise when we consider applying to human reproduction the new powers of selective breeding and genetic engineering. Does God want us to try to improve the human race not only through education and medicine but also by recombinant DNA experiments? Such rapid advances in science prove the urgent need for equal efforts toward spiritual progress and the need for new theologies. As St. Paul warned us:

Things beyond our seeing, things beyond our hearing, things beyond our imagining, all prepared by God for those who love him. These it is that God has revealed to us through the Spirit. For the Spirit explores everything, even the depths of God's own nature. (I Corinthians 2:9–10 NEB.)

Teilhard called for a new theology that would incorporate the modern scientific discoveries of the "immensity of space, which imbues our accustomed way of looking at things with a strain of Universalism" and the progressive "duration of time which . . . introduces . . . the idea of a possible unlimited Progress (Futurism)." Because of these two concepts, universalism and futurism, Teilhard believed we now possess a higher, more organic understanding of the cosmos which could serve as a basis for a new, unprecedented religion.

The twentieth century after Christ may very well represent new renaissance in human culture, a new embarcation into future cultures. Persons born in this century can hardly imagine the small amount of knowledge and the limited concept of the cosmos man had when the scriptures of all the five major religions were written. Do old scriptures need reinterpreting to accommodate an expanded notion of the universe?

More important for theology is the expanded concept of history. When all the scriptures of all major religions were written, the history of the universe was conceived as only a few thousand years. Now geologists and paleontologists who think in hundreds of millions of years read history in visible form sometimes more reliable than history books or scriptures. And cosmologists think in billions of years. Because light travels only a hundred and eighty-six thousand miles a second, we can see the sun not as it is now, but as it was some eight minutes ago. We see some stars as they were when Christ was born. We see some galaxies as they were six million years ago. Such a revolution in our conceptions of time and history is beginning to shape our theology.

What existed before this universe began? What will exist after the sun has grown cold? After minerals there emerged plants, and after plants animals, and after animals there emerged minds; and minds began to participate in the creative process. What comes next? Is there evidence that minds are developing into even more miraculous spirits and souls? These are not only questions of science but also of theology—a new type of theology not yet taught in the seminaries.

Consider the cold, inert world of minerals, the throbbing world of life, the curious, searching realm of the intellect. What next? This may be the most important question facing us at the end of the twentieth century. To answer it, scientists are daily engaged in new scientific experiments that will help us know more about the vast unseen. Theologians, too, answering Chardin's call for a new religion, must begin to explore the vast unseen dimensions of our evolving universe; they must plumb the very "depths of God's own nature."

V   Humble About What?

Humility is a misunderstood virtue. It can mean serving others, as when Jesus said, "Among you, whoever wants to be great must be your servant, and whoever wants to be first must be the willing slave of all." (Matthew 20:26–27 NEB.) But, humility toward men is not the subject of this book. Nor do we mean any belittling of the talents and blessings God has given us.

The word humility is used here to mean admission that God infinitely exceeds anything anyone has ever said of Him; and that He is infinitely beyond human comprehension and understanding. A prime purpose of this book is to help us become more humble and thereby reduce the stumbling blocks placed in our paths toward heaven by our own egos. If the word heaven means eternal peace and joy, then we can observe that some persons have more of it already than others. Have you observed that these are generally persons who have reduced their egos, those who desire to give rather than to get? The Holy Spirit seems to enter when invited and to dwell with those who try to surrender to Him their hearts and minds. "Behold, I stand at the door and knock; if any man hear my voice and open the door, I will come in to him and sup with him, and he with me." (Revelation 3:20, KJV.) As men grow older and wiser, they often grow in humility.

The humble approach has much in common with but is not the same as natural theology, process theology, or empirical theology, whose horizons are all too narrow. They often attempt to give a comprehensive or systematic picture of God in keeping with human observations. But the humble approach teaches that man can discover and comprehend only a few of the infinite aspects of God's nature, never enough to form a comprehensive theology. The humble approach may be a science still in its infancy, but it seeks to develop a way of knowing God appropriate to His greatness and our littleness. The humble approach is a search which looks forward, not backward, and which expects to grow and learn from its mistakes.

All of nature reveals something of the Creator. That golden age of creation is reached as the Creator reveals Himself more and more to the minds of men. Men cannot learn all about God, the Creator, by studying nature because nature is only a contingent and partial manifestation of God. Hence Natural Theology which seeks to learn about God through nature is limited. Recently a new concept of theology has been born which is called the Theology of Science. This denotes the way in which natural scientists are meditating about the Creator on the ground of their observations of the astronomic and subatomic domains, but also on the ground of investigations into living organisms and their evolution, and such invisible realities as the human mind.

Experimental theology can reveal only a very little about God. It begins with a few simple forms of inquiry, subject to little disagreement, and proceeds to probe more deeply in thousands of other ways. Spiritual realities are not quantifiable, of course, but there may be aspects of spiritual life which can be demonstrated experimentally one by one even though there be hundreds of failures for each success. This approach is similar to that of experimental medicine.

As with experimental theology, the humble approach implies that there is a growing body of knowledge and an evolving theology not limited to any one nation or cultural area. The truly humble should be so open-minded that they welcome religious views from any place in the universe that is peopled with intelligent life. Seekers following the humble approach are never so zenophobic that they reject ideas from other nations, religions, or eras. Because the humble approach to theology is ongoing and constantly evolving, it may never become obsolete.

When learning about God, a world-wide approach is much too small. Even a universe-wide approach is much too small. The "picture" ninety-nine percent of people have of God is small. Have you heard anyone say, "God is a part of life"? Would it not be wiser to say of humanity that it is only an infinitesimal speck of all that has its being in and through God? Our own ego can make us think that we are the center rather than merely one tiny temporal outward manifestation of a vast universe of being which subsists in the eternal and infinite reality which is God. Have you heard the words, "the realm of the Spirit"? Is there any other realm? Humanity on this little earth may be an aspect of all that is upheld by the Spirit, but the Spirit is not an "aspect" of humanity. To say that God is a "part" or an "aspect" of life is as blind as for a man, standing on a shore looking at a wave, to say, "The ocean is an aspect of that wave."

The ocean-wave analogy is helpful in approaching God with more humility. A wave is part of the ocean, having no existence apart from the larger body of water. The wave is temporary, whereas oceans are relatively permanent. Each wave is different from each other wave. In a sense, the wave is created by the ocean and is a child of the ocean. When it dies, it returns to and continues to be a part of the surging oceans creating ever new breakers on the beach. It is this keen sense of proportion and relationship that those advocating the humble approach seek to encourage.

The humble always respect the hierarchy of being evident in creation. Consider a tree. The tree is alive, having been created just as we were. Like us, it consists of billions of cells and atoms. It ages, dies, and hopefully produces seeds after its kind. But the tree cannot describe us. It has no ability to comprehend us or the complex culture of which it is a mere part. It may be a beautiful addition to our garden. We may nourish and care for it. But the difficulty the tree would have in describing us is perhaps similar to our difficulty in writing an account of God. If any person were to say he knew all about God, it would be like a tree claiming to know all about its gardener. Those following the humble approach maintain a belief in the great ladder of being.

Similar to the chain of being, with its unending variations and surprises, is the mosaic of human opinion about God. The sheer variety of opinions concerning the nature of God should give us pause. We should admit humbly that other theologies contain valuable insights into God that our own may lack. In many ways, men attempting to describe God encounter the same difficulties as the proverbial blindmen describing an elephant. No one sees the entire picture, yet each feels and understands a part necessary for the full description.

To have all men believe alike would be a great tragedy. Progress would cease. The spiritual struggle would be over. Life would hardly be life. The more we know, the more we know we do not know. This is what gives life spice. In fact, in order to grow, we must daily become more humble and honest in admitting the paucity of our knowledge. This humble admission of ignorance is what produces progress, what keeps man searching, what makes life as we know it exciting and challenging.

Gaining knowledge is like working a quarry. As we chip out bits of information, the mining face gets larger and larger. The more knowledge we gain the more we can see the extent of the unknown. As we grow in knowledge, we grow in humility. This may be just as true in studying the soul as in the investigations pursued by natural sciences.

A man or woman pursuing the humble way to God could adopt a credo similar to the following:

God is billions of stars in the Milky Way and He is much more.

God is billions of billions of stars in other galaxies and He is much more.

Time and space and energy are all part of God, and He is much more.

The awesome mysteries of magnetism, gravity, light, knowledge, imagination, memory, love, faith, gratitude, and joy are all part of God and He is much more.

God is four billion people on Earth and He is much more.

God is untold billions of beings on planets of millions of other stars and He is much more.

God is all the things seen and also the vastly greater abundance of things unseen by man.

Men who dwell in three dimensions can comprehend only a little part of God's multitude of dimensions.

God is the only reality—all else is fleeting shadow and imagination from our very limited five senses acting on our tiny brains.

God is beginning to create His universe and allows each of His children to participate in some small ways in this creative evolution.

God is the infinitely large and also the infinitely small—He is each of our inmost thoughts, each of our trillions of bodily cells, and each of the billions of wave patterns which are each cell.

God is all of you and you are a little part of Him.

By constant reminders such as this, we might avoid the most common pitfall of theology: the attempt by man to put limits on God.

Throughout all history, the gods created by men's minds have been too small. All concepts knowable to man have the specific characteristics of the human thought which formulates them. How often have we heard someone deny the existence of God because good people suffer. It is as if that unbeliever attributes to God "man's inhumanity to man" and assumes that "God's inhumanity to man" disqualifies Him from being God! Does not God work in mysterious ways? Cannot what appears to us as "God's inhumanity" or injustice be part of a more perfect picture that we do not see? God's love is not as small as ours. It is infinite. In fact, if we can never fully understand even another human being, how will we ever understand God?

It is a great mystery that evolution has provided us with the mental ability to think about our Creator. As far as we know, only humans among all of God's creatures on earth have the ability to think about God. But all concepts we can form are limited by our five senses and by the smallness of our minds. Therefore we can never totally know God. We really only know our attempts to know Him; we devise theologies hoping they in some way adequately represent Him. And yet they are always inadequate. If God were small enough to fit our human reason, He would not be God at all but only another human. In some ways, we are like radio receivers that can receive music, voices, and wonderful sounds from hundreds of sources but are hopelessly blind to the sunsets and flowers.

To each of us has been given free will and a mind which is itself a creative power. We can create only in a very limited way. However, because our ability to create and to understand appears vastly greater than that of any other kind of earthly creature, we are thought of as made in the image of God.

Many religions hold that knowledge about God comes not so much from human reasoning as from God choosing to reveal Himself to us. The Church of Christ of Latter Day Saints, for instance, is based on revelation, translated in 1828, from books of gold. The Prophet Muhammad (570–632 A.D.) received revelations which were memorized and later written down by his disciples.

Christians believe God came into the world two thousand years ago and revealed Himself in the life of Jesus of Nazareth. But none of His words and no accounts of his life were evidently written down until a generation after his ascension into heaven.

Men could write down only what they understood. Communication reduced the revelations to the mental development of the messengers. If God had revealed the General Theory of Relativity two thousand years ago, no one would have been able to write it down. Maybe God is ready to reveal Himself more and more. Maybe by evolution each generation is able to comprehend a little more. Ninety-nine percent of God's universe has become known only in the latest half-century. Nuclear physicists and geneticists and astronomers are earnestly seeking with open minds and with humility. Can you say the same for all churches and all theologians?

There are clear scriptural bases for advocating the need for an inquiring and open mind. According to St. Luke, Jesus said, "Ask, and it shall be given you; seek, and you shall find; knock, and it shall be opened unto you. For everyone who asked, receives, and he who seeks, finds; and to him who knocks it shall be opened." Maybe God reveals Himself where He finds an inquiring mind—an open mind. In the Acts of the Apostles (17: 24–28, NAS) St. Paul said:

The God who made the world and everything in it . . . made from one every nation of men . . . that they should seek God, in the hope that they might feel after Him and find Him. Yet He is not far from each of us, for "In Him we live and move and have our being"; as even some of your poets have said, "For we are indeed His offspring."

Christ came to reveal God to men. But because of the limitations of human minds and human language, maybe less than one-hundredth part has been handed down to us. It is easy for us to realize how ignorant and primitive were the Jews of two thousand years ago and the Hindus of three thousand years ago. We should be humble enough to admit that if they had only perhaps one-tenth of one percent of all knowledge, we may have only one percent, even though the little glimpses we do have are indeed awesome.

One following the humble approach thinks it possible that God may want to reveal Himself further than He has done to date in any major or minor religion. He may be ever ready to give us new revelation if we will but open our minds to seek and inquire, but first we must rid ourselves of that rigidity and intellectual arrogance that tells us we have all the answers already. Like natural scientists who already assume the humble approach in their studies, maybe we should recognize that the law of creation is a law of accelerating change. Human language has always been too inadequate and restricted to utter all truths once and for all. The human mind has never been ready to receive all knowledge.

Time, space, and energy are the limits of our lives as they are the limits of our knowledge. God, of course, is not bound in these ways. He is the Creator of the awesome vastness of His cosmos. He knows each person's most fleeting thought just as

He knows the power of a quasar and the intricate complexity of a DNA molecule. His most marvelous and mysterious creation on earth is the human brain with its indwelling mind. With the use of our minds, we can participate in some small ways in the creation of matter and even life itself. It should be clear to us that even though we are seriously hampered by our human weaknesses, we are meant to share with God his readiness to reveal Himself to us. We have a duty of humility, the duty to be open-minded.

In humility, we should try to be continually creating our own personalities and souls by learning more about the Creator. St. Paul says in I Corinthians (2: 9–12, NEB):

But in the words of scripture, "Things beyond our seeing, things beyond our hearing, things beyond our imagining, all prepared by God for those who love Him," these it is that God has revealed to us through the Spirit. For the Spirit explores everything, even the depths of God's own nature. Among men, who knows what a man is but the man's own spirit within him? In the same way only the Spirit of God knows what God is. This is the Spirit that we have received from God, and not the spirit of the world, so that we may know all that God of His own grace has given us.

The human body is even more awe-inspiring than the stars of the universe. We recall again that astronomers now think that the Milky Way galaxy contains over 100 billion stars and that the universe contains over 100 billion galaxies. The number of stars in the universe is truly astronomic: but the number of atoms in our body is even greater, about 5 million times as great.

An average cell may be made of 50 thousand billion atoms. The average human may have 100 thousand billion cells. So the atoms in our body may total 5,000,000,000,000,000,000,000,000,000. We each have about thirty billion cells in our brain alone. Some cells are spheres, some spirals and rectangles, others have tails. Some nerve cells are star-shaped with tiny bodies trailing wispy arms. Consider the astronomer Carl Sagan's description of the human brain:

If each human brain had only one synapse—corresponding to a monumental stupidity—we would be capable of only two mental states. If we had two synapses, then $2^2 = 4$ states; three synapses, then $2^3 = 8$ states, and, in general, for N synapses, 2^N states. But the human brain is characterized by some 10^{13} synapses. Thus the number of different states of a human brain is 2 raised to this power, i.e. multiplied by itself ten trillion times. This is an unimaginably large number . . . . It is because of this immense number of functionally different configurations of the human brain that no two humans, even identical twins raised together, can ever be really very much alike. These enormous numbers may also explain something of the unpredictability of human behavior. The answer must be that all possible brain states are by no means occupied; there must be an enormous number of mental configurations that have never been entered or even glimpsed by any human being in the history of mankind. From this perspective, each human being is truly rare and different and the sanctity of individual human lives is a plausible ethical consequence.[10]

Thus, if as humans we continually surprise ourselves, should we not be prepared to be surprised by God?

So what is it we are to be humble about? Our experience of God, our experience of ourselves? Perhaps the experience of God that we overlook most easily is the experience of Him through science. Being humbled before science is a good first step toward the humility we should have before God. As Vannevar Bush puts it:

Science here does things. It renders us humble and it paints a universe in which the mysteries become highlighted, in which constraints on imagination and speculation have been removed, and which becomes ever more awe-inspiring as we gaze . . . on the essential and central core of faith. Science will be the silence of humility not the silence of disdain.[11]

Just as we need the humility to live with conflicting scientific theories, we also need the humility to accept conflicting religious attitudes. Friedrich Schleiermacher wrote in 1799, "Nothing is more unchristian than to seek uniformity in religion." He argued that instead of being segregated behind ecclesiastical walls, differences of opinion should be allowed to work upon, enrich, and define each other. He claimed that lack of appreciation for other religions has no basis in religion itself. The more adequately one learns about the infinite, the more humility and openness one will have for the unlimited range of its manifestations.

Maybe the Creator's plan (not only for the physical universe but also for the metaphysical) is ever-increasing revelation, growth, change, and variety.

VI Benefits from Humility

Humility is the gateway to understanding. As thanksgiving opens the door to spiritual growth, so does humility open the door to progress in knowledge and also to progress in theology. Humility is the beginning of progress. Humility leads to open-mindedness. It is difficult for a person to learn anything more if he is sure he knows it all already. When we realize how little we know, we can begin to seek and to learn. Unless we recognize our ignorance, why should we investigate?

For each of us to grow in spirituality, we should be humble in worshiping God. If we free ourselves of self-will and surrender to God's will, we can become channels for God's love and wisdom to flow to others. Theologians have long proclaimed this; but sometimes, when formulating creeds or describing God, they seem to deny it. Some sound as if they think they know it all. This can lead to statements that make God appear limited and anthropomorphic, rather than truly infinite and majestic in His divine power.

For any theologian or minister to claim he knows all about God, when he really knows less than a minute amount of what may be known, makes him appear arrogant and obscurantist to educated listeners or readers. And worse, it acts as a closing of the doors so that the fullness of God's light cannot flow freely through him to others. A closed mind does not produce progress. An atheist who is sure there is no God is really a pitiful person because he is too egotistical to admit his limitations and insignificance. Because his small concept of God may not seem to fit with facts observed by scientists, he denies that God exists rather than admit that his own concept is too small. How small is a man who says, "If God does not conform to my thoughts, then He does not exist"? Before he can receive the Holy Spirit he must surrender his pride and "become as a little child."

Some people have said that religion causes wars, that the diversity of religious beliefs will always be divisive. But the fact is that such wars were brought about for a number of reasons, not the least of which was egotistical and unwarranted claims to proprietary rights over the knowledge of God. History reveals that great havoc and suffering were caused not by religion, but by men who thought their concept of God was the only one worthy of belief. "He that is of a proud heart stirreth up strife," it says in the book of Proverbs (28:25, KJV). The verbal and physical violence in religion could be reduced by believers who claim nothing more than a minimal knowledge of the infinity of God.

Ralph Waldo Trine has said, "Let us not be among the number so dwarfed, so limited, so bigoted as to think that the infinite God has revealed himself to one little handful of his children, in one little quarter of the globe, and at one particular period of time."[12] In fact, at the heart of true religion is the willingness to see truths in other religions. The Persian scriptures claim, "Whatever road I take joins the highway that leads to Thee . . . . Broad is the carpet God has spread, and beautiful the colors he has given it." A Buddhist believes that, "The pure man respects every form of faith. My doctrine makes no difference between high and low, rich and poor; like the sky, it has room for all, and like the water, it washes all alike." A Chinese sage has said, "The broad-minded see the truth in different religions; the narrow-minded see only the differences." And a Hindu holy man has written that only the narrow-minded ask, " 'Is this man a stranger, or is he of our tribe?' But to those in whom love dwells, the whole world is but one family." Lastly, the Christian witnesses to this with the following words: "Are we not all children of one father? God has made of one blood all nations to dwell on the face of the earth."

Differing concepts of God have developed in different cultures. No one should say that God can be reached by only one path. Such exclusiveness lacks humility because it presumes that we can and do comprehend God. The humble person is ready to admit and welcome the various manifestations of God.

Jesus quoted Isaiah thus: "But in vain they do worship me; teaching for doctrine the commandments of men." (Matthew 15:9, KJV.) Schism in religions is caused by intolerance; and intolerance is a form of egotism. However, tolerance is not the same as the humble approach. We should seek to benefit from the inspiring highlights of other denominations and religions, not just to tolerate them. We should try our very best to give the beauties of our religion to others, because sharing our most prized possessions is the highest form of "Love thy neighbor." Let us not water down the diverse religions into a know-nothing soup; but rather let us study enthusiastically the glorious highlights of each. An old Chinese precept is, "The good man does not grieve that other people do not recognize his merits. His only anxiety is lest he should fail to recognize theirs." It is a mistake for people of different religions to try to agree with each other. The result is not the best of each but rather the watered-down, least-common denominator. What is more fruitful is a spirit of humility in which we recognize that no one will ever comprehend all that God is. Therefore, let us permit and encourage each prophet to proclaim the best as it is revealed to him. There is no conflict unless the restrictive idea of exclusiveness enters in. We can hold our ideas of the Gospel with the utmost enthusiasm, while humbly admitting that we know ever so little of the whole and that there is plenty of room for those who think they have seen God in a different way. The evil arises only if one prophet forbids his audience to listen to any other prophet. The conceit and self-centeredness of such restriction—the false pride of saying that God *can* be only what we have learned Him to be—should be obvious.

The human ego has been the curse of religious denominations for thousands of years. In every major religion wars have been fought about differences of creeds. Nations or tribes have exterminated others because they worshiped different gods or the same god as taught by different prophets. This is human ego run wild. Let us humbly admit how very small is the measure of men's minds. This realization helps to prevent religious conflicts, and obviates attacks by atheists against religion. Moreover, humility of this kind opens more minds to the idea that science supports and illuminates religion.

If a person concentrates only on his progress or enlightenment, he is essentially self-centered; for he should also help others, and share what he has learned with others by speaking, writing, broadcasting, and disseminating his ideas. Such new evangelists should be welcomed and respected for their generosity.

Influenced by humanism, some clergy in Christian churches unknowingly encourage religious strife by working for political or social goals rather than purely spiritual ones. They strive too much to create an earthly, material, man-made kingdom in contradiction to the spiritual, internal kingdom that Jesus preached. In Third World nations, for example, churches sometimes advocate armed force by governments, or even violence by terrorists for the sake of social justice. They neglect to teach their members that enduring improvement must begin with self-improvement and voluntary improvements in our own hearts. Compulsory brotherhood is a contradiction in terms.

Christians have sometimes derived their compulsory, intolerant attitudes from a statement such as this one in St. John. Jesus said, ". . . no one comes to the Father except by me. If you knew me you would know my Father too." (John 14: 6–7, NEB.) But is this an intolerant and exclusive claim? At first glance, it is. But perhaps we can see what Jesus meant by recalling a similar statement in Matthew, "No one knows the Son but the Father, and no one knows the Father but the Son and those to whom the Son may reveal him." (Matthew 11:27, NEB.) Jesus prefaced this comment with the words, "I thank thee, Father, Lord of heaven and earth, for hiding these things from the learned and wise, and revealing them to the simple." What he seems to be saying is that there are frontiers to human knowledge of God, but these frontiers are open to the lowly and simple of any age or culture. Proud and overbearing egotism prevents knowledge of the Father, and is clearly opposite to the teachings of Jesus.

Christians believe that God came into the world in human form to reveal Himself. But human intelligence is so limited that we could understand only a little. Missionaries have difficulty revealing all the gospel to primitive natives, so that they reveal just what the natives can comprehend. Jesus, Himself, we are told, taught the multitudes only as they were able to hear and understand. He found human language and philosophy two thousand years ago so inadequate that He used symbolism, metaphor, living examples, parables, and so on. Maybe the reason why He wrote nothing is that writing was and is inadequate to convey truth without warping and constricting it. For example, suppose a man so loved the forest that he transformed himself into a tree and then tried to use the limited language of trees to teach them about man. The trees could form only small concepts of man and their contact with humans in various ways could produce merely a variety of small concepts. Is not the superiority of man over trees infinitely less than the superiority of God over man?

Some people do appear to come closer to God when they pray in Jesus' name, possibly because they have progressed more in that upward path of the humility and meekness of Jesus than others. But on the other hand, some appear more spiritual when they pray as disciples of Buddha or Mohammed or Abraham. Theodore Parker taught that the doctrinal formulations of Christianity have changed and will change from age to age and what is sometimes called heresy at one time is accepted as orthodox and infallible in another age. Old forms, Parker says, give way to new, and each new form will capture some of the truth but not the whole. "Transient things form a great part of what is taught as religion. An undue place has often been assigned to forms and doctrines, while too little stress has been laid on the divine life of the soul, love to God and love to man." [13]

Religious advance springs from deep humility. Therefore, it comes most easily to a person who is aware of his ignorance and his need to learn. It is more difficult for a man highly educated in theology to comprehend how infinitely minute his knowledge is compared to God's knowledge. It is significant that Jesus was not trained as a scribe or pharisee. St. Luke recorded:

Jesus looked at him and said "How hard it is for those who have riches [or education or intellect] to make their way into the kingdom of God! Yes it is easier for a camel to pass through the eye of a needle than for a rich man [or an intellectual] to enter the kingdom of God." (Luke 18: 24 and 25, JB.)

Intellect and wealth both seduce men into self-reliance. Of course some theologians do know ten times as much about religion as the average layman or minister. But if they claim to have more than one percent of knowledge of God, they are ridiculous in their pride. St. Paul said:

Make no mistake about this: if there is anyone among you who fancies himself wise, I mean by the standards of this passing age—he must become a fool to gain true wisdom. For the wisdom of the world is folly in God's sight. Scripture says "He traps the wise in their own cunning"; and again, "The Lord knows that the arguments of the wise are futile"; so never make mere men a cause for pride. (I Corinthians 3:18–21 NEB.)

The human ego makes people try to solve problems by human effort alone without turning to seek assistance in God's wisdom. Rigid creed is a form of pride, for it means we think we understand all about God. Both the Old and New Testaments are critical of the proud. "Everyone that is proud in heart is an abomination to the Lord," it says in Proverbs (Proverbs 16:5, KJV), and St. James warns, "God resisteth the proud, but giveth grace to the humble." (James 4:6 KJV.) "A man's pride brings him humiliation; he who humbles himself will win honor." (Proverbs 9:23, KJV.) "Pride goeth before destruction and a haughty spirit before a fall." (Proverbs 16:18 KJV.) "By humility and the fear of the Lord are riches, and honour and life." (Proverbs 22:4, KJV.) "Before honour is humility." (Proverbs 15:33, KJV.) "With the lowly is wisdom." (Proverbs 11:2, KJV.) "Humble yourself in the sight of the Lord and he shall lift you up." (James 4:10 KJV.)

Sometimes large councils of churches make exclusive dogmatic pronouncements, even in fields where they are poorly informed, such as economics and politics. This can create division, hatred, or strife. Perhaps results would be better if they expressed love for all, welcomed diversity, and avoided the sin of self-righteousness.

Becoming "unselfed" opens the door to communication with God. He who relies on his own wisdom or beauty or skill or money shuts God out. But he who is humble and grateful for such God-given blessings opens the door to heaven on earth here and now. For each of us to grow in spirituality, we should be humble in worshiping God. We should free ourselves of self-will and surrender to God's will. If we get rid of ego-centeredness, we can become clear channels for God's love and wisdom to flow through us, just as sunlight pours through an open window. In the language of electronics, man is a receiver and transponder; but when his pride causes him to conceive of himself as a transmitter instead, he naturally cuts himself off from God who is his source of supply for both love and wisdom.

We should be as humble as the scientist investigating nature, limiting himself to those parts of nature which can be observed. In fact, we should take as our models those careful scientists, conscientiously differentiating between the few aspects of reality that they can observe and those vast uncharted areas for which they have not yet devised technologies and methodologies for research. We should imitate those scientists who are not deluded by intellectual pride and doubt and who do not deny the metaphysical aspect of life. Scientists following the humble approach to science as well as to God would never assert that what they cannot comprehend is for that very reason nonexistent. The scientists, however, who have surmounted this barrier of human egotism are beginning to investigate and learn about unseen realms, including the spiritual.

As we have seen earlier, perhaps both scientists and theologians should pool their humility and explore together the distant corners of the universe. Why should either group, in its arrogance, design a small pattern of thought and insist that God and His creation fit into it? For example, in the distant future it may be regarded as incredible that in those dark ages called the twentieth century some medical doctors were so limited as to deny that any benefits could come from the prayers of Christian Science practitioners; and that some Christian Scientists were so limited as to deny that God might choose to work through the hands and minds of medical doctors. Such narrowness is the opposite of the humble approach. More and more healing and health seems to come from the inside as well as the outside; but why not use spiritual and material remedies both together.

When the disciples of any cause, sacred or secular, stop seeking and claim they have the answer, the movement ossifies. It appears that God's creative method is movement, change, continuing search, ongoing inquiry. Those who seek are rewarded. Those who are sure they already have the answers gradually become obsolete. Perhaps "built-in" obsolescense is God's plan for keeping the world of ideas forever young, fresh, and invigorating. The self-confident proud grow old and die, and with them die their ideas.

Instead of burning the heretic at the stake, we may benefit more if we listen to him and carefully observe whether his ideas bear good fruit or not. If his message is not holy, it will fade away when subjected to the free competition of ideas. The open-minded approach is to look for God in a multitude of ways, in the kind of empirical questioning pursued by natural scientists and those theologians who recognize that some of tomorrow's spiritual heroes may be among those considered today as heretics.

Progress occurs most often in a condition of free competition. God gave us free will. He might have chosen to create us as angels with all the knowledge we would ever need or want.

But in His wisdom He chose to give us free will with which to desire and long for, to try, to fail, to succeed, and finally to progress. It is contrary to this divine purpose for any church or national government to dictate that we must all fit into one mold, to take away free will, to eliminate the free competition of ideas. Any large government enforcing regimentation retards progress and change, and reduces souls to machines.

New discoveries come mainly from free minds. The worship of God is not weakened by keeping an open mind any more than cosmology was weakened when Ptolemaic theories were replaced by those of Copernicus. Maybe one of the attributes of God is change. Did He decree the survival of the fittest? Maybe God intends us in some way to use the new power He has put into our hands in relation to selective breeding and recombinant DNA, to improve the human race. Why else does He give us this awesome new knowledge and the free will to use it?

By learning humility we find that the purpose of life on earth may be far different from what anyone now supposes. Diligently each child of God should seek to find out and obey God's purposes. If we encourage free and friendly competition of ideas, the truth may more easily emerge. It may be God's plan that any organization that tries to maintain its "truth" as the status quo is headed for extinction. No matter how well protected, every willow tree grows old and dies. But if, before it dies, a little limb is snipped and put in good moist soil, it will take root, flourish, and grow into another tree. This principle seems to apply to plants, animals, people, nations, churches, and even to ideas. From a little sprig of an idea, the world's great bodies of thought grew year by year until they were fully mature. For example, despite harsh persecution the early Christian church grew rapidly like a young willow tree for five centuries. Likewise for five centuries, the ideas of Mohammed swept the world like wildfire. Which religions and denominations are growing most rapidly today? Many with the most rapid growth are those which are still young, still exploring, still taking risks, still experimenting with the meaning of life.

Secular ideas and institutions also show this tendency toward the life cycle. Communism, for example, captured a quarter of the world's people in one century for many reasons, a primary one being its youthful promise to sweep away the stifling patterns of older societies. But in many nations, socialism and communism have become so restrictive and coercive that a growing number of dissidents refuse to tolerate it. They criticize or leave their countries for other places that permit and encourage free expression of thought.

Youthfulness is an important principle of life whether considered from a biological or spiritual viewpoint. The young at heart or the young in mind are humble and open-minded and welcome new ideas. Jesus' admonition to become like little children may have been His way of telling us to experiment, explore new ideas, test things, admit our lack of knowledge and know-how, and to be humble. Yes, change and progress require a youthful attitude. Ideas and institutions which remain rigid for generations tend to wither.

Christians think God appeared in Jesus of Nazareth two thousand years ago for our salvation and education. But we should not take it to mean that education and progress stopped there, that Jesus was the end of change, the end of time. Is such notion compatible with God's law of the universe? To say that God cannot reveal Himself again in a decisive way because He did it once years ago seems sacriligious. We should be gentle, kind, and sympathetic toward God's new prophets even though they bring strange new ideas. We should not forbid religious expression, however misguided we think it to be. No useful purpose was served when the Inquisition forced Galileo to recant in 1633. Jesus, too, was considered unorthodox by the learned religious establishment of his day. Those with the humble approach invite the new evangelists to share what they think they have learned with others by speaking, writing, broadcasting, and publishing their ideas.

Just as each tree or child or soul can grow in the correct nourishing environment, so too, could the world-soul of humanity grow and flourish if we had global toleration and inquiry. Religious leaders in every nation could increase spiritual understanding just as fast as scientists increase our understanding of the physical world. A lot, of course, depends upon our willingness to love those who are strange and different from ourselves even though they cling to their strange and new ideas. As Ella Wheeler Wilcox put it:

A thousand creeds have come and gone
But what is that to you or me:
Creeds are but branches of a tree
The root of Love lives on and on.

Humbly to admit that we know only a very little of God's truth does not make us agnostic. If a medical doctor can admit with an open mind that he does not understand all diseases, symptoms, and cures, surely we can be equally humble and honest, not agnostic, by admitting we each have more to learn about God. We ought not to brand every skeptic as a godless materialist, any more than we would have skeptics accuse every believer of being a dogmatic roadblock to progress. There is room for many branches on the tree. The life-sap of love lives on and on.

VII   Creation Through Change

Creation is just beginning. We are just starting to understand that God has given us talents so we can participate in His creative process. The old ways of structuring and ordering institutional religions may not apply to the future. Often they are too rigid, too traditional. New, freer, more imaginative and adaptable creeds will have to be devised in order that man's God-given mind and imagination can build the kingdom of heaven.

If, as Teilhard said, the universe is "a huge psychic phenomenon," an upward evolution toward increasing consciousness made possible by ever more complex structures, we must somehow encourage our more gifted individuals to dedicate their time and talents to this ongoing work of creation. We will need the best minds and hearts. In the whole sweep of evolution we see movement from the simple toward ever richer complexity and variety. So, too, human creators must represent the wide variety of human thought and invention. Men should try to produce creations that truly reflect the talents God gives us. Just because man *seems* to be the highest species of creation, the end of cosmogenesis, we should not be deluded into thinking we are the lords of creation. We are the servants of creation. We are a new beginning, the first creatures on earth allowed to participate consciously in the evolving creative process.

Today the world urgently needs new breakthroughs for man's basic understanding of God. Theologians need to be humble and open-minded. It is good for churches to have creeds, doctrines, dogmas, liturgy, and the hierarchies of layman and clergy. This helps the church to exist as an organization of people whose ideas are compatible. This gives continuity to the development of the church; and it helps outsiders to see what each church denomination represents. However, because of a lack of humility, there is today and always has been throughout the history of all churches a tendency for dogma or hierarchy to stifle progress. If the members and clergy were more humble, they could use dogma in a more open and inquiring way as a beginning point for continual revision and improvement. If a family (or a corporation or church) prepares a good budget but never changes it for a century, such a budget will surely become obsolete and gradually change from being a help to being a millstone hung round the family's neck. Budgets are helpful only if they are continually revised and improved. Like budgets, church structures are more helpful if they are continually revised and improved. John Calvin taught that "to be Reformed is to be always reforming."

It is interesting that throughout history religion has developed and progressed most often by the work of those who were first regarded as heretics. The pharisees were learned and holy men, but most of them seemed to have regarded Jesus as a heretic. Other heretics were Buddha, Paul, Zoroaster, Mohammed, Wycliffe, Hus, Luther, Calvin, Wesley, Fox, Smith, Emerson, Bahaullah, and Eddy. Christians believe God chose to enter the world in human form but not as a traditionalist urging merely restudy of Abraham and Moses but rather as a progressive with a new revelation. Rarely does a conservative become a hero of history. Rather, it is usually a progressive, far-reaching thinker, one who breaks out of a traditional mold. In other words one who, according to the accepted customs of his time, would be branded a heretic. The opening chapters in the life of most good heretics are usually about humility; the desire to learn more, and eventually the growing awareness that something innovative should be tried.

The earth needs a new Columbus, a new Galileo, a new Copernicus, a genius who can enlarge the global vision of mankind to reveal how tiny and temporary we are in comparison to the infinity and eternity of God. Who can make us humble enough to comprehend that mankind may not be the end of the creative process, nor the earth the center of the universe?

Dr. Robert Hilliard has said that if the growth of knowledge continues at the present rate, then when a baby born today graduates from a university, the quantity of knowledge on earth will be four times as great. By the time such a child is fifty years old the amount of knowledge will be thirty-two times as great; and ninety-seven percent of everything known to man will have been learned since the day the child was born.

This is the blossoming time in the creation of man. Evolution is accelerating. Progress is accelerating. One of God's great blessings to man is change, and the present acceleration of change in the world is an overflowing of this belssing. Those who love God should devote as much manpower and as many resources to research in spiritual subjects as corporations and governments devote to research about material things. Seminaries need to do as much research as universities.

Only about one child in a million is born with a mind that is superhuman in one or more ways. Why does God's process of evolution produce these rare geniuses on earth? Is it His plan that they should help all people to progress? The one in a million who contributes a new idea to humanity can be a blessing to millions, so that God's creation can continue to progress. God gave each oyster the ability to have a million children of which only one, on the average, reaches maturity. Is it the purpose of the million to ensure that one will preserve the race? In addition to the geniuses given more-than-human minds, God also creates saints and prophets with more-than-human souls. A prophet is a pioneer in the uncharted regions of the spirit. No two persons are equal or identical in body or mind, and it is probable that no two persons are equal in soul. However much we may yearn for equality, it does not seem to be part of God's plan.

Sören Kierkegaard taught that the human race advances on

the backs of those rare geniuses who venture into realms that most of us are afraid of. Arend van Leewin has said, "Ninety-nine percent of people, irrespective of race, play a passive as opposed to a creative role; and even the creative section are passive with regard to ninety-nine percent of their civilization."[14] And Huston Smith, the masterful chronicler of world religious thought and practice, wrote:

The average man is no more capable of forming his imagination in ways that resolve his feelings nobly than he is capable of being his own scientist. Both tasks require genius. Geniuses in the art of shaping man's imaginings are artists, philosophers, prophets, and seers. Over time their creations coalesce and distill into cultures. As the religious forms of traditional Judaism and Christianity are losing their powers to inform the contemporary mind, the West desperately needs religious geniuses who can create new imaginal forms, convincing to the contemporary mind, which consummate man's needs for home, vocation, and transcendence.[15]

Any tendency to stifle religious genius by adopting excessively detailed religious laws or unchanging doctrines, liturgies, or structures is the result of a lack of humility. Histories of all religions show that traditionalists are eventually hopelessly out of touch with life, and that their position usually passes away. Fixed dogma and bureaucracy are similar. Both squelch progress. Both may ultimately impede the path of each human soul into heaven. If a purpose of man on earth everywhere is to be a co-creator with God, it is presumptuous or egotistical for any one group to say that there is only one kind of believer whom God can use as a tool in His continuing creation of the universe.

In our own times we have witnessed several brave religious pioneers who have marched into old areas of religious endeavor with a new, bold spirit and program. Brother Roger Schutz, the founder of the Taizé community in France, has answered one of the greatest spiritual needs of the post-war world. His quiet monastic community attracts architects, printers, theologians, lawyers, and countless professional people who, after submitting themselves to his program of prayer and reflection, return to the world to pursue their careers more fully committed to creating a more decent world of love and joy. His efforts to organize the worldwide "Council of Youth" in 1970 inspired thousands of young people to go to Taizé and then return to their own countries to work for religious renewal.

Mother Teresa of Calcutta, often called by people of many faiths "a living saint," has demonstrated to the world yet another way that God's creation can change through human (or in her case, superhuman) effort. Mother Teresa formed a new order of religious women that has lived among and served the poorest of the poor in India and many other nations, while at the same time demonstrating divine love. Public as well as private charitable organizations could follow her example and methods of providing human services and love to the outcasts of modern society. Malcolm Muggeridge said about Mother Teresa and her Missionaries of Charity:

When I think of them in Calcutta, as I often do, it is not the bare house in a dark slum that is conjured up in my mind, but a light shining and a joy abounding. I see them diligently and cheerfully constructing something beautiful for God out of the human misery and affliction that lies around them.[16]

Another pioneering woman in the struggle for Christian renewal in the world is Chiara Lubich. Her Focolare, or Fireside Movement, begun in Italy in 1943, has become a successful international means of providing spiritual community to people for whom the church as a system and institution is not enough. Living in lay communities structured as families, and imbued with the loving ethos of family life, architects, doctors, engineers, nurses, carpenters, secretaries, and others find a sense of spiritual belonging that run-of-the-mill society does not provide. Her innovative program, now adopted by thousands of people the world over, infuses vigorous inspiration into volunteers who seek to reanimate the world in the spirit of Christ. Her New Family, New Humanity, and New Parishes movements are all creative changes in the traditional concept of church organization.

It is through people like Brother Roger, Mother Teresa, and Chiara Lubich that great blessings flow from the church. More freedom should be given to people like these three who take seriously the challenge to be humble co-creators with God. Their messages should be studied. The next stage of human divine progress on the evolutionary scale needs dedicated men and women, geniuses of the spirit, blazing trails for the rest of us to follow.

In recent centuries, hundreds of protestant denominations have been born from new concepts and new revelations. Multitudes of cults and sects have arisen in other major religions, also. But how many of these sponsor research for more new ideas? The New Thought Movement, which includes The Unity School of Christianity and The Church of Religious Science, is a rare exception, one which strives for continuous innovation.

Charles S. Braden writes,

New Thought as now taught is the creation of a perpetually advancing mind. It is not satisfied with any system originating in other ages because systems do not grow while mind does. Indeed, change and growth are the silent mandates of Divinity.[17]

This is the kind of spirit the humble approach encourages, the spirit that puts no limits on our quest for more understanding of God. Elmer Gifford, a New Thought minister in Pasadena, writes:

The term New Thought is used to convey the idea of an ever-growing thought . . . man is an expanding idea in the mind of God . . . . As mind advances, the old forms die, because they no longer serve or satisfy men's needs . . . . New Thought can never therefore be a finished product and if it remains truly New Thought, it will never be completed enough to creedalize it . . . . Thought can never be final and still remain thought.

The well-known scientist and Christian, Vannevar Bush, said, "A faith that is over-defined is the very faith most likely to prove inadequate to the great moments of life."[18] Certainly the great moments of life include those crises in which imaginative responses are needed. Marceline Bradford has said:

What is explicit here is the fact that millions of intellectuals the world over have become disenchanted with backward-looking religious institutions . . . . In order to recapture the great thinking minds of the world, the clergy must turn their heads 180 degrees from past to future. With feet planted squarely in the present and eyes directed to the future, religious leaders can find factual bases in science for viable, solid, dynamic doctrines. For science and rationality are enemies not of religion—only of dogmatism.[19]

Even the best doctrines can affect some men like blinders on a horse. They can create a kind of tunnel vision. One unfortunate aspect of dogma is that it tends to belittle the infinite variety and nature of God. Dogmas are, after all, written by men; and men's apprehension of God is always limited. A serious danger in this is that the great new advances and breakthroughs in religion may come mainly from persons outside traditional church denominations. It would be unfortunate and a great waste of human energy if every advance or reform in the church had the nature of being a rival from the outside. Those well-meaning people within the church would naturally be more resistant, would tend to side with the conservatives, thus strengthening the forces behind the status quo and ultimately making change even harder to effect.

Most church concepts come directly or indirectly from ancient scriptures. The problem with scriptures is that they were written in a world of men whose minds were limited by cosmologies long since discredited. Today, we imagine the universe to be billions of times larger and older and more complex than the one conceived by the ancients. The Bible, for example, is a most wonderful collection of God's revelations. But, we should seek to interpret it not as containing and constricting within its statements all that there is to be known about God, but rather as directing each generation of God's people to far, far more of God than can ever be contained in the language and thought patterns of any age. To interpret the Bible in a narrow and restricted way, in accordance with the smallness of our mental grasp, is to make God smaller than our human minds. Two thousand years ago human minds were inevitably restricted to the range of their knowledge of the universe at that time, and they tended to confine their expression of divine revelation within that range. But, should we not be able to give a fuller and wider interpretation of divine revelation today, now that the range of our understanding of the universe God has created is so vastly enlarged by the discoveries God has allowed us to make? Why should we always try to express spiritual truths in obsolete words and ancient thought patterns? The fact that Jesus himself wrote nothing suggests that what he had to teach could not be frozen into words, even in his own age. Thus, he did not limit for future generations their range of human expression.

God has given us free will for new interpretations of eternal truths so that in our limited way we can be creative. But of course, free will gives us also the awesome power to build our own individual hells and heavens here on earth as well as for eternity. God knew free will would lead to problems, evils, and much suffering; but His divine plan seems to be that out of adversity we learn how to create; out of struggle we become more spiritual. Out of our desire to change the world for the better, we learn that the principle of creation is change and that through change will God's creations continue.

In conclusion, we might consider the description of reality given by Harold K. Schilling, a physicist:

I want to call attention to one more of the fundamental, constitutive characteristics of reality that provides, I feel, a criterion for the acceptability of values. Reality is historical and developmental, rather than merely inert and fixed; and it is creative and productive, rather than sterile and only conservative; and it is open, rather than closed, to new possibilities, and thrusts toward the future. Reality seems not to have come into being full-blown, but gradually, and over a long period of time.[20]

Schilling claims that matter and most likely all other forms of reality (forces? energies? spirits?) are fundamentally developmental. Reality is a continuing creative process in an unmistakable direction, "from the simple to the complex, from the small to the large, from the isolated individual entities to combina-

tions and integrated systems, and to community." Links between people, between churches, and between nations need to
be forged as a Mother Teresa or a Brother Roger or a Chiara
Lubich would forge them. From the study of both physics and
theology, the long-range cosmic trends seem obvious. In the
words of Schilling:

In any case, it seems clear that if our values are to be in harmony with long-range trends—and divine intent—they must be
such as not to hinder or inhibit development and change, and
the emergence of the utterly novel, but to facilitate them, and
thus to contribute to the building of a mankind and world
characterized at its ground by development . . . .

Let us have no quarrel with any theologian. Let us happily
admit that his concepts and doctrines may be right. But let us
listen most carefully to any theologian who is humble enough
to admit also that he may be wrong—or at least that his great
insights do not close the door to great insights by others. Let us
seek to learn from each other. Let us always keep trying to
increase our humility.

VIII   Spiritual Progress

The idea of progress became a major goal in human thinking only a few centuries ago in the West, and less than a century ago in Asia and Africa. Men thought that the world (universe) was static or moved in cycles, not in an upward curve called progress. Therefore there was little if any urge towards scientific research. There was no concept of evolution for the earth, for the universe, or for living things. Therefore men lacked the urge to try by research to speed up or increase the course of evolution. Until clear concepts of progress and evolution were formulated in the eighteenth and nineteenth centuries, people felt no need to use scientific research to understand the laws of nature and society.

This static viewpoint still hinders most religions. Neither the Koran, the Bible, nor the ancient scriptures of Asia say much about progress, and they say even less about research. Even now in the United States, the hotbed of research and progress, church bodies do little to help in the evolution of religious thought. They do almost nothing resembling the forward-looking research being done in the great scientific laboratories of corporations and universities. Within the different religious denominations of the church, the minor activities called research are essentially archeological, concerned with the excavations of ancient cities, the search for lost scriptures, or another modern translation of an ancient book. In the United States alone over forty billion dollars are spent yearly on scientific research, but almost nothing on spiritual research.

It is small wonder, then, that some people believe religion is gradually becoming obsolete. Mankind is racing forward in harnessing energy and understanding the nature of matter, but in spiritual growth the human race sometimes appears to be stuck in the stone or perhaps iron age. For thousands of years, numerous wise men and women have meditated and speculated about God. But so far there have been almost no experiments connected with spiritual realities in the same way that experiments are conducted by chemists and physiologists. Suppose chemistry were still dominated by alchemists searching ancient scriptures for lost secrets. What scientific breakthroughs would be produced by that thought pattern? Does this resemble in some ways the mental pattern of our churches and seminaries today?

We should listen to the warning implied in the anthropological studies of Anthony Wallace, who claims that in the last hundred thousand years of human history more than one hundred thousand different religions have flourished and disappeared. Wallace points out that this is surely evidence that in human nature there is always an abiding "sense of God." But, it is also a clear indication that concepts of God which are too small do become obsolete and vanish. History is replete with little gods who died. Herbert Menken compiled a list of over a hundred deities whose names now appear only in history books or as inscriptions on old monuments. Most likely they were much too finite to be gods at all. Belief in them died out because they were too statically or narrowly conceived; and they did not keep pace with the growth of men's minds, with the new knowledge, and the revelations the universal creative spirit continually gives to His children.

Often we read the words "religious revival" or "church renewal." Both are desirable; but they are not enough. What would it mean if people spoke in this way about astronomy, physics, chemistry, or medicine? Would "renewal of medical science" signify a lack of progress in the past needing new ideas? Would "revival of chemistry" imply a dying science in need of reviving or a need to restudy the ideas in the ancient books? To revive the old is not enough to keep theology in the vanguard of the knowledge explosion.

Religious thought should progress along with the social, political, economic, and scientific environment, or people will grow dissatisfied and abandon belief systems that appear to have little basis in reality. A *New York Times* study covering 1957 to 1970 chronicled Americans' replies to the question, "At the present time do you think religion as a whole is increasing its influence in American life or losing its influence?" The percentage who thought religion was indeed losing influence increased from fourteen percent in 1957 to seventy-five percent in 1970. Reasons given for this decline in religious influence included statements that religion was "outdated" or "not relevant in today's world." The report stated that these results revealed one of the most dramatic reversals in opinion in the history of polling.[21]

The Gallup organization has found even greater religious decline in Europe. Every nation in Europe has lower church attendance percentage-wise than in America. In some nations still considered heavily Christian, church attendance by adults now averages below ten percent. Such shrinkage appears in practically all the large, older Christian denominations. Also in the twentieth century, the percentage of practicing Buddhists and Hindus in the world population has decreased. As yet, the major denominations have rarely hired impartial scientists to study the causes of decline or the possible remedies.

Along with the decline in regular religious attendance at older chruches, hundreds of new religious groups have formed in recent times, and many of them have grown like wildfire in the last ten years. When the twentieth century began, for instance, there were no major denominations called "pentecostal" or "charismatic." Yet, beginning without any formal organization in dozens of nations, more than a hundred new denominations of these kinds have sprung up full of zeal and missionary outreach. In the United States alone, over fifty million people now describe themselves as "born again Christians." The first

World Congress of Charismatics drew over fifty thousand dele-
gates to Kansas City in 1977 from all over the earth.

Television programs run by churches in the United States
draw audiences ten times greater than similar programs of
thirty years ago. At least a dozen church programs on television
and radio enjoy audiences in the millions every week. More
new church buildings are being erected than ever before. Cir-
culation of church newspapers and magazines in the United
States is breaking all-time records. In South Korea, the number
of Christians doubled in the latest ten years and also in the ten
years before that. Another doubling is expected in the next
ten years.

Young people are responding with enthusiasm to new inter-
denominational and international youth clubs and organizations. Youth for Christ, Young Life, Inter-Varsity, and Campus
Crusade have become very influential. In fact, Bill Bright's
Campus Crusade has recently announced a campaign to raise
one billion dollars for religious revival. This is the largest goal
ever set for public donations by any charity of any kind any-
where in the history of man.

With this sudden upsurge in new religious activities, and with
the need to keep religion relevant to the times, churches and
foundations should now appropriate manpower and money for
joint theological-scientific research. Governments should spon-
sor such impartial research just as they do science and cultural
research. Because natural scientists understand the scientific
method better than most theologians, they should undertake
research projects independent of religious denominations and
develop suitable methods of scientific inquiry into spiritual matters.

Recently scientific associations for this purpose are springing
up, such as the Institute on Religion in an Age of Science and
the Center for Advanced Study in Religion and Science, both at
Rollins College, Florida, and the American Scientific Affiliation
at 5 Douglas Avenue, Elgin, Illinois (60120), and the Christian
Medical Society at 1122 Westgate, Oak Park, Illinois (60301).
Also, there is in Brussels the International Academy of Re-

ligious Sciences affiliated with the International Academy of the Philosophy of Sciences. Similar institutes concerned with science and theology have sprung up in recent years in Heidelberg and Munich in Germany, and in Strasbourg and Metz in France, not to mention others.

Even more exciting is the vision of a new theology now being born called the Theology of Science. Professor Ralph Wendell Burhoe waxes poetic about this vision:

. . . it is still my bet that at several points in the next few years and decades the traditional theological and religious communities will find the scientific revelations a gold mine, and that by early in the third millennium A.D. a fantastic revitalization and universalization of religion will sweep the world. The ecumenical power will come from a universalized and credible theology and related religious practices, not from the politics of dying institutions seeking strength in pooling their weaknesses . . . .

. . . I cannot imagine a more important bonanza for theologians and the future of religion than the information lode revealed by the scientific community . . . . It provides us with a clear connection between human values, including our highest religious values, and the cosmic scheme of things.

. . . My prophecy, then, is that God talk, talk about the supreme determiner of human destiny, will in the next century increasingly be fostered by the scientific community.[22]

Another striking phenomenon is the number of books on theology being written by mathematicians, physicists, biologists, and other natural scientists. Many are listed in the bibliography of this book. Some scientists are reporting the results of their research on the observable effects of divine activity in the world. For example, Sir Alister Hardy, the marine biologist at Manchester College, Oxford, is publishing a six-volume series on the nature of religious experience. Journals, such as *Zygon*, a quarterly published by Rollins College, Winter Park, Florida (32789), were founded to publish articles on the relationship between science and religion. To paraphrase slightly William James, "Let empiricism once become associated with religion

. . . and I believe that a new era of religion as well as of science will be ready to begin." Perhaps it already has.

An age of "experimental theology" may be beginning. This term is used to indicate the study of unseen spiritual realities by concentrating on observable data resulting from spiritual events, changes, and differences in physical phenomena. Religious researchers should discuss ideas and propositions as openly as philosophers, and devise appropriate experiments to uncover new data about spiritual laws in the same way that scientists study the laws of nature. The great challenge at the present moment is to distinguish the real differences between the methodologies used to study the nature of physical phenomena and the methodologies to be used in inquiry into the nature of spiritual reality. The astronomer Carl Sagan wrote:

It was an astonishing insight by Albert Einstein, central to the theory of general relativity, that gravitation could be understood by setting the contracted Riemann-Christoffel tensor equal to zero. But this contention was accepted only because one could work out the detailed mathematical consequences of the equation, see where it made predictions different from those of Newtonian gravitation, and then turn to experiment to see which way Nature votes. In three remarkable experiments—the deflection of starlight when passing near the sun; the motion of the orbit of Mercury, the planet nearest to the sun; and the red shift of spectral lines in a strong stellar gravitational field—Nature voted for Einstein. But without these experimental tests, very few physicists would have accepted general relativity. There are many hypotheses in physics of almost comparable brilliance and elegance that have been rejected because they did not survive such a confrontation with experiment. In my view, the human condition would be greatly improved if such confrontations and willingness to reject hypotheses were a regular part of our social, political, economic, religious and cultural lives.[23]

It is generally acknowledged today in scientific circles that the so-called immutable laws of matter are merely descriptions of the way things usually happen. But every few years some scientist collects new data or proposes a new theory that requires some old law to be rewritten. We frequently hear of doctors proving that a certain treatment used in medicine a generation ago was worse than useless. In general, scientists are ready to test and accept new ideas that support the foundation of science and build on it, while repenting of inadequate theories and ideas that more recent evidence tends to discredit. A difference between scientists and theologians seems to be that whereas scientists and doctors are humbly admitting error, some theologians resent their pet ideas being challenged or criticized. In earlier, more barbaric days, religious authorities occasionally burned at the stake or crucified "upstarts" who claimed to have new revelations or alternative spiritual insights, even when they did not strike at the foundation of faith. Why should men of God be less willing to listen sympathetically to new ideas than scientists?

The possibility of a great new reformation depends upon scientists humble enough to admit that the unseen is vastly greater than the seen, and upon theologians humble enough to admit that some older concepts of God may need to grow. By using the humble approach, both can develop a vastly larger cosmology and a wider, deeper theology. Scientists, who are usually ready to have their theories rigorously tested, should undertake joint research projects with theologians in studying the relationship between science and religion. Their major contribution may be to show theologians the value of being open-minded, and the benefits that can be derived from a methodology that is willing to include new hypotheses rather than to excommunicate new hypothesizers. It would be a fabulous start if more religious leaders would encourage or merely allow their followers to read literature that challenges some older concepts. After all, a church whose doctrine cannot survive the fire of experimentation may lose its ability to set its members on fire with zeal and devotion. It may become as one of the dead churches which are now only a forgotten name in a dusty book.

No one can foresee exactly which research projects for spiritual progress should be undertaken or even the specific form that empirical inquiry may take in this realm. Nor can anyone foresee which experiments will prove fruitful. When research in electricity began in the eighteenth century, no one could have possibly predicted it would lead to telephones, X rays, and television. Research in the physical sciences shows that the great majority of projects result in no useful invention. Dr. Paul Ehrlich experimented with six-hundred-and-six chemicals before finding Salvarsan, the first cure for syphilis, called the "magic bullet." In natural science, research is largely a matter of trial and error. In empirical science it is only through multitudes of experiments that one new fact can be established.

No one can say in advance just what discoveries will be made by proper research in the science of the soul. Just as most medical experiments produce nothing immediately useful, very few empirical attempts to determine laws of the spirit will yield verifiable truth. Institutions willing to finance research can only accept project proposals and then select the few that seem to offer the best in terms of cost-benefit ratio. Where and how to undertake research will be learned from earlier research and from the free flow of information between researchers. This process of ongoing self-inquiry must become the normal method of spiritual studies since everything is so new and there are so few models to imitate. For example, experiments in natural science that produce the same results each time, like those in gravity, may not provide the paradigm for experiments appropriate to spirit. It is possible, however, that a statistical approach may yield limited results in a range of spiritual matters, just as sociological patterns are determined by studies of large groups of people or aggregates of similar events. For example, recent statistical experiments have convinced most people not that every smoker dies of lung cancer but rather that lung cancer is ten times more likely for cigarette smokers than other people.

At first, not all church dignitaries may welcome experimental questioning of this kind. They may not foresee the benefits from new discoveries in experimental theology. Many will find it easy to point out errors in the humble approach and this line of experimental inquiry, for there are sure to be multitudes of errors, as with all new projects. But if ninety-nine percent of spiritual experiments were failures and only one percent were to yield enduring benefits, this measure of success would be higher than that of the natural scientists.

Must it always be that resistance to progress is more often found in churches than among scientists or businessmen? Can breakthroughs in religion and great new advances come only from persons outside the hierarchies of church denominations? Why are more persons desiring progress attracted to careers in physiology or electronics rather than the ministry? Why are dictatorial "pronouncements" frequent in church councils but almost unknown in conventions of physicians or physicists? Is the basic cause a lack of humility? The smaller a man is the more likely he is to deny God altogether or to claim he knows all about God. Bigger men are usually more humble. God promises to reveal Himself to those who seek. If the seekers are physicists, then physics progresses more in its own realm than the church does in its realm. Can theology, once called the queen of the sciences, also use appropriate empirical methods of research? Can theology learn anything from the statistical methods of science? If that is possible, maybe it can become an adventure in the invention of research projects leading to the discovery and proof of facts about life in the spiritual universe. Likewise, researchers in spiritual matters should try out many different forms of inquiry and not be easily discouraged either. Researchers in relatively limited fields like biology have discovered only a little fraction of what may be known: hence, researchers about the Infinite could not expect to produce a systematic theology which is comprehensive and unchanging. With proper humility, they may hope to discover only a little more about man's relation to his Creator. Open-minded questioning and open-minded faith are quite similar. Both derive from humility. Both affirm that most is unknown and thereby keep the door open to further investigation and progress. Worshipers of every faith should seek and welcome opportunities to give proof and to determine the laws of the spiritual life which may convince the skeptics. Over six centuries ago, John Duns Scotus taught that the human intellect can know God through natural reason only up to a point, for knowledge about the Infinite cannot itself be infinite. Mere human intellect can discover a few spiritual truths without any miraculous illuminations, and even then it can take in relatively little of the living God and His ways.

As we have said, theological researchers must learn general theory as well as methodologies from scientists. Whatever their special field of interest, theologians should become to some extent theologians of science. Scientific revelations may be a gold mine for revitalizing religion in the twenty-first century.

The scientific concepts that appear inimical to religion at a primitive level of analysis may in the end contribute to the development of new universal symbols and languages that will keep human values and religious truths viable. Only by ongoing dialogue between theologians and scientists will the new patterns of culture emerge and preserve a sense of meaning to human life in the new age. Burhoe agrees with Anthony Wallace that religion

is the very center of man's most advanced evolutionary thrust to find order or organization, governing his overall attitudes and behaviors with respect not only to himself and his fellow men but also with regard to the ultimate realities of that cosmos in which he lives and moves and has his being.

In general, discussion about God in the next century will have to take place within the scientific community if it is to be widely relevant to the future society. It may be wise to begin those discussions now. Theologians following the humble way should now invite biologists, behaviorists, psychologists—scientists in all related fields—to offer courses in their seminaries and divinity schools.

However much we may agree or disagree with such a program and its predictions, it seems apparent that the scientific approach can rapidly produce a theology of such cosmic dimensions that it may resist the historic trend of obsolescence. Leaders of older religions should humbly recognize that God may be vastly greater than their earlier concepts of Him. Scientists should humbly recognize that they have gained very little insight into the nature of infinite God who creates universes both seen and unseen. God transcends and upholds all of nature, physical and spiritual. Nothing is separate from God. Human scholars participating in God's creative process can do so only by working in concert with the natural and spiritual laws of the universe.

The possibility that the earth may enter a new era of spirit beyond the noosphere is even more exciting than Burhoe's prediction regarding the theology of science. In fact, theology of science may be one step toward that era of spirit. As we have said earlier, the development of man on earth may not be the end of evolution, but only the beginning of it. It has always been difficult to imagine what would come next. However, the multitude of discoveries in this century related to things previously unseen, points toward the likelihood of even more amazing discoveries aiding human evolution in the future.

Sixty years ago, Professor Charles P. Steinmetz, director of General Electric Laboratories in Schenectady, said that when the great discoveries of the twentieth century go down in history, they will not be in natural science but in the realm of the spirit. Sixty years later we see little evidence of these discoveries. Could the reason be that we have poured more money and manpower into the natural sciences? Are we still blind to the possibility that the ever-new discoveries in natural sciences are actually data revealing the nature of the universal creative Spirit?

Let us try to devise some possible research projects in religion that might resemble current research in the physical world of science, medicine, economics, and politics. To serve as illustrations, here are a few various possibilities:

THE MINISTERIAL LONGEVITY PHENOMENON

Records kept for two hundred years by the Presbyterian Ministers' Fund, one of the oldest life insurance companies in the world, show that Christian ministers live ten years longer than other men. Why? A research team of ministers, theologians, psychologists, and physicians might discover interesting information on this phenomenon. Has any scientist yet collected statistical data relating to whether medical doctors live longer than Christian Science practitioners?

HEALING AS MIRACLE

Several church denominations have collected thousands of well-documented cases of divine healing, but they have not yet been subjected to scientific studies by critically minded doctors, historians, and sociologists. Such studies may reveal how, why, when, and to whom divine healing most likely occurs.

THE RISE-UP-AND-WALK PROBLEM

Some doctors agree that the patients' rate of healing, after having the same operation, varies as greatly as three hundred percent among different people. In addition to studying the biological, anatomical, chemical, and psychological reasons for this, studies into the religious attitudes of patients might show a correlation between spiritual conviction and physical recovery.

THE JOY-TO-THE-WORLD QUESTION

St. Paul says that joy is one of the fruits of the spirit. Recent research has been conducted by psychologists on this question of why some people experience unexpected, intense rushes of joy while others do not. A theological consultant to these studies might be able to discover what *spiritual* factors contribute to the experience of joy. Are people who trust wholeheartedly in God generally more joyous than a control group of agnostics? Which groups of people describe themselves as happy most of the time? Which do not? Which groups radiate happiness? A scholar or researcher could raise interesting and pertinent issues on these questions that psychologists might otherwise overlook.

THE "BORN AGAIN" QUESTION

When people are "born again," or "filled with the spirit," they say they are no longer the same. Has anyone yet subjected such changes to rigorous testing? Scientists might be able to detect visible evidence about how the Holy Spirit alters or improves the lives of people who say they are filled with it. What characteristics "before and after" do these people exhibit? Maybe certain changes can be determined and described in science journals. What might be the outward aspects of the indwelling Holy Spirit?

PSYCHIATRIC HEALTH

Do persons who become charismatic Christians through the experience of Pentecost need psychiatric help less than they did before? Maybe scientists could collect statistics on the frequency of visits to psychiatrists before and after the charismatic experience. Studies of Catholics who see psychiatrists reveal that a great number of them no longer go to confession. Is there something about professing one's religion or confessing one's sins, i.e., discussing one's interior life openly with others, that eliminates the need for a psychiatrist's couch? Studies on this topic might be conducted.

GOD AND THE PSYCHOTIC

Psychiatric teams which include pastoral theologians might embark on new studies of patients in mental institutions to correlate types of insanity or psychoses with previous religious convictions. Are there significantly larger or smaller percentages of mental patients who were Christian ministers, atheists, Christian Science practitioners, doctors, nuns, or scientists?

THE PRODIGAL-SONS-AND-DAUGHTERS PROBLEM

It should not be left solely to sociologists, social workers, and parole officers to collect statistics on young criminal offenders in our society. Sunday schools, churches, mosques, and synagogues have been traditionally hailed as bulwarks of decent societies. Do youthful offenders come from families in which religious worship is strong, mediocre, or weak? Ministers and theologians should participate in these kinds of studies. It should be possible to collect statistics on young persons indicted for crimes to discover what proportion attended Sunday schools or were reared by parents who regularly attended church or mosque or synagogue.

FAITH AND HEALTH

> Is it a fact that godly men have less heart trouble (or stomach trouble) than atheists? Has anyone bothered to make a careful investigation of this? Does any learned journal report such investigations?

These are but a few examples of the type of research projects in science and religion that institutes, academies, and seminaries might undertake. These examples are meant to be only thought-provoking. It is hoped they will suggest multitudes of other similar research projects.

Experiments with unquestionable scientific controls are convincing to educated leaders. Therefore people who love God should diligently work to devise thousands of appropriate, theologically and scientifically acceptable "experiments." Also, they should write articles for science journals and collect bibliographies of experimental research of this kind in the study of spiritual laws and observable effects of the unseen Spirit. Experiments by scientists who have earned the respect of other scientists can be especially influential. If the results of these inquiries prove to be convincing to college teachers, journalists, and government policy-makers, then the course of human history could be basically influenced towards bringing to all peoples "the fruit of the spirit."

To advocate experiments that would provide concrete evidence in religious issues is very different from advocating "free thought." The difference involves imagination and speculation versus critical testing and verification. Those who love God should participate in experiments related to spiritual matters and not leave them to researchers in psychic phenomena or extrasensory perception. The serious, conscientious researchers in those fields may be outnumbered by multitudes of the fuzzy-minded or opportunistic.

The better religious journals should publish articles discussing how far discoveries of astronomers and physicists may really be old revelations by God newly understood by man. Wherever truth is found, God is speaking. If the voice of science, however indirectly, is one of the voices of God, it should be listened to with reverence. If laws of the spirit are fragments of knowledge about God, so also in their way are the laws of nature. Churches and other religious groups should honor scientists who are committed to studying the divine as it manifests itself in the physical world. Seminaries should invite more scientists to lecture, and offer courses on topics related to theology of science, cosmology, and experimentation. We may be in for some surprising discoveries.

We may reaffirm what Henry Drummond discovered in the 1850s, namely that the supernatural is more natural than strange. He suggested that:

What is required to draw Science and Religion together again—for they began the centuries hand in hand—is the disclosure of the naturalness of the supernatural. Then, and not till then, will men see how true it is, that to be loyal to all of Nature, they must be loyal to the part defined as spiritual . . . . And even as the contribution of Science to Religion is the vindication of the naturalness of the Supernatural, so the gift of Religion to Science is the demonstration of the supernaturalness of the Natural. Thus, as the Supernatural become slowly Natural, will also the Natural become slowly Supernatural, until in the impersonal authority of Law men everywhere recognize the Authority of God.[24]

If Drummond was correct, we might find that members of both the scientific and religious communities have a common base from which to speak to each other.

Hence, the humble approach can be put into practice in a concrete way beginning now. The only requirement is that scholars in all fields recognize the mutual dependence and interrelationship of their disciplines. The next step is to bridge those mythical chasms that encourage experts in one field to talk only to other experts in that field. It may not be as difficult as some people have previously thought. Henry Margenau, professor of physics at Yale, has said:

Science now acknowledges as real a host of entities that cannot be described completely in mechanistic or materialistic terms. For these reasons the demands which science makes upon religion when it examines religion's claims to truth have become distinctly more modest; the conflict between science and religion has become less sharp, and the strain of science upon religion has been greatly relieved. In fact, a situation seems to prevail in which the theologian can seriously listen to a scientist expounding his methodology with some expectation that the latter may ring a sympathetic chord. It is not altogether out of the question that the rules of scientific methodology are now sufficiently wide and flexible to embrace some forms of religion within the scientific domain.[25]

Mutual dialogue between studies of the natural and of the supernatural should begin in earnest, and we might put to rest once and for all those vague and damaging old claims that science has no soul and the soul has no basis in scientific fact.

IX The Benefits of Competition

The humble approach does not promise security; it is risky, strenuous, and dangerous. It will not be adopted by the weak of heart or will. Its advocates will be the strong-hearted and clear-minded, those who are unafraid of competition and struggle. Only those with a healthy faith in God and confidence in themselves will survive in this arena of ideas. The humble approach demands of its followers a dedication to freedom and a vigilant suspicion of security. As Benjamin Franklin put it in America's revolutionary days, "Anyone who gives up a little freedom for a little security does not deserve either."

The greatest development in human history has been the increasing possibility of each separate individual having the personal freedom to learn, to grow, and to design his or her own life. This is a relatively new phenomenon. Throughout recorded history most governments have been authoritarian, characterized by the rule of a few over the many. Such governments allowed little popular influence on decision-making in domestic laws or foreign policy, and little freedom of religion or speech. Most societies have not been "open" for the great majority of the populace.

Beginning around the time of the Renaissance, more emphasis was given to the expression of individual personality, to the notion that opportunity was a vital human concern, and to the idea that personal truth was more important that collective truth dictated from on high. Such notions led to the Reformation—a great breakthrough in religious freedom. The libertarian revolutions of the eighteenth century, coupled with the new scientific discoveries, produced the free world as we know it, a world where the individual is important, where a man's or woman's opinion should be listened to, where each person has a right to choose the basics of a decent life: career, marriage partner, school, religion, place of residence, and free speech.

Freedom fosters competition which yields progress. When the creativity and ingenuity and competition of individuals were set free, the result was progress and prosperity beyond anything ever imagined before. In the free world, amazing progress was made in the areas of education, religion, production, science, art, and literature. Inventions multiplied and culture was enriched. In God's ongoing creation, He seems to favor free, tolerant, open-minded individuals as His helpers. This individual freedom is enhanced by other freedoms—those of worship, free speech, free enterprise, and the right to own property. It is interesting that God does not force His good upon us. Instead He gives us the free will to claim or reject the blessings of life.

Only God knows whether the bounteous acceleration of progress and increase in knowledge over the past five hundred years will end. But if it does, most likely it will be halted by the greatest road-block to human progress and happiness: authoritarian government. Freedom requires government. As Jefferson put it, government is instituted to "secure" our liberties. But excessive government, the author of the Declaration of Independence warned, is the chief destroyer of freedom. Government maintains freedom to the extent that it gives each person freedom from domination by others, but unrestrained government intervention in the economic, cultural, or spiritual life of its citizens reduces that freedom. More research needs to be done on which government activities protect, and which restrict, freedom. Lincoln believed that government should do for its people those things that they could not do for themselves. But what are these activities?

Without going into detail, a democratic government by enacting clear and impartial laws usually protects freedom, whereas governments which respond to the whims of a dictator, an elite, or a bureaucracy lead to fear among the citizenry and domination of the people by the government instituted to serve them.

A most basic protection against bad government is the freedom to criticize and defy it. Those who can write or speak against those in government without fear of reprisal, are relatively free. But when the government is allowed to harass its citizens without due process of law, then freedom is a myth. Another safeguard of freedom is the right to ownership of property. People who have assets to own, use, and sell are much freer than those wholly dependent on assets owned by government or others.

No one knows for certain, but most people in the world are probably uneasy with the idea of individual freedom. In Erich Fromm's phrase, they seek an "escape from freedom." These people feel comfortable only under strong authority, as, for instance, when a dictator of some sort tells them exactly what to do and think. This is why democracy has not proven to be a popular form of government in every nation. It is why many of America's Founders thought a democratic experiment would be short-lived. This history of democracies is that they don't last. Most people hunger for a demagogue to give them bread and circuses, fix their status, and give them a cog-role in the machinery of society. Such persons are only half alive. They seldom seek or achieve much progress, for progress comes only from the free, the pioneering innovators who take advantage of life's opportunities. It is difficult to imagine that God's creative purpose is served by those half-alive persons content to be only cogs in the regimented society.

Calvin held that people will instinctively worship, but if not taught to worship God they will create idols to worship. Today more people worship idols than God, and those idols are often the institutions and governments created by men themselves. A good example can be found in the communist world. Eight hundred million Chinese communists venerated Mao Tse-tung as if he were a god. For many years more copies of his "little red book" were sold than either the Bible or the Koran. In general, communist dedication and devotion to government resembles religion. Demanding total surrender and total loyalty, communism, like a political religion, formulates elaborate and inflexible doctrines to control every aspect of life. It resembles slavery. It may claim to be revolutionary but in actual fact it is reactionary, a regress to the kind of serfdom typical of the Dark Ages when government and church dictated the details of each individual's daily life.

No one knows why God allows his people to fall into captivity, as has happened so often in history. Perhaps He allows communism to establish a place in people's minds and hearts because of the vacuum created by religions that failed to develop and progress with the "knowledge explosion." Maybe the communist threat serves the purpose of challenging the increasing religious and social rigidities that occur when there are no great challenges to face. Adversity does seem to serve a creative purpose. An omnipotent God might permit dictators to stamp out religion for hundreds of millions of people—for an ultimately useful purpose: to awaken and challenge the faithful. It may be a "call to arms" for His children to take a stand against tyranny and fight for freedom so that progress might continue. Tyranny of any kind hinders the great creative process of evolution.

Communism, too, will eventually become obsolete, because after the first revolutions, its doctrines became rigid and forbade change. In the rise of any new ideology, rigid doctrine leads to the triumph of rigidity itself. Then it causes decay and obsolescence. Decay seems already evident in many communist countries because their governments forbid freedom in so many areas of personal life—economic, religious, intellectual, and artistic. Being so earth-centered, communism is as narrow-minded as the cosmologies of the ancients who pictured the universe extending for only a few thousand miles and enclosed within the star-studded spheres of heaven.

Communism was founded on hatred between the classes and envy of those to whom God gives more talents. So it is unlikely to uplift human nature. Communism substitutes the collective structure of government for the individual as the giver of welfare to the poor. But the greater blessing from giving goes not to the receiver but to the loving giver. Jesus said, "It is more blessed to give than to receive." (Acts 20:35 KJV.) The giver is the one who is uplifted and spiritualized by the gift. When giving is channeled through government by force, it has an opposite effect on the producer whose produce is forcibly given. Forced charity does not uplift either the giver or the receiver. It dehumanizes and hinders the spiritual growth of all the people. Forced charity may be better than no charity, but it is a pitiful substitute. Never did Jesus advocate government welfare! Never did the disciples or prophets of other religions either, except those who were earthly dictators themselves.

Based on man's vices rather than virtues, communism is unlikely to uplift human nature. All in all, communism seems to be one of those worldviews out of step with our modern notion of progress, a notion that includes personal freedom and a humble acceptance of scientific data suggesting a spiritual realm beyond material reality.

People who like "all-pervasive" government seem to be attracted to careers in government offices, whether of churches or nations. Perhaps this explains why so many in church headquarters advocate expansion of government regulations. Moreover, advocates of policies leading to more regimentation seem to form multitudes of lobbying organizations; whereas those who like more freedom for each individual are less likely to get organized. It is strange how rarely church leaders speak out today against dictatorial governments or atheistic regimes. Why are they so silent on great moral issues, such as personal freedom?

Rather than advocate more individual freedom, some religious leaders, particularly the bureaucratic-minded ones, support a union of all Christian denominations. At first, union sounds desirable. Such advocates say it is a scandal that Christ's churches are divided among themselves. One slogan often heard is that "united we stand but divided we fall." But should reconciliation in Christ mean the institution of a centralized authority?

Some leaders once hoped that the World Council of Churches would lead to a world union of churches. Many writers, especially some Hindus, advocate a union of all religions. We should make every effort to tolerate each other, listen to each other, and eventually love each other. Many benefits flow from sharing literature and information with each other and from facilities to help us lovingly listen to each other.

But centralized authority from a bureaucracy of united world churches is the prelude to stagnation. Religion will grow not in union but through freedom and competition. Originality and discovery derive from variety, not uniformity. If each denomination of every faith sent missionaries to every other denomination lovingly to explain and share their vision with others, then we would all learn more. If our concepts are divine truths, then they will not suffer in competition with other concepts. What a happy competition it will be if each of us is lovingly trying to give to the other his holy treasures. How selfish it would be for us not to witness to others and send missionaries abroad! But likewise, other religions or denominations want lovingly to witness to us and we should receive their unselfish missionaries with gratitude and brotherly joy.

Among scientists there is friendly rivalry between those holding different theories and those belonging to different schools of thought; and if churches do not foster something similar, they will appear old-fashioned and then irrelevant. God's long creative process has always led to greater diversity. Let us rejoice in diversity and avoid establishing any monolithic church. By spirited and loving competition, the truth will be purified and strengthened.

Progress comes from competition and this is what churches need most. Competition between religions may be an advantage. By free competition the wheat is gradually separated from the chaff. The true religions should welcome competition because then they are put to the test, and if they are true, they will survive. Only an inferior religion needs to prevent competition, lest its inferiority should be exposed. The long history of the evolution of plant and animal varieties seems to show that competition is God's chosen method of developing his creation. Why should it be different in the realm of spirit and religion?

Tolerance is a divine virtue but can become a vehicle for apathy. Millions of people are thoroughly tolerant toward diverse religions; but rarely do such people go down in history as creators or benefactors or leaders of any religion. The use of tolerance is mainly to keep us humble so that we may listen with an open heart and an inquiring mind. We want our neighbor to share and try to convey to us the brilliant light which transformed his life—the fire in his soul—not his least-common denominator. More than tolerance, we need competition. When men on fire for a great gospel compete lovingly to give their finest treasures to each other, then everyone benefits. If we enthusiastically share the inspiring highlights of each faith and church, then we are all richer. On our daily upward struggle toward communion and union with our Creator, we need all the inspirations and revelations which every child of God can give us.

In summarizing the views of Teilhard, Wildiers said there are two ways of unifying mankind, by coercion and by sympathy and affection. The truly creative force is a combination of sympathy and affection. Even at lower levels than the human, these forces operate to unify and create the universe. They are

the constructive forces in the cosmos as a whole. The atoms were impelled towards one another by an intrinsic affinity; and so the molecules came into being. The cells coalesced; and thence the great diversity of organisms appeared.[26]

Another area in life where the law of competition is being undermined is in the lack of teaching of religion in our schools. In recent years American schools have come to teach mainly secular rather than religious knowledge. No wonder misbehavior is increasing. Where are the schools and colleges which still consider it their first duty to teach honesty, ethics, character, morals, self-control, philosophy of life, and religion? Most churches seem content to devote only one hour a week in Sunday school to teach our children principles governing spiritual growth. Many Sunday schools rely only on amateur teachers and require no homework, no grades, and no tests. How woefully ignorant our children would be if we relied on such methods to teach history or science! It is no wonder that we are said to be rearing generations of moral and spiritual weaklings.

Until the last century, most colleges and universities were founded and supported by religious groups. Often the main purpose was to prepare priests and ministers for their lifework. Most schools for children were founded and taught by religious people. Now, most of these schools and colleges, in the name of impartiality, have abandoned responsibility for teaching religion in favor of secular subjects. The desire for impartiality does not mean we should eliminate religion from the curriculum.

In the name of equality or social justice, governments increasingly dominate educational policies and squeeze out the church-supported schools. In the United States, the courts rule today that the Constitution forbids religion in public schools, even though the authors of the Constitution had no such intent. The men who framed the Constitution of the United States would be dumbfounded by the Supreme Court decision that forbade worship in public schools. The founders of our nation intended to ensure free and fair competition between religions, not to stamp out religion. Their efforts to separate church and state were not efforts to abolish religious education in the classroom. Total omission of religion from schools prevents free competition. The net effect is to imply that only secular, not spiritual knowledge is respectable. New generations are being educated to be intellectual and cultural adults but spiritual and ethical infants.

Various methods have been devised to allow each child, or its parent, to choose from the broad spectrum of religious studies—from traditional world religions to atheism. There are ways to keep religion in our schools without favoring one denomination over the others. For example, each school could provide a room which could be used for thirty minutes a day by any religious or nonreligious group to present their beliefs or worship. Students or their parents could then choose which room they will study in.

Competition is God's law of the universe because through it the useless are gradually weeded out and change for the better occurs. God's law of evolution means progress. If we do not have free competition among ideas, even religious ideas, old and established theories will never be improved. They will never have to defend themselves. They may survive long after their time of usefulness. We should not abolish the discussion of religion in the classroom anymore than we should ban the discussion of political or biological theories.

We should not even ban worship. Rather, let us have different forms of worship in schools and allow our children to inspect and experience them all. Those which are most meaningfull will be well-attended. Those that students find worthless will eventually be discontinued. If we did this, there would be healthy and lively rivalry among various denominations and intense discussion about the Spirit. Some students might even discover their future careers as ministers or theologians or religious scholars because of exposure to religion at the lower levels of education. This is the humble approach: an open mind, a willingness to admit there might be alternative truths just as valuable as ours, and the fortitude to compete with others—to search, to discover and create the societies and religions of the future.

Another technique for providing free public education and religious instruction for those who desire it, would be for the government to compute its cost of educating each child for a year and then give to parents a voucher with which they could pay tuition costs at any school of their choice. The selected school would then redeem the voucher for cash from the government. Not only would such a system provide both free education *and* religious education; it would also introduce competition between schools which would lead to better teaching methods. Recently, certain churches in many nations have founded and financed church schools for the children of their members. At present, parents who want their children to learn character and religion in schools must pay twice; first in cash to the church school and then in compulsory taxes to the government for schools to which they will not send their children.

The wisdom of God is beyond the measure of men's minds. To most of us, the "survival of the fittest" seems cruel. God allows big fish to eat little fish, and he also allows millions of insects to die every hour. For many people, the idea that "survival of the fittest" builds stronger species does not justify the suffering. However, maybe God in his infinite wisdom and mercy so regulates the course of His creation that the suffering involved in this harsh law is the best way to build and enrich souls.

We should remind ourselves once more that to embark upon the humble approach is to ask for competition in the battle of ideas. To assure that the competition is fair, no church, no school, no government should seek to impose its system upon others who do not share their beliefs. Church-goers, students, and citizens need absolute freedom so that unfettered they might examine the rich variety of ideas in God's universe. We need to be constantly vigilant against any person, group, institution, or political party that would tyrannize our lives. To assure free competition, Thomas Jefferson proposed "eternal enmity over every form of tyranny over the mind of man."

X   Earth as a School

What is the purpose of life on earth? Many philosophers have said that God created the earth as a school for souls. Some say human souls are created out of the thoughts of God. God may have invented and created each body and mind as the temporary shell to house a soul during its childhood.

Rev. Earnest O. Martin said in 1962:

. . . spiritual development, the formation of a heavenly character. This is the purpose of life on this planet, which Swedenborg spoke of as a seminary for heaven. It is here that we grow into angelhood and begin to develop the potentialities that God sees within us. Heaven is essentially a quality of life, an inward condition or state in which men live in harmony with the will of God. And yet it is also a place—a real, tangible, substantial existence. Swedenborg's answer is that life is one. The natural world and the spiritual world are not two distinct, separate existences that have no relationship. We are spirits and from the day of our conception we are citizens of the spiritual world. Love, understanding, loyalty, friendship, patience, mercy,— these are spiritual realities the Lord seeks to instill in our lives here and now. The natural world is the theater in which our spirits operate and develop and grow. It is here that our loves, our attitudes and our desires are molded and find expression. That is why God has placed us here.

An omnipotent God could have created us all as angels instantly. But, He did not choose that method. A lifetime on earth may seem a slow way to create a soul. And eighteen billion years may seem a slow way to create the school building; but, let us remember that God also created time. Nels F. S. Ferré (1908–1972) used to remind us that God is not bound by time, for He created not only our universe but also both space and time. Time may have been created as the means and medium for learning, for growth, and for building the ability to give love. William Adams Brown (1865–1906) taught that the purpose of God in creating the world is to develop the Kingdom of God, or more specifically:

. . . the production of beings like the good God, and their union with Himself in the fellowship of love. . . . I is because the world as we know it today ministers to such a spiritual end that we believe it had its origin in the will of the holy and loving Father whom Christ reveals.[27]

The great question is this: How much progress can our soul make before our body becomes uninhabitable? To progress is to increase our love of God, our understanding of God, and our love for His children. Our body has a physical reality, but it is only a temporary shell. Death destroys only that which is fit for destruction. The butterfly developing in the chrysalis in due time splits and abandons the dead chrysalis and flies away on wings of amazing beauty undreamed of by the chrysalis or the caterpillar.

Various major religions have described earth as a school. The *Bhagavad-Gita* ("Song of God") teaches:

Whatever a man remembers at the last, when he is leaving the body, will be realized by him in the hereafter, because that will be what his mind has most constantly dwelt on during this life. Therefore you must remember me at all times and do your duty. If your mind and heart are set upon me constantly, you will come to me. Never doubt this . . . I am the Atman that dwells in the heart of every mortal creature; I am the beginning, the lifespan, and the end of all . . . one atom of myself sustains the universe.

Buddhism, teaching that the life of the spirit transcends the life of a man on earth, emphasizes that this life of the spirit is the only true reality and that on earth people should strive to grow spiritually through exercising free will, reason, love, and meditation.

Rev. Charles Neal, in 1976, expressed it in this way:

"Who then are we?" We are God's perfect children in the making. Each of us is evolving to perfection. But at this stage we do not yet have it made. Let us recognise that the Universe is a Cosmos. It is not slaphappy, disorganized, haphazard or accidental. It is an orderly system and its nature is to evolve. That is, to bring into the open through endless and infinitely slow degrees that which is already involved in it, namely Perfect Creation. God-mind moved on itself; It got an idea, to express Itself. It went to work, and out of the formless it created form. How did it all start? The "big bang" theory is as good as any. Possibly eons ago all space was filled with whirling gasses, minute particles of matter. Then drawn together by some force (love?) until they became compressed generating heat, then exploded into suns and stars. Eventually cooling through millions of years and forming various layers: the central core, the barysphere; the crust or lithosphere; then the waters forming the hydrosphere; then the atmosphere and finally the stratosphere. . . .

The nature of the Universe is to evolve. This is true of every part including rocks, minerals, plants, animals and man. This is also true of the very essence of the Universe, which is consciousness. Consciousness has been present in every stage. It is God-Mind seeking to express Itself as perfection. Consciousness evolves along with every other element. A rock is more limited in consciousness than the mineral it contains. A vegetable with its ability to grow is a still more highly evolved expression of consciousness. As the Persian poet wrote: "God sleeps in the mineral, dreams in the vegetable, stirs in the animal, and awakens in man." [28]

Earlier in the century, Teilhard, speaking from long years as a scientist, priest, and poet, said, "It is a law of the universe that in all things there is prior existence. Before every form there is a prior, but lesser evolved form. Each one of us is evolving towards the God-head." This evolving toward God may be our purpose on earth.

If earth is a school, who are the teachers? One teacher is called adversity. Why did God put souls into a world of tribulations? Why did He not just make souls perfect in the first place? Is not God vastly more far-sighted and infinitely wiser than we are? Maybe from God's perspective the sorrows and tribulations of this earth are the best way to educate souls.

Growth can come through trial and self-discipline. There is a wealth of evidence indicating that too much prosperity without work weakens character and causes us to become self-centered rather than God-centered. Spiritual growth and happiness do not come from getting but from learning to give. The great souls are the most rapidly growing souls. Trees and human bodies are limited in growth both in space and time, but is there any evidence that the individual soul is limited in its growth?

How could a soul understand divine joy or be thankful for heaven if it had not previously experienced earth? How could a soul comprehend the joy of surrender to God's will, if it had never witnessed the hell men make on earth by trying to rely on self-will or to rely on another frail human or on a soulless man-made government?

Maybe the earth was designed as a place of hardship because it is the best way to build a soul—the best way to teach spiritual joy versus the bodily ills. Why was it said that into every life some rain must fall? It is apparent that sometimes a great soul does not develop until that person has gone through some great tragedy. Let us humbly admit that God knows best how to build a soul. If the soul were born perfect, how would it understand or appreciate the absence of pain and sorrow? As a good father does not do his son's homework for him, so our Heavenly Father does what helps us to grow, not what we ask for. We should be thankful that God does not always give us the stupid things we ask for. St. Paul wrote:

More than this: let us even exult in our present sufferings, because we know that suffering trains us to endure, and endurance brings proof that we have stood the test, and this proof is the ground of hope. Such a hope is no mockery, because God's love has flooded our inmost heart through the Holy Spirit he has given us. (Romans 5:3-5 NEB.)

As a furnace purifies gold, so may life purify souls. When a man is born into the world, he is like a piece of charcoal. It is soft and amorphous so when rays of the sun fall upon it, it reflects nothing. Then in the crucible it is subjected to such intense pressure and heat that it is born again as a diamond. Next, it is cut with many facets by the master craftsman. Now when the sun's rays fall on it, it reflects the colors of the rainbow, creating a symphony of beauty and radiance. So it is with a man between the time he is born into the material world where he is cut and chipped and then born again into heaven when he begins to reflect the divine light of God. Maybe this was God's purpose for creating the crucible called earth.

How does a soul grow? Spiritual growth takes place through human reason and divine revelation, through communing with nature and God, and by diligent use of the talents He gives us as well as from learning how to make studied and wise choices. Man's capacity for choosing good over evil must be developed. In exercising our free will and choosing good, we demonstrate that we are created in the image of God. Each time we consciously prefer evil over good, we have failed another test in becoming more God-like. By being a positive creator in nature, rather than a destroyer, we become more and more like the infinite Creator.

Just as politics is essentially control over others, so is religion essentially control over, or overcoming of, self. Those who have learned to put aside completely their selfish egos become as a little child and enter into the kingdom of heaven. Our job is to be pure like a clean windowpane so that the truth and light of God can shine through—a radio receiver through which God's music enters the world. When we know this, we become constantly grateful to God and good things are attracted to us as to a magnet. St. Paul wrote, "For we are God's handiwork, created in Christ Jesus to devote ourselves to the good deeds, for which God has designed us." (Ephesians 8:10, NEB.)

There are many similarities between the Exodus story of forty years' wandering by the chosen people in the Wilderness of Sin before reaching the promised land "flowing with milk and honey," and the forty years wandering by each person between birth and the time when some learn the spiritual laws and reach heaven on earth. Often it takes forty years for a self-centered little animal to become a God-centered little angel. What are the marks of spiritual maturity? Do we put our trust in God or in man? Do we desire more to give than to get? These are marks of a mature soul.

Spiritual growth can be achieved in part by knowledge—by overcoming our ignorance and self-centeredness until we are in tune with the divine. Since God possesses all knowledge, any additional knowledge or understanding we can acquire makes us more like Him. As followers of the humble approach, we must always be alert to new discoveries and new insights into both spiritual and natural phenomena. We should never imagine we know enough. That would be like saying we know God in his totality, which would border on the blasphemous. Ralph Waldo Trine put it this way:

Great spiritual truths—truths of the real life—are the same in all ages, and will come to any man and any woman who will make the conditions whereby they can come. God speaks wherever He finds a humble listening ear, whether it be Jew or Gentile, Hindu or Parsee, American or East Indian, Christian or Bushman. It is the realm of the inner life that we should wisely give more attention to. The springs of life are all from within. We must make the right mental condition, and we must couple with it faith and expectancy. We should also give sufficient time in the quiet, that we may clearly hear and rightly interpret.[29]

Of course all of us should work for self-improvement by prayer, worship, study, and meditation. But one of the laws of the spirit seems to be that self-improvement comes mainly from trying to help others—especially from trying to help others to enjoy spiritual growth. Growth comes by humbly seeking to be a more useful tool in God's hands. Giving to others material things helps the growth of the giver, but often injures the receiver. It is better to help the receiver to find ways to grow spiritually himself. It is more far-sighted to give advice and instruction, like a wise father to the son whom he loves. If, following Jesus, we teach "Seek ye first the Kingdom of God," then the other material things will follow. Helping the poor to grow spiritually and to become givers themselves is the real road to permanent riches, including material riches. Over and over it has been proved that there is magic in tithing.

Charles Grandison Finney, the great revivalist of the nineteenth century, taught that insofar as people can be brought to obey God, economic and social troubles will fade away. After a person is born again, he or she is twice as useful in the world, helping to bring salvation to others. Finney's great belief was that for every opportunity missed, a soul is lost. Hence the lives of Christians ought to be lived at fever-pitch like those of a rescue party during a disaster. We should not sing, "The great church victorious will be the church at rest."[30] This is like saying graduate from the university so you can stop learning. Spiritual growth does not result from rest. If the earth is a great classroom for souls, troubles and strife are the examinations. God counts not whether we live or die, but how we meet the tests. We receive blessings in proportion as we use the talents and blessings already given us. But the work most often neglected is the work of spiritual education. If God created the earth as a school for souls, then most of us are very lazy pupils. Most of us may fail the test. Life on earth is brief. We are in this school only a few years. Why should we waste even one day? Each night when we lie down to sleep can we say we have learned to love God more or helped our neighbor to love God more?

One of the major lessons to learn while on earth is that building our heaven is up to us. Emanuel Swedenborg wrote that we will not be in heaven until heaven is in us. Here on earth we can begin to receive the life and spirit of heaven within us. Swedenborg also believed that heaven is a kingdom of "uses," where everyone is challenged to his or her full potential, where contributing to the welfare of others brings happiness. Heaven is glimpsed on the day we realize that each of us has a unique and valuable gift to benefit the world.

In the gospels, of course, there are two differing views of the kingdom of God. The apostles themselves did not seem to ever get it clear. One is the external rule of God predicted as a purely future event. The other is the internal rule of God already present here and now. Jesus spoke more often about this internal condition whereby a person is born again and his or her whole existence is permeated by the living God. It is this concept of the kingdom that makes more sense for those adhering to the humble approach.

More and more theologians agree that heaven and hell should be spiritually interpreted, "as conditions in consciousness and not as geographic locations" or "areas of awareness in which the soul or psyche or spirit continues its development nearer to the reality of God than (is) possible on this four-dimensional physical plane." This was Charles Fillmore's view. "The 'many mansions' are no longer etheric apartment dwellings, but, according to modern theology, states of mind or of being."

The concept that heaven only comes after death or is located elsewhere fails to encourage us to build heaven on earth. However, if we view the earth as God's garden for nurturing souls, then we should follow Jesus' example of witnessing to that kingdom of God on earth now. In each miracle of healing, Jesus did not say, "I will heal you after you die or when I come again." He said, "Rise up now and walk." In and through Jesus' example, God helps people to grow spiritually. Such teachings are important for showing us more of the nature of God. They instruct us in ways to become more God-like, and assure us we can reach heaven during this life as well as after death.

The idea that heaven is a locality situated on the other side of death and that we must be either wholly in heaven or wholly in hell, has stunted progress in religion and caused it to march out of step with the rapid progress of business and science. Should we not see all around us that heaven is like sanity or wisdom? Few are totally without it. It usually comes gradually, not all at once. Some travel back and forth between heaven and hell. Those who are most deeply in heaven radiate happiness, but their circumstances vary greatly in health, wealth, and intellect. Heaven may be in the union of our spirit with God's spirit, in a constant striving and studying to become like Him. When Jesus said that His kingdom was not of this world, He may have meant that it is within our mind and soul, not in outward material surroundings. As St. Paul told the Corinthians, "Well, now is the favorable time; this is the day of salvation." (II Corinthians 6:20 JB.) St. Luke 17:20–21, KJV, reads: "And when he was demanded of the Pharisees, when the kingdom of God should come, he answered them and said, The kingodm of God cometh not with observation. Neither shall they say, Lo here! or, lo there! for, behold, the kingdom of God is within you." Luke 13:18–21 tells us that Christ said: " 'What is the kingdom of God like?' He continued, 'what shall I compare it with? It is like a mustard seed which a man took and sowed in his garden; and it grew to be a tree and the birds come to roost among its branches.' Again he said, 'The kingdom of God, what shall I compare it with? It is like yeast which a woman took and mixed with half a hundred-weight of flour till it was all leavened.' " How should we understand what Christ said in Matthew 16:28 (KJV)? "Verily, I say unto you. There be some standing here, which shall not taste death, till they see the Son of Man coming in His kingdom."

If a man's soul grows until it reaches heaven on earth, then for him individually there has been a "second coming of Christ"—for him individually "the end of the world" has come and gone. He or she is "in the world but not of it." Much of the eschatological prophecy of the Bible can be interpreted in this spiritual way to apply inwardly to the individual human soul rather than to earthly locations or to the end of humankind as a whole. We who advocate the humble approach should be open to the possibility of reaching heaven on earth. Standing for spiritual progress, as it does, the humble approach is always "in" this world but not "of" it. It is always moving into the next world or the next phase of human development.

Who are the happiest people you have ever met? Let us write down the names of ten persons who continually bubble over with happiness, and we will probably find that most are men and women who radiate love for everyone. They are happy deep inside themselves because they are growing spiritually and fulfilling God's laws. Jesus said: "Thou shalt love the Lord thy God with all thy heart, and with all thy soul and with all thy mind. This is the first and great commandment. And the second is like unto it, Thou shalt love thy neighbor as thyself."

Each human can only study and strive toward such divine love. Even the saints need to work daily to maintain continuous overflowing love for friends and foe alike. But the more we love, the easier it becomes to love even more. Love given multiplies. Love hoarded disappears.

This is a law of love. If we radiate love, we will receive back joy, prosperity, happiness, peace, and long life. But if we give love only to gain one of these rewards, then we have not understood love. Love in expectation of any reward is not love. When we learn to radiate love, we are fulfilling God's purpose—bringing God into expression on earth. When we learn to radiate love, we are gaining that mind which was in Christ, and are becoming fruitful sons of God, opening the door to heaven on earth.

Thus, through personal adversity, service to others, study of the natural and supernatural cosmos, prayer, and meditation, we can advance in the spiritual journey. We will find, however, that the journey does not lead to some atmospheric cloud-land of harps and haloes. It leads within. The search for God, as Carl Jung has pointed out, will take us through our own unconscious into the kingdom of heaven that is at hand, the state of perfection that lies in embryo within each of us.

From the variety of nations on earth, would we find it more pleasant to live in a nation of atheists or a nation of theists? What differences could we expect to find? From any community, select the dozen most beloved men or women. Will they be mostly God's men? Because they radiate love, love returns to them twofold. The reality of God is shown by the gifts He leaves with those who open their hearts to Him, gifts such as joy, mercy, and love. This distinguishes spiritual communion from hallucination and superstition which rarely leave such gifts. Let us think over the people we know to see which have come closest to heaven on earth. Are these mostly God-centered persons? One way to prove the existence of God is to see what results for those who put their faith in Him.

Samuel Taylor Coleridge (1772–1834) said that the truth of

religion is found in the way it answers the deepest needs of a man's spirit. In America it has been estimated that one out of every twenty adults suffers from alcoholism, and more in some other countries. But among the fifty million Americans who now claim to have been born again, alcoholism is very rare. God cures them when they turn to Him. This is a blessing for their families also. When we "get religion" even our dog or cat can see a change in us.

XI   Creative Thinking

Frequently people say, "I'm going out of my mind" or "my mind is playing tricks on me" or "I'm losing my mind." The mind is certainly an elusive component of every human being. It is the link between our bodies and our souls. With it we can think about our nature, other people, our bodies, and our souls. We can even think about thinking; that is, we can use our minds to think about our minds. Most likely, this is what distinguishes our mental capacity from that of animals. Animals are at a less evolved level than man precisely because they do not seem to be able to step back mentally and think about themselves. Animals have instincts, some level of primitive thought, and even emotion. They can build environments and communicate with each other, even with us. But as far as we can tell, animals cannot philosophize about anything.

As human beings we have been given by God a highly developed, extremely sophisticated mind. According to His plan, evolution has produced us for a purpose: possibly to be co-creators with Him in His on-going creation of the cosmos. He endowed us with the mental capacity to know, learn, evaluate, solve problems, and improve our selves and our societies. In this way we are created somewhat in His own image and likeness. With minds attuned and receptive to His revelations, both spiritual and natural, we can be a help in future progress.

God has given each person a mind capable of creative activity in the maturation of the universe, as well as the maturation of the soul. By following the humble approach, we will keep our minds as open and receptive as possible because we never know what contingencies await us. We should also keep our minds strongly linked to our souls and our souls linked to God. In this way, the creative process in which we are engaged will flow from the mind of God through our souls to our minds where creative thinking will produce creative results in the physical world.

We will see the divine effecting changes in the external culture we humans create within our homes, families, schools, churches, businesses, and governments. We will also be aware of spiritual evolution in our own personalities. On the other hand, if we let slip our control over our thoughts, we might produce disastrous effects, much like persons who think or feel their way psychosomatically into illness. Our minds are powerful. They can bring on physical sickness and determine the rate of recovery. If they can unconsciously produce such results within the cover of our skin, imagine what they could achieve with conscious effort in our exterior world!

Many people, however, are as self-centered as little children. Gradually they learn to love more selflessly and thus reach spiritual maturity. Such persons begin their entry into heaven while on earth. They can make the most of their years on earth, to develop their spiritual talents, as well as to serve the needs of others. For example, each person can learn in many ways to radiate love. One of the simplest ways is by thanksgiving. A heart full of gratitude is ready for love. If, before arising, we say a prayer of thanksgiving each morning—naming five of our blessings—we are ready that day to radiate love. God surrounds us each day with so many thousands of blessings and miracles in His universe, that it is easy to start each day with deep thanksgiving.

Since we have the gift of self-consciousness, we should examine our lives from time to time to see how we are using our mind, imagination, and will to build God's kingdom through love. One way is by creative control of our thoughts. Each word or action begins as a thought. We can say loving words and do loving deeds only if our minds and hearts are full of love. So it is good to stand watch over each thought which sprouts in the mind. If it is a loving thought, let us cultivate it. If it is not, let us crowd it out by filling our mind with loving thoughts. Try this experiment: Think of any person you envy or resent. Then free the mind of that poison by seeing that person as a child of God, and pray for that person's happiness as an experiment in self-discipline. God dwells in some way in every human being, and it is easy to find good qualities in any person if we lovingly try. As Jesus said, we should pray for those who irritate us. Our mind is very much like a garden, fertile with good soil, water, sunlight, and drainage. We, as the gardeners of our minds, can cultivate whatever thoughts we choose; we must nourish good thoughts, weed out the bad ones, and ensure that evil thinking does not overshadow and block out the radiance of the good. By years of careful thought control, your mind can become a garden of indescribable beauty. "As a man thinketh so is he."

For the sake of clarity and simplicity, let us think of each person as composed of four basic components: *God, soul, mind,* and *body.* Philosophers, cosmologists, theologians, and poets have used a great variety of words, synonyms, and analogies to describe these distinctive realities. But the multitude of terms tends to obscure exact meanings. Of course this quartet is an oversimplification. Reality is vastly more complex and infinite.

However, for the sake of simplicity, we will consider *God* to be the infinite creator of the cosmos. If He is truly infinite, then nothing exists apart from Him, and all other realities are created reflections of Him. *Soul* signifies that divine infusion which is unique to each human being. Most major religions teach that each soul is immortal and can be educated. *Mind* is defined as the strategic link between soul and body. Mind is complex and miraculous but temporary. The human *body* is defined as a temporary physical dwelling for the mind and soul. In the light of scientific analysis, all bodies, human and subhuman, are only evanescent arrangements of forces and wave patterns.

Obviously the human body, especially the brain, has great effect on the mind. When we are tired or sick, for instance, we often think less clearly. But basically the determining influence flows in the other direction, from the unseen to the seen, from God to soul, to mind, to body. These four are realities; but probably the lesser three derive from the first.

When we look at a person, we see a body and recognize a mind. When God looks at a person he sees first and foremost an immortal soul. We should never forget that the body is only a temporary configuration of wave patterns. First appearances seldom reveal the underlying truths. The earth appears to be flat but actually is round. It appears to be still but is actually moving in various directions at incredible speeds. The egg looks dead and inert until the day the bird breaks out. As Emerson said, "Things we see are out-picturing more basic realities that we do not see." The ultimate causes, forces, and purposes of things are invisible. We usually see only a few outward manifestations, not the causes and forces themselves, but only their effects.

Our body is like our house. So is our mind. Let us take care of it while we live in it, using our mind to develop our soul. God gave it to us not in fee but as a temporary trust. Why worry if our mind is feeble, if it is good enough to connect our soul with the world while we develop our soul? The life lived in the open is only a surface reflection of the life lived in closed sessions with our God. The laws which govern the realm of soul can be learned, but not always in the way we learn the laws of arithmetic or physics or human logic.

Ramakrishna once said:

It is the mind that makes one wise or ignorant, bound or emancipated. One is holy because of his mind, one is wicked because of his mind, one is a sinner because of his mind and it is the mind that makes one virtuous. So he whose mind is always fixed on God requires no other practices, devotion or spiritual exercises.

Unfortunately, most of us do not possess the Hindu claim that allows total concentration on God. We need to work at controlling our minds and channeling our thoughts. Norman Vincent Peale's approach—"positive thinking"—is a good one to follow.

Ella Wheeler Wilcox (1855–1919) wrote in her poem, "Attainment":

Use all your hidden forces. Do not miss the purpose
of this life, and do not wait for circumstances to mold
or change your fate!

And, in "You Never Can Tell", she wrote:

"You never can tell what your thoughts will do in bringing
  you hate or love,
For thoughts are things, and their airey wings
Are swifter than carrier doves
They follow the law of the Universe,
Each thing must create its kind,
And they speed o'er the track to bring you back
Whatever went out of your mind."

Marcus Bach wrote:

. . . to dwell upon goodness is to become the recipient of all
that is good. To be joyful is to attract more joyfulness.
To meditate on love is to grow lovely in the inner self.
To think health is to be healthy. To put life into God's
love is to put God's love into your life.

There is an intimate relationship between what we think and
what we are. The Dhammapada scriptures, attributed to the
Buddha, put it this way:

All that we are is the result of what we have thought: it is
founded on our thoughts, it is made up of our thoughts. If a
man speaks or acts with an evil thought, pain follows him, as
the wheel follows the foot of the ox that draws the carriage.
. . . If a man speaks or acts with a pure thought, happiness
follows him, like a shadow that never leaves him. . . . Hatred
does not cease by hatred at any time; hatred ceases by love
—this is an old rule. . . . As rain breaks through an ill-
thatched house, passion will break through an unreflecting
mind. . . . If one man conquer in battle a thousand times a
thousand men, and another conquer himself, he is the greatest
of conquerors. One's own self conquered is better than all
other people conquered; not even a god could change into de-
feat the victory of a man who vanquished himself.

As co-creators with God, we must control our thoughts, directing them toward creativity, toward evolution, toward progress. If our thoughts are not in this direction, we will be impediments in God's plan.

Why do not all people learn to benefit from mind-control which is probably the most useful tool we will ever possess. Some people allow their minds to run as loose and as uncontrolled as a spilled cup of mercury. Some are not even aware that they can control their minds. Some are just too lazy. In fact, the mind is only an instrument. Each person can guide thoughts and even emotions into any paths he wishes. We can each learn to be the pilot of our mind. A ship without a pilot leads to disaster. So does a mind and body without a pilot. Even ordinary people wield extraordinary power in the words that leave their lips. Jesus was addressing each of us when he said:

For the words that the mouth utters come from the overflow of the heart. A good man produces good from the store of good within himself; and an evil man from evil within, produces evil. I tell you this: there is not a thoughtless word that comes from men's lips but they will have to account for it on the day of judgement. For out of your own mouth you will be acquitted; out of your own mouth you will be condemned. (Matthew 12:35–37, NEB.)

God has given each person a mind capable of creative activity in the ongoing expansion of the cosmos, which includes the expansion of his own soul. The creative process goes from thoughts to deeds. Our words are our thoughts crystallized. The objects we build and the deeds we do emanate from our thoughts and our words.

Obviously, to build a house we begin with thoughts, then words, then deeds. Every good object produced by man is created by this process. Nations are formed in this way, and so are sciences and all the organizations and institutions of human society. Even more awesome is the fact that thoughts build not only outwardly but inwardly. By thoughts we create not only our possessions but also our personalities and our souls. By long practice of thought control we can each make of ourselves the kind of person we want to be. Our thoughts and attitudes can even help to bring about physical sickness, but they can also influence the rate of healing in our bodies as well as our minds.

It cannot be repeated often enough that we can learn to radiate love; but first we must practice using loving words and loving thoughts. If we keep our minds filled with good thoughts of love, giving, and thanksgiving, they will spill over into our words and deeds. If we are not very careful to weed out all evil thoughts such as envy or hate or selfishness they, too, will overflow into our words and deeds. To produce beautiful music requires long practice and so does the production of a beautiful mind. With practice both come more easily. We must beware of entertaining whatever pops into our minds. Rather, let us think thoughts we may be proud of, controlling and using them as divinely provided tools. If we really do not want to worry, then we must fill our minds with thoughts of thanksgiving, not fear. This takes self-control and practice; but the more we practice, the easier it is.

Charles Neal said in 1978:

One would think therefore that intelligent men and women, particularly prayerful ones, would be meticulous in their choice of words, speaking only those which are helpful and are constructive. And above all things, let us avoid negative and destructive words. But as we know very well, this is not what usually happens, for people still do not really believe that they may have dominion over their own lives, and fail to exercise that dominion through the right use of their minds and through the right use of selected words. While their minds have creative power, people do not seem to realize this, despite the fact that it is clearly implied again and again in our scriptures. . . . Our casual words reflect what we truly believe deep down within ourselves. They express what our thoughts have been over long periods of time and they come through spontaneously, unimpeded by deliberate and considered thought. Our so-called thoughtless words are reckoned to be true expressions of what actually is in our minds. Thus we begin to see that what some people call slips of the tongue or Freudian slips are not slips at all. Detail of sickness, disharmony and woe, that every counsellor and New Thought minister hears over and over again, are the products of minds that have made wrong choices in the use of ideas. Surely the cure for sickness, disharmony and woe of this kind lies in a complete change in the disciplined management of our thought process, including the very words that we utter, day by day.[31]

Our thoughts and words have power. We should discipline and manage them wisely. They can be what separate us from the rest of creation. They can also be what connect us to God.

XII   Love and Happiness
The True Test

Happiness sought eludes. Happiness given returns. The pursuit of happiness is never successful because happiness is always a by-product. Ralph Waldo Trine (1866–1936) has said:

A corollary of the great principle already enunciated might be formulated thus: there is no such thing as finding true happiness by searching for it directly. It must come, if it come at all, indirectly, or by the service, the love and the happiness we give to others. So there is no such thing as finding true greatness by searching for it directly. It always, without a single exception, has come indirectly in this same way, and it is not at all probable that this great eternal law is going to be changed to suit any particular case or cases. Then recognize it, put your life into harmony with it, and reap the rewards of its observance, or fail to recognize it and pay the penalty accordingly; for the law itself will remain unchanged. Life is not, we may say, for mere passing pleasure, but for the highest unfoldment that one can attain to, the noblest character that one can grow and for the greatest service that one can render to all mankind. In this, however, we will find the highest pleasure, for in this the only real pleasure lies.[32]

If we endorse the humble approach, we should radiate love and happiness as faithfully as the sun radiates light and warmth. As sunlight is a creative source, so can our love be a creative source of new life and ideas. God is the source of love. Love cannot flow in unless it also flows out. The Spirit of God is like a stream of water and His disciples are like many beautiful fountains fed by this river of waters. Each one of us is such a fountain, and it is our task to keep the channel open so that God's Spirit can flow through us and others can see His glory. Without God, we are not likely to bring forth any good. If we think too much of the visible world or trust in our own ability, we become like a clogged fountain. We will never learn to radiate love as long as we love ourselves, for if we are characterized by self-concern, we will radiate self-concern.

Jesus then said to His disciples "If anyone wishes to be a follower of mine, he must leave self behind; he must take up his cross and come with me. Whoever cares for his own safety is lost; but if a man will let himself be lost for my sake, he will find his true self. (St. Matthew 16:24–5, NEB.)

God loves us all equally and unceasingly. It is His nature to do so. We should seek always to let God's love shine forth like the light inside an electric bulb illuminating all our habitation. Emil Brunner wrote:

Every human relationship which does not express love is abnormal. In Jesus Christ we are told that this love is the whole meaning of our life, and is also its foundation. Here the Creator reveals Himself as the One who has created us in love, by love, for love. He reveals to us our true nature, and He gives it back to us.[33]

Rufus Matthew Jones taught that those who worship God are empowered by the Spirit, and that religion is not a burden but rather a matter of being lifted up to new heights of joy and philanthropic achievement. The divine spirit moves into your life and makes it over from within so that all things are seen in a new light, and love for all becomes the spontaneous expression of a Spirit-filled soul. If we think too much of the visible world, or trust too much in our own ability, or love ourselves inordinately, we will never learn to radiate love. Instead we will radiate self-concern, egotism, arrogance. Ironically, egotism will not allow us to find our true selves. We miss the true self of grace and spirit, and thus sever our links with God. The self we admire so greatly is a diminished version of the total self. Often in the name of humanism, egotism obscures the divine life in our souls. It substitutes the worship of men for the worship of God. In its extreme form, godless humanism becomes idolatry, denying the existence of the infinite creator and exalting the limited intellect of the human race so recently evolved on one small planet, earth.

The ultimate conceit is that no mind is greater than the human mind. How could humans be so egotistical as to believe that no other being in the universe can be purposeful and consciously creative? Or that creatures on other planets may not have learned more about God than we? Surely man's multitudinous creations are tiny and few compared to what the mind which created man has created in other galaxies and in unseen realms and dimensions undreamed of.

Humanists claim they promote science and progress. However, we must not immediately assume that they espouse the humble approach. In his recent work on humanism, *Architects of Moral Anarchy,* John Howard has discussed the dangers to society when traditional moral precepts, such as hard work and respect for the property of others, are discarded for an ethic of selfishness. He decries the moral vacuum created in the last forty years in which the structure of a hard-working society is ridiculed. The work ethic and other virtues of free competition may not survive in a moral vacuum. To prosper, society needs citizens deeply convinced of the value of earning one's way from "rags to respectability." Howard writes:

Nowadays, anyone who ventures into the territory of moral judgments, declaring certain conduct right or wrong, is simply ignored, or in the case of an influential spokesman, will have scorn heaped upon him by the public commentators. When a Solzhenitsyn describes with chilling accuracy the moral rot that has debilitated America, he must be chastised, belittled, and declared incompetent to judge such things.[34]

Before remedial action can be undertaken, the forces causing this situation should be clearly understood. Possibly the leading force in the so-called "new morality" lies in the twentieth-century humanist movement as expressed in The Humanist Manifesto, proclaimed by thirty-four respected Americans in 1933. (The present humanist movement, Howard warns, is not to be mistaken for its historical forerunner which dates back to Renaissance humanism. Erasmus, Melanchthon, Luther, and More were poles apart from modern humanists. The crucial difference, of course, is faith in God.) In Howard's analysis, the 1933 document

asserted that science and economic change had rendered old beliefs invalid and that conscientious people needed to recognize that new circumstances required a formulation of a value system appropriate to the new knowledge. The cornerstone of the new doctrine was to be an acknowledgement that there is no Supreme Being, with the obligations, hopes and taboos of traditional religion set aside. Man was declared the measure of all things, so there needed to be a hierarchy of commitments to give human beings the best chance for satisfaction and joy in life. In short, a new humanistic religion was declared.

Howard maintains that these modern humanists convinced themselves that a socialized, cooperative order should be established for the sake of redistributing more equitably the means of life. He said:

The moral fervor of this movement and its categorical rejection of traditional beliefs made humanism the seedbed of, and the rallying point for, many of the new thinkers in education, psychology and the other social sciences, as well as the activist leadership in most of the civil rights and liberation movements.

For four decades, ideologies stripped of God provided a sufficient formal agenda for the energetic and increasingly influential humanist movement. Then in 1973, *Humanist Manifesto II* was published in *The Humanist,* the official journal of the American Humanist Association. Atheism was reaffirmed, and traditional religion identified more specifically as an obstacle to the complete flowering of the human psyche. Ethics were proclaimed to be "autonomous and situational," and traditional codes of morality were decried. A guaranteed annual income was requested. There were endorsements for an international redistribution of wealth, pacifism, and a world government.

In 1969, Dr. Carl Rogers, officially designated "Humanist of the Year," gave the Sonoma College commencement address entitled "The Person of Tomorrow." In it, Rogers said the person of tomorrow has no use for religion and marriage as institution. He is "passionate" and "spontaneous" but for no concrete, humanitarian goal. He trusts only his own experience, obeys only the laws he chooses, and exhibits "a profound distrust of all authority." It appears that this person is the epitome of self-centeredness. By definition, humanism is man-centered and therefore egotistic.

Such a person could hardly be a follower of the humble approach that encourages us to use our open-mindedness and our inventiveness to advance God's evolving creation. This "person of tomorrow," admired by Rogers and others, is too egotistical, too dogmatic, too selfish to achieve his stated goal (which, again, is far removed from that of the humble approach) "bringing to all the people of the world the maximum joy and satisfaction as defined by the scientific knowledge of the moment." But there is more than the knowledge of the moment. Unfortunately, a self-directed, situational ethic admits of no eternal truth, no infinite divine creator, no enduring obligations.

The degree to which this philosophy has been accepted and woven into the institutions, the life-styles, and the expectations of society will determine the size of the task confronting anyone seeking to re-establish the habit of viewing the world in moral terms and thus preserving the system of competition, freedom, and advancement through healthy rivalry. Whereas many humanists have very genuinely believed that the new morality to which they are committed constitutes a higher set of virtues than that which has prevailed in the past, the editor of *The Humanist* resorted to sensationalism by placing an advertisement for that journal in *Hustler* magazine. Bragging that, "For more than three decades *The Humanist* has chased almost every sacred cow in the country," the ad claimed that *The Humanist* is "one of the most irreverent, most quoted and most influential magazines of social commentary in America."

How much respect can one have for a movement that demeans the long line of sincere humanists stretching back to the great names of the Renaissance by using a pornographic magazine as an invitation to others to "learn more about us and our jousts with sacred truths"?

The humble approach rejects all self-centered philosophies, especially those brands of humanism teaching that man is the end purpose of evolution. In humility let us admit that God's awesome creative process is likely to continue even if humans should disappear from the face of the earth. Humanism is egotistical because it encourages men to think that mankind is, itself, the ultimate concern. Rather than worshiping the universal Spirit creating the universe, humanists worship the creatures. Communists go even further to worship governments which are created by creatures. Today we wonder why the children of Israel in the wilderness worshiped a golden calf which they themselves had created. Is it any wiser to worship a government created by men?

Many people in this generation—including some intellectuals and academics attracted to humanism—have turned away from God because of the traditionalism of so many churches. They think of the church authorities as old-fashioned or even small-minded. But is not that very turning away equally small-minded?

The humble search for God continues in new ways, and seeks to recreate and revitalize the churches. Have we ever met a person who was helped to grow spiritually by turning away from all religion? Do those who turn away become better persons, more useful, or more high-minded? Would it not be more beneficial for humankind, if persons to whom God has given keen intellects use their talents for increasing our understanding and love of God?

Rejecting religion is negative and self-centered. Even the disillusioned could become positive, generous forces for reform if they did not retreat into their private worlds of pessimism and despair, like Jean Paul Richter, Friedrich Nietzsche, and Albert Camus, the trio who laid the foundation for the current idea that "God is dead." If we accept such a ridiculous notion that God died, we must then accept the notion that there is no more revelation, no new guidelines; that man is now on his own as he moves into the next era of change. Those adhering to the humble approach cannot accept a position that replaces the primary active source of all knowledge, God, with weak human intellect. The humble approach includes a vision of progress as limitless, unending—a vision that calls us to do our best work, to serve others, to love, to aspire beyond the merely human.

By their fruits you will know them: the egotists, the humanists, the immoralists, those who despair. And by the fruits of faith, hope, and love, you will know the humble children of God. Let us explore the ways that these traditional virtues should be reflected in those who follow the humble approach.

Faith

University students often give up their faith mistakenly thinking "faith" is similar to a kind of blindness. Some become self-styled atheists believing in only the visible or tangible. Later, after much more experience in life, most of them turn back to religion. Life and experience teach that things visible to humans are ultimately unexplainable and unknowable without an understanding of underlying spiritual realities. The know-it-all attitude is often found among the young. As people grow older, however, most acquire a deeper faith in God and more religious fervor. Egotistical arrogance often comes from a lack of experience, and humility comes with maturity. The gullibility and credulousness of some young persons is not at all the same as the broadmindedness and humility of the humble approach.

Faith does not imply a closed, but an open mind. Faith means "having respect for" or "standing in awe of." Quite the opposite of blindness, faith appreciates the vast spiritual realities that materialists overlook by getting trapped in the purely physical. Where the Bible says "fear of God," possibly a better rendering in many passages would be "respect for God" or "admiration for the great power of God." Gabriel Marcel claimed that "an open and expectant state of mind . . . either implies faith or is faith."

How does scripture define faith? In the New Testament we learn that "Faith gives substance to our hopes and makes us certain of realities we do not see." (Hebrews 11:1, NEB.) The faith which Jesus requested of us differed in some ways from what was later called faith by the church. Jesus taught personal loyalty or faithfulness. The church later sometimes seemed to mean something more like credulity. Mere credulity ought to be replaced by a conception of faith as an attitude of humility and loyalty which results in expectancy and bestows a quiet confidence.

Hope

Basically, hope is trust. In what or whom do we trust? The humble approach bases its hope on the eternal, not the transient. Understand the transient and utilize it, but do not place eternal hope in it. Can there ever be any question more basic than this: "Do we put our trust in God or in some temporary thing?" God will never fail us. A father may fail us. A son may fail us. Possessions may fail us. But God's love never fails. God's love is always unconditional and unlimited even for the worst sinner. If we put our trust (faith) in God, we are opening the door for abundant blessings.

The man who trusts in himself, thereby cuts himself off from God and from other men. Trust in self (egotism) leads to worry, tension, and even to insanity. No man can solve all the problems which sometimes come into a human life. Subconsciously he knows he is not equal to the task and may crack under the strain. But to trust in God does not mean that we should not work hard and use to the utmost each of our talents. Jesus made this duty plain in the parable of the talents. A man who is not productive becomes unhappy. To trust in God (faith) means that we should remember that each of our talents is a gift from God. If we are strong in mind or in muscle, that, too, is a gift from God. If we have honors or titles or possessions, they, too, are God's gifts. It is a form of idolatry (and egotism) to put our trust in any of these. Our knowledge may be famous among men; but compared to God's knowledge, it is infinitesimal. Therefore, the truly wise and humble man prays, "Not my will but thine be done." Trust in others weakens; trust in self isolates; but trust in God magnifies our life and our soul.

Charity

What is charity according to the humble approach? It is not the same as welfare. Giving welfare to the unemployed, although good for the soul of the giver, is not good for the soul of the receiver. The greater charity is to help a person join the ranks of the givers rather than be forever trapped in the position of receiver. When the desire to give replaces the desire to get, a person exchanges an attitude of childishness for one of maturity. Just as when one nation gives food to another nation, it does no spiritual good for the recipient nation. In fact, human nature is such that the receivers often become envious, demanding, and resentful. This is bad for the souls of people.

The greater charity is to help the people of a poor nation to learn the traits which lead to prosperity, such as trustworthiness, hard work, free competition, thrift, and the Golden Rule. Any poor nation can be converted to amazing prosperity rather quickly and lastingly if its people and government adopt wholeheartedly these five virtues. Not only is this the way to material prosperity but also to spiritual growth. The godly gift to the poor is not money but the gospel.

The wealth of a nation comes not from natural resources but from what is in the minds and hearts of its people. People pursuing the humble approach express their love in charity in order to both alleviate suffering and elevate the recipients of their love. Feeding the hungry, caring for the sick, clothing the naked are necessary in the short range; but in the long range, the real charity is to help the poor learn the spiritual traits which lead to prosperity, dignity, and happiness. Besides bestowing technology and know-how on people in poor nations, we should also support the self-sacrificing missionaries who live among the less fortunate as loving human helpers in their development. Technology and know-how are spiritless. People, however, can radiate love and joy as they teach the spiritual realities which are creating the material universe.

XIII   Laws of the Spirit

Everyone now understands the term, "the laws of nature," the multitude of principles discovered by scientists, primarily in the last four centuries, explaining or describing the physical universe. Our faith in their immutability has been shaken in recent years as we see them being revised, reformulated, and replaced because of new data. Nevertheless, we now know that such laws exist and from time to time we experience their effects in our daily lives.

Not everyone, however, yet understands the phrase, "the laws of the spirit." There is a difference between laws of the spirit and religious laws such as those formulated by Moses, Hammurabi, Mohammed, and other ancient law-givers. Early civilizations adopted complex and rather rigid systems of religious laws. Some of these religious teachings may have reflected underlying laws of the spirit, but most were not themselves laws of the spirit. Some tended to legitimize social and religious customs of ancient cultures. By "laws of the spirit" we mean universal principles of the unseen world that can be determined and tested by extensive examination of human behavior and other data. Partly for lack of clearly defined methodology and a body of research material, this field appears about as disorganized and controversial as the natural sciences were in the milleniums before Galileo. In the days of Moses or Mohammed, there was very little knowledge of the principles of physics, chemistry, or biology, and little appreciation among the average people of the progress and rich rewards that could be achieved through successful research in these fields.

Just as people of earlier times were ignorant regarding the physical sciences, we today are ignorant about the principles of spiritual progress. In addition to having as yet little under-standing or agreement as to what spiritual laws are, we do not seem to recognize that God's purpose is not some permanent status quo, but change, process, and progress based upon the laws of the spirit. The spiritual dimensions of the cosmos are dynamic, changing, ceaselessly interacting. Surely the time has come for us to concentrate our resources on the kind of inves-tigations which will enable us to understand the patterns and laws governing spiritual growth and development. Ceaseless seeking may be a part of the growth of souls as well as minds. It may be possible through research that some agreement may be reached on laws of the spirit. This field of research may yet become as bounteously fruitful as the natural sciences were in the last four centuries.

Church leaders often are not yet aware of the need to spon-sor wide-ranging open-minded research into the laws of the spirit. History records innumerable crises in which some tradi-tional leaders of established churches did not welcome innova-tive suggestions for religious renewal and advancement. Many accused these "researchers" of being heretics, self-seekers, or insane. Indeed, some were, just as today some studies in psy-chic research are conducted by fuzzy-minded or poorly trained psuedo-scientists. If a new renaissance is to begin now, research into laws of the spirit should be undertaken largely by persons rigorously trained in many fields of science: physical, mental, and spiritual. Already, some leaders in these exact sciences are beginning to speak and write about their religious concepts. We hope they will help to clarify or verify some of the laws of the spirit, as in recent years some medical investigations into an-cient herbal remedies have proved many of them to be useful.

We should first become comfortable with the concept of spir-itual laws and not fear that research into them violates some static condition of God's universe. We may indeed discover that some laws are eternal verities, never to be altered. But with an open-minded humble approach, let us begin. The Book of Psalms opens with these words:

"Blessed is the man . . . (whose) delight is in the law of the Lord; and in his law doth he meditate day and night and he shall be like a tree planted by streams of water, that bringeth forth its fruit in its season, and whose leaf doth not wither; and in whatsoever he doeth he shall prosper." (Psalms 1:1–3, KJV.)

Of course, it is not very apparent at this moment in history exactly how each law of the spirit could be discovered, tested, and utilized. Nor can we predict what laws will be discovered by generations of scientists sifting data for evidence of the effects of the unseen. It would have been impossible five hundred years ago to predict anything of the laws of thermodynamics or nuclear physics, let alone the devising of experiments to test and establish them as laws. The difficulties of bringing to light, of describing and testing the laws of the spirit, are not any less than those which faced chemists two hundred years ago.

Studying and teaching the laws of the spirit should benefit humanity in even greater measure than did, for example, the laws of chemistry. Matthew Arnold thought that the decreasing influence of the Bible in the nineteenth century could be reversed if the ideals and hopes and laws expressed in the poetic and allegorical language of the scriptures could be explored experimentally. He hoped that dogmatic theology could be succeeded by empirical theology or experimental theology. If people could understand religious principles in their own everyday language rather than in ancient metaphors, they might take them more seriously. Likewise, if we could see the effects of spiritual laws operating in our modern world rather than read about their effects in ancient Israel, we might try to live our lives in closer harmony with them.

Possibly there are some laws of the spirit on which all major religions agree? For example, ancient Hindus taught that hate is never overcome by hate, but hate can be overcome by love. Does any religion now disagree? Such agreements might be useful in providing a starting point for further inquiry, experimental testing, and formulation.

It is not necessary, however, or even desirable that everyone should agree on a fixed code or list of laws. Natural scientists are not in absolute agreement about laws of nature. Some diversity of judgment and opinion can be beneficial because that induces progress. Maybe the amazing acceleration of discoveries and progress in the twentieth century is due in part to increasing diversity and rivalry in the domains of the sciences. If a world government were to codify a list of laws, perhaps progress and advance in research would slow down dramatically.

More benefits may result in the domains of the spirit if each individual were to draw up his own personal list of the laws governing spiritual matters. Of course, this would be easier if he first studied the books and articles of scientists engaged in investigating possible laws of the spirit. However, only when we understand and claim as our own some actual laws of the spirit do we begin to build our own heaven. What could be more uplifting than for each human to write in his mind and heart, as well as on paper, the various laws by which he ought to live? He may measure his spiritual growth if every year he revises and rewrites his own personal list of laws. How beneficial it would be if every school each day devoted a few minutes to help each pupil study the laws of the spirit as they are brought to light and formulated by great scientists, so that each person could improve his own written list. The supreme moments in the life of each of us occur whenever we grasp a new inspiring truth and appropriate it so that it revitalizes our personality and becomes a part of our life.

When any field of research is begun, no one can possibly predict what may be discovered eventually. Astronomers before Copernicus could not have predicted or even imagined galaxies, or supernovas, or pulsars. Even so, no one can yet say what laws of the spirit will be formulated and proven eventually. But to give some idea of laws of the spirit which might be researched, here are a few examples taken mostly from the wisdom of the centuries expressed by the world's major religions.

1. Religions generally agree that, "As a person thinks, so is that person." If this is a true law and it can be taught con-

vincingly, especially to young people, it might be the basis for new generations much more disciplined in the control and management of their minds and lives than current generations.

2. Happiness comes from spiritual wealth, not material wealth. Happiness is always a by-product, never a product. Happiness comes from giving, not getting. If we pursue happiness for ourselves, it will always elude us. If we try hard to bring happiness to others, we cannot stop it from coming to us also. The more we try to give it away, the more it comes back to us multiplied. If we try to grasp happiness, it always escapes us; if we try to hand it out to others, it sticks to our hands like glue.

3. The more love we give away, the more we have left. The laws of love differ from the laws of arithmetic. Love hoarded dwindles, but love given grows. If we give all our love, we will have more left than he who saves some. Giving love, not receiving, is important; but when we give with no thought of receiving, we automatically and inescapably receive abundantly. Heaven is a by-product of love. When we say "I love you," we mean that "a little of God's love flows from us to you." But, thereby, we do not love less, but more. For in flowing the quantity is magnified. God's love is infinite, and is directed equally to each person, but it seems to gain intensity when directed to sinners. This is the wonder and mystery of it, that when we love God we get an enormous increase in the quantity flowing through us to others.

4. It is better to give than to receive. Giving is a sign of psychological and spiritual maturity. There are few diseases so childish and so deadly as the "gimmies," a disease that separates us from friends and from God, and shrinks the soul. The secret of success is giving, not getting. To get joy we must give it and to keep joy we must scatter it. The greatest charity is to help a person change from being a receiver to being a giver.

5. Loneliness is the punishment for those who want to get, not give. Helping others is the cure for loneliness. If we feel lonely, we are probably self-centered. If we feel unloved, we are probably unloving. If we love only ourselves, we may be the only persons to love us. Whatever we give out, we get back.

6. Thanksgiving opens the door to spiritual growth. If there is any day in our life which is not thanksgiving day, then we are not fully alive. Counting our blessings attracts blessings. Counting our blessings each morning starts a day full of blessings. Thanksgiving brings God's bounty. From gratitude comes riches—from complaints poverty. Thankfulness opens the door to happiness. Thanksgiving causes giving. Thanksgiving puts our mind in tune with the Infinite. Continual gratitude dissolves our worries.

7. To be forgiven, we must first forgive. Forgiving brings forgiveness. Failure to forgive creates a hell for the unforgiver, not the unforgiven.

8. When Jesus was asked what is the greatest law, He said:

Thou shalt love the Lord thy God with all thy heart, and with all thy soul, and with all thy mind. This is the first and great commandment. And the second is like unto it, Thou shalt love thy neighbour as thyself. On these two commandments hang all the law and the prophets. (Matthew 22:37–40 KJV.)

This can be researched as a basic law of the spirit. A person who applies this law finds his life revolutionized. Opening our heart to God allows His love to flow through us like a mighty river. If we love God totally as He loves us, we will love each of His children without exception as Jesus Himself described. (Luke 6:27–36, KJV.) The happiest people on earth are those who love God totally.

9. Surrender to God brings freedom. It is in dying to our selfish selves (self-denial) that we are born to eternal life.

10. St. Matthew reports that Jesus enunciated another law of the spirit: "But seek ye first His kingdom and His righteousness, and all these things shall be yours as well." (St. Matthew 6:33, RSV.) Do we not have daily evidence of this in the confirmation of the proverb, "Honesty is the best policy"? Honesty leads to prosperity. Those who are trustworthy are the ones entrusted with great blessings. Even in the lives of nations this law of the spirit is manifest, for any nation whose people are steadfast in religion, fair play, hard work, thrift, and trustworthiness will automatically grow in prosperity also.

More and more manpower and resources are being devoted to the forces of nature—discovering, proving, understanding, using, and teaching these forces. But almost everyone agrees that one of the greatest forces on earth is *love*. Should churches finance constant research into this force of love? Should schools offer courses for credit (with homework, tests, and grades) on the force of love? The real wealth of a nation does not come from mineral resources but from the way it develops and harnesses the lovepower in the minds and hearts of its people.

In the New Testament an account of this force of love is presented very vividly and clearly:

Dear friends, let us love one another, because love is from God. Everyone who loves is a child of God and knows God; but the unloving know nothing of God. For God is love; and His love was disclosed to us in this, that He sent His only Son into the world to bring us life. The love I speak of is not our love for God, but the love He showed to us in sending His Son as the remedy for the defilement of our sins. If God thus loved us, dear friends, we in turn are bound to love one another. Though God has never been seen by any man, God Himself dwells in us if we love one another; His love is brought to perfection within us. (I John 4:7–12 NEB.)

God is love; he who dwells in love is dwelling in God, and God in him. This is for us the perfection of love, to have confidence on the day of Judgement, and this we can have, because even in this world we are as he is. There is no room for fear in love;

perfect love banishes fear. For fear brings with it the pains of judgement, and anyone who is afraid has not attained to love in its perfection. We love because He loved us first. But if a man says, "I love God," while hating his brother, he is a liar. If he does not love the brother whom he has seen, it cannot be that he loves God whom he has not seen. And indeed this command comes to us from Christ Himself; that he who loves God must also love his brother. (I John 4:12–21, NEB.)

If you love only those who love you, what credit is that to you? Even sinners love those who love them. Again, if you do good only to those who do good to you, what credit is that to you? Even sinners do as much. And if you lend only where you expect to be repaid, what credit is that to you: Even sinners lend to each other if they are to be repaid in full. But you must love your enemies and do good; and lend without expecting any return; and you will have a rich reward; you will be sons of the Most High, because He Himself is kind to the ungrateful and wicked. Be compassionate as your Father is compassionate.

Pass no judgement, and you will not be judged; do not condemn, and you will not be condemned; acquit, and you will be acquitted; give, and gifts will be given you. Good measure, pressed down, shaken together, and running over, will be poured into your lap; for whatever measure you deal out to others will be dealt to you in return. (St. Luke 6:32–38, NEB.)

And now I will show you the best way of all. I may speak in tongues of men or of angels, but if I am without love, I am a sounding gong or a clanging cymbal. I may have the gift of prophecy, and know every hidden truth; I may have faith strong enough to move mountains; but if I have no love, I am nothing. I may dole out all I possess, or even give my body to be burnt, but if I have no love, I am none the better.

Love is patient; love is kind and envies no one. Love is never boastful, nor conceited, nor rude; never selfish, not quick to take offence. Love keeps no score of wrongs; does not gloat over other men's sins, but delights in the truth. There is nothing love cannot face; there is no limit to its faith, its hope, and its endurance.

Love will never come to an end. Are there prophets? Their work will be over. Are there tongues of ecstasy? they will cease.

Is there knowledge? it will vanish away; for our knowledge and our prophecy alike are partial, and the partial vanishes when wholeness comes. When I was a child, my speech, my outlook and my thoughts were all childish. When I grew up, I had finished with childish things. Now we see only puzzling reflections in a mirror, but then we shall see face to face. My knowledge now is partial; then it will be whole, like God's knowledge of me. In a word, there are three things that last for ever: faith, hope and love; but the greatest of them all is love. (I Corinthians 12:31 to 13:13, NEB.)

As can be seen in these few passages from the Christian scriptures, many psycho-spiritual truths might be discovered by researching these age-old maxims about love. Maybe we will discover that love is indeed the basic force in the spiritual world. Maybe school children can be taught some laws of the spirit rather than slowly learning them later through suffering.

Are our prayers answered? On earth we will never know the reason why. Maybe it is an evidence of God's unlimited and undeserved love? God's love is its own ultimate reason. What is our response? Should it not be an overwhelming feeling of gratitude and desire to grow in some small way more like Him—to seek to be an open channel loving God and radiating God's love to all His children?

Love of God comes first and makes it easier to love in other ways. If we want our enemy to see only our good qualities and not our flaws, then lovingly look for and see only his good qualities. He, too, is a child of God. God loves us both even though neither of us is yet perfect. Above all, we should not only radiate love but also help others to become alive with love.

Throughout our discussion of the humble approach, we have been calling for and encouraging the expression of the highest and noblest qualities of the human spirit. Have we been asking too much? Is this plea for the humble approach too unrealistic to be achieved? We don't think so. It has always been our firm belief that human potential is far greater than most of us realize.

What are we—no more than creatures constituted by the possession of bodies and minds? Bodies and minds are only our tools. To the question *who are we* in ourselves, the answer should be given that the real self is a *soul*. Most people go to school for twelve long years just to educate the mind which lives only briefly. Can we not discover equally effective methods to educate the soul for eternity?

Two thousand years ago more time was devoted to spiritual education than to mental education. The same was true two hundred years ago. Most old universities were founded by ministers, to train ministers. But in the last two centuries we have increased mental education enormously, so that now twenty times as many hours are spent on mental as on spiritual improvement. No wonder the world is out of joint. Let us not work less for mental education; but could we not expect both children and adults to study at least seven hours a week for spiritual growth? The results might be rewarding.

It is not surprising that our world has problems. Many churches are no longer "relevant" because so little planning is devoted to spiritual education and so little time is actually set aside for it. If we tried to teach chemistry by such methods, there would be very few able chemists and few new discoveries in chemistry. Should not schools include in the curriculum courses in ethics, philanthropy, character-building, self-denial techniques, freedom from envy, joy of giving, thought-control, philosophy of life, etc.? To say that religion should not be included in university studies because it cannot be seen or accurately measured seems as questionable as saying that love should not be studied for the same reason.

New teaching methods could be tried. Maybe besides using only books and traditional classrooms we could teach effectively through newspapers, comics, radio, television, etc. At least church teachers could try to identify and warn against movies, magazines, and plays which are degenerate. Probably the new techniques of "programed learning" and "programed textbooks" could be adapted to teach spiritual growth at various ages, both in daily schools and Sunday schools.

Animals rely on instinct, so their mental development is slow. Many homes and many schools do not go much beyond instinct in their methods for teaching spiritual growth. For rational humans, education ought to be far more than merely a drawing out of what is somehow already embedded in the child as if by instinct.

By learning humility, we find that the purpose of life on earth is vastly deeper than any human mind can grasp. Diligently, each child of God should seek to find and obey God's purpose, but none be so egotistical as to think that he or she comprehends the infinite mind of God.

As we become more and more humble, we can learn more about God. Let us recall once more that man is able to observe only a tiny part of reality and his observations are often misleading because he is self-centered.

Scientists have steadily been changing their concepts of the universe and laws of nature, but the progression is always away from smaller self-centered or man-centered concepts. Evidence is always accumulating that things seen are only one aspect of the vastly greater unseen realities. Man's observational abilities are very limited, and so are his mental abilities. Should we not focus our lives on the unseen realities and not on the fleeting appearances? Should we not kneel down in humility and worship the awesome, infinite, omniscient, eternal Creator?

Every person's concept of God is too small. Through humility we can begin to get into true perspective the infinity of God. This is the humble approach. Are we ready to begin the formulation of a humble theology which can never become obsolete? This would be a theology really centered upon God and not upon our own little selves.

REFERENCES (FOOTNOTES)

1. *The Key to the Universe,* by Nigel Calder, 1977.

2. *In the Center of Immensities,* by Sir Bernard Lovell, 1978.

3. *Sartor Resartus,* by Thomas Carlyle, 1858.

4. *The Universe and Dr. Einstein,* by Lincoln Barnett, 1957.

5. *Natural Law in the Spiritual World,* by Henry Drummond, 1883.

6. *In Tune with the Infinite,* by Ralph Waldo Trine, 1897.

7. *Physics and Reality,* by Albert Einstein, 1936.

8. *An Introduction to Teilhard de Chardin,* by N. M. Wildiers, 1963.

9. *In the Center of Immensities,* by Sir Bernard Lovell, 1978.

10. *The Dragons of Eden,* by Carl Sagan, 1977.

11. "Science Pauses," by Vannevar Bush, *Fortune Magazine,* May, 1965.

12. *In Tune with the Infinite,* by Ralph Waldo Trine, 1897.

13. *The Transient and the Permanent in Christianity,* by Theodore Parker, 1841.

14. *Christianity in World History,* by Arend van Leewin, 1964.

15. *Empiricism: Scientific and Religious,* by Huston Smith, 1964.

16. *Something Beautiful for God,* by Malcolm Muggeridge, 1971.

17. *Spirits in Rebellion,* by Charles S. Braden, 1963.

18. "Science Pauses," by Vannevar Bush, *Fortune Magazine,* May, 1965.

19. "The Downfall of Communism," by Marceline Bradford, *The Freeman,* May, 1962.

20. *What is the Future of Man?* by Harold K. Schilling, 1971.

21. *New York Times,* March 5, 1970.

22. *Science and Human Values,* edited by Ralph Wendell Burhoe, 1971.

23. *The Dragons of Eden,* by Carl Sagan, 1977.

24. *Natural Law in the Spiritual World,* by Henry Drummond, 1883.

25. *Truth in Science and Religion,* by Henry Margenau, 1960.

26. *An Introduction to Teilhard de Chardin,* by Norbert M. Wildiers, 1968.

27. *Masterpieces of Christian Literature,* by Frank N. Magill, 1963.

28. *A Sermon at Unity Church, Miami,* by Charles Neal, 1976.

29. *My Philosophy and My Religion,* by Ralph Waldo Trine, 1896.

30. "The Church's One Foundation," by Samuel J. Stone, *Hymnal,* 1949.

31. *Sermon at Unity Church, Miami,* by Charles Neal, 1978.

32. *What All the World's A'seeking,* by Ralph Waldo Trine, 1896.

33. *The Divine Imperative,* by Emil Brunner, 1932.

34. *Architects of Moral Anarchy,* by John Howard, 1978.

KJV = King James Version

RSV = Revised Standard Version

NEB = New English Bible

JB   = Jerusalem Bible.

Bibliography

Books

Abdul Hamid, S. M.
Science Follows the Divine Qur-an
Karachi, 1972

Abele, Jean
Christianity and Science
Translated from French, R. F. Trevett
New York, Hawthorn, 1961; London, Burns & Oates. A. Clarke
    Books

Agar, William M.
Catholicism and the Progress of Science
New York, Macmillan, 1940

Alexander, Denis
Beyond Science
Philadelphia and New York, A. J. Holman Company, 1973; London,
    Lion Publishing, 1976

Akbar Ali, M.
Science in the Quran
Dacca, Malik Library, 1972

Alexander, Samuel
Space, Time and Deity
The Gifford Lectures at Glasgow, 1916–1918
London, Macmillan, 1920

Ali, Md. Wajed
Scientific Proofs of the Existence of God
Dacca, Society for Pakistan Studies, 1970

American Scientific Affiliation
Modern Science and Christian Faith: a symposium on the relationship of the Bible to modern science, by members of the American Scientific Affiliation
Wheaton, Illinois, Van Kampen, 1950

Ames, Thomas
A Spiritual Universe: the living garment of God
London, Arthur H. Stockwell, 1933

Anderson, James A.
Natural Theology: The metaphysics of God
Milwaukee, The Bruce Publishing Co., 1962

Arnold, Charles London
Cosmos, the Soul, and God: a monistic interpretation of the facts and findings of science
Chicago, A. C. McClurg & Co., 1907

Atkinson, David J.
"The Theological Method of T. F. Torrance"
M. Litt. Dissertation, Briston University, 1973

Aubert, Jean Marie
A God for Science? Tr. Paul Barrett
Westminster, Md., Newman P., 1967 154p. Bib. footnotes. Tr. of Recherche scientifique et foi chrétienne

Austin, William Harvey
The Relevance of Natural Science to Theology
London, Macmillan, 1976

Ayres, Clarence Edwin
Science, the False Messiah
Indianapolis, Bobbs-Merrill, c. 1927

Barry, William Francis
The Triumph of Life; or, Science and the Soul
London, Longmans & Co., 1928

Barth, Karl
Church Dogmatics III. *The Doctrine of Creation,* Volumes 1–4
Edinburgh, T. and T. Clark, 1958–1961

Bavink, Bernhard
Science and God
London, G. Bell, 1933

Bayne, Stephen F., Jr. (ed.)
Space Age Christianity
New York, Morehouse, 1963

Beasley, Walter J.
Creation's Amazing Architect
Melbourne, Australian Institute of Archaeology, 1968

Beck, S. D.
Modern Science and Christian Life
Minneapolis, Augsburg, 1970

Belcher, James E.
Scripture, Science and the Scientific Method
New York, Carlton Press, 1970

Belton, Leslie James
Religion and the Scientists
London, Lindsey Press, 1944

Benson, Clarence H.
Immensity; God's Greatness Seen in Creation
Chicago, Scripture Press, 1937

Baerg, Harry J.
Creation and Catastrophe: the story of Our Father's World
Washington, Review and Herald Pub. Assoc., 1972

Baillie, J. et al.
Science and Faith Today
London, Lutterworth Press, 1953

   *Natural Science and the Spiritual Life: Philosophical Discourse before the
   British Association for the Advancement of Science at Edinburgh,* 12
   August 1951
   Oxford University Press, 1957

Balthasar, Hans Urs von
Science, Religion and Christianity
London, Burns and Oates, 1958

Barbour, I. G.
Christianity and the Scientist
New York, Association Press, 1960

   Issues in Science and Religion
   Englewood Cliffs, N.J., Prentice-Hall, 1965

   *Myths, Models and Paradigms: a Comparative Study in Science and
   Religion*
   New York, Harper and Row, 1974

   Science and Secularity: the Ethics of Technology
   New York, Harper and Row, 1970

Barbour, Ian Graeme (ed.)
Science and Religion: New Perspectives in Dialogue
New York, Harper and Row, 1968

Barnes, E. W.
Scientific Theory and Religion: the World Described by Science and its Spiritual Interpretation
New York, Macmillan; Cambridge, University Press, 1933

Barnes, Kenneth
Has Science Exploded God?
Nutfield, Surrey, Denholm House Press, 1976

Benson, Purnell H.
Christ and the Scientific Road
Madison, N.J., Religion Through Scientific Study, 1954

Bettex Frédéric
Science and Christianity
Cincinnati, Jennings and Pye; New York, Eaton and Mains, 1901

Bingham, Charles T.
Christianity and Medical Science
Farmington, Conn., Salem Books, 1960

Birch, Louis Charles
Nature and God
London, SCM, c. 1965

Bivort de la Saudée, Jacques de (ed.)
God, Man and the Universe: A Christian Answer to Modern Materialism
London, Burns and Oates, 1954

Black, John Nicholson
The Dominion of Man: the search for ecological responsibility
Edinburgh, Edinburgh University Press, 1970

Blaikie, Robert J.
Secular Christianity and God Who Acts
London, Hodder and Stoughton, 1970

Boodin, John Elof
God and Creation
New York, Macmillan, 1934

Booth, Edwin P. (ed)
Religion Ponders Science
New York, Appleton-Century, 1964

Boutroux, Emile
Science and Religion in Contemporary Philosophy
(Tr. Jonathan Nield)
Port Washington, N.Y., Kennikat Press, 1970

Bower, Samuel Aethel
"The Contribution of Modern Science to Religion"
S.T.D. dissertation, Temple University, 1935

Bowman, John Wick
The Student of the New Testament and the Faith of the Church in a Scientific Age
Pittsburgh, Pa., John Gwyer, 1938

Bragg, William Henry
Science and Faith
London, Oxford University Press, 1941

Brain, Walter Russell
Science, Philosophy, and Religion
Cambridge, University Press, 1959

Braithwaite, Richard Bevan
An Empiricist's View of the Nature of Religious Belief
Cambridge, University Press, 1955

Branford, Victor
Science and Sanctity
London, Leplay House Press, and Williams and Norgate, 1923

Brock, Fred R. (ed.)
The Biblical Perspective of Science: Readings in Physical and Biological Science
New York, MSS Information Corp., 1972

Browne, Laurence Edward
Where Science and Religion Meet
Wallington, Surrey, Religious Education Press, 1950

Brunner, Emil
The Christian Doctrine of Creation and Redemption, Dogmatics
London, Lutterworth Press, 1952

Babe, R. H.
The Human Quest: a New Look at Science and the Christian Faith
Waco, Texas, Word, 1971

   The Encounter between Christianity and Science
   Grand Rapids, Eerdmans, 1967

Buber, Martin
The Eclipse of God. Studies in the Relation between Religion and Philosophy
New York, Harper Torchbooks, 1957

Budhananda, Swami
Can one be Scientific and yet Spiritual?
Calcutta, Advaita Ashrama, 1973

Burhoe, Ralph Wendell (ed.)
Science and Human Values in the 21st Century
Philadelphia, Westminster Press, 1971

Burroughs, John
The Light of Day: Religious Discussions and Criticisms from the Naturalist's Point of View
Boston and New York, Houghton Mifflin, 1900

Burtt, Edwin A.
The Metaphysical Foundations of Modern Science
New York, Harcourt Brace, 1925

Butterfield, H. B.
The Origins of Modern Science
London, Bell, 1949

Butterworth, Robert
The Theology of Creation
Notre Dame, Indiana, Fides Publishers, 1969

Buttrick, George Arthur
The Christian Fact and Modern Doubt: a Preface to a Restatement of Christian Faith
New York, London, Scribner's, 1934

Cantore, Enrico
Scientific Man. The Humanistic Significance of Science
New York, ISH Publications, 1977

Capra, Fritjof
The Tao of Physics: an Exploration of the Parallels between Modern Physics and Eastern Mysticism
Berkeley, Shambhala, 1975

Canther, K.
Science. Secularization and God: Toward a Theology of the Future
Nashville, Abingdon, 1969

Charon, Jean
Man in Search of Himself
London, George Allen and Unwin, 1967

Chatfield, Herbert Walter
A Scientist in Search of God
Croydon, England, Chatfield Applied Research Laboratories, 1964

Chauchard, Paul
Science and Religion
(Tr. S. J. Tester)
New York, Hawthorn Books, 1962

Chauvin, Rémy
God of the Scientists, God of the Experiment
(Tr. Salvator Attanasio)
Baltimore, Helicon Press, 1960

Clark, Cecil H. Douglas
The Scientist and the Supernatural
London, Epworth Press, 1966

Clark, Gordon Haddon
The Philosophy of Science and Belief in God
Nutley, N.J., Presbyterian and Reformed Pub. Co., 1965

Clark, John Ruskin
The Great Living System: New Answers from the Sciences to Old Religious Questions
Pacific Grove, California, Boxwood P., 1977

Clark, Robert Edward David
The Universe and God: a Study of the Order of Nature in the Light of Modern Knowledge
London, Hodder and Stoughton, 1939

    Scientific Rationalism and Christian Faith, with particular reference to the writings of Professor J. B. S. Haldane and Dr. J. S. Huxley
    London, Inter-Varsity Fellowship, 1945

    The Universe: Plan or Accident? The Religious Implications of Modern Science
    London, Paternoster Press, 1949

    The Christian Stake in Science
    Exeter, Paternoster Press, 1967

    Science and Christianity—a Partnership
    Mountain View, California, Pacific Press Pub. Assoc., 1972

    God Beyond Nature
    Mountain View, California, Pacific Press Pub. Assoc., 1977 (Revised edition of 1960)

Clarke, William Kemp Lowther
Doubts and Answers
London, SPCK, 1968

Cioran, Emile M.
The New Gods
(Tr. Richard Howard)
New York, Quadrangle, 1974

Cobb, J. B.
God and the World
Philadelphia, Westminster Press, 1969

Coder, S. Maxwell, and Howe, George F.
Bible, Science and Creation
Chicago, Moody Press, 1966

Coffin, Harold G.
Creation: Accident or Design?
Washington, Review and Herald Pub. Assoc., 1969

Collingwood, Robin George
Speculum Mentis, or, the Map of Knowledge
Oxford, Clarendon Press, 1924

> *Faith and Reason: a Study of the Relations between Religion and Science*
> London, Ernest Benn, 1928

> *An Essay in Metaphysics*
> Oxford, Clarendon Press, 1940

> *The Idea of Nature*
> Oxford, Clarendon Press, 1945

> *The Idea of History*
> Oxford, Clarendon Press, 1946

Combaluzier, Charles
God Tomorrow
(Tr. Matthew J. O'Connell)
New York, Paulist Press, 1974

Compton, Arthur Holly
The Freedom of Man
New Haven, Yale; London, H. Milford, Oxford, 1935

> *Religion of a Scientist*
> New York, Jewish Theological Seminary of America, 1938

> *The Human Meaning of Science*
> Chapel Hill, University of North Carolina, 1940

Corcoran, Patrick (ed.)
Looking at Lonergan's Method
(M. Hesse, W. Pannenberg, T. F. Torrance et al.)
Dublin, Talbot Press, 1975)

Cotton, Edward H. (ed.)
Has Science Discovered God? A Symposium
New York, Thomas Y. Crowell, 1931

Coulson, Charles Alfred
Christianity in an Age of Science
London, G. Cumberlege, Oxford, 1953

> *Science and Christian Belief*
> London, Oxford University Press, 1955

Science and the Idea of God
Cambridge, University Press, 1958

Science, Technology and the Christian
New York, Abingdon, 1960; London, Greenwood Press, 1979

Crommett, Eugene Earl
God, Creation and Man as Scientist
Ph.D. dissertation, The General Theological Seminary, 1960

Cross, Frank Leslie
Religion and the Reign of Science
London and New York, Longmans, Green, 1930

Culp, G. Richard
Remember thy Creator
Grand Rapids, Baker Book House, 1975

Cupitt, Don
The Worlds of Science and Religion
New York, Hawthorn Books, 1976; London, Sheldon Press, 1976

Curtis, Heber Doust
One Scientist's Religion
From articles synthesized and edited by Will Carl Rufus
Ann Arbor, Michigan, Wesley Foundation, 1944

Dalton, Matthew W.
The Period of God's Work on this Planet: or, How Science Agrees with the Revelation of our Beloved Redeemer: a Key to this Earth
Willard, Utah, 1906

Dahlke, Paul
Buddhism and Science
London, Macmillan, 1913. Translated from German, Bhikkhu Silacāra

Dampier-Whetham, William Cecil Dampier
The History of Science and Its Relations with Philosophy and Religion
Cambridge, University Press, 1929

Dandekar, Ramchandra Narayan
Universe in Hindu Thought
Bangalore, Dept. of Pub. and Extension Lectures,
Bangalore University, 1970

Darrow, Floyd Lavern
Through Science to God
Indianapolis, The Bobbs-Merrill Co., 1925

Davies, Paul
The Runaway Universe. The Ultimate Catastrophe—from the big bang to final heat death
London, J. M. Dent, 1978

Davies, P. W. C.
Space and Time in the Modern Universe
Cambridge, University Press, 1977

Davidheiser, Bolton
Science and the Bible
Grand Rapids, Baker Book House, 1971

Davis, W. H.
Science and Christian Faith
Abilene, Texas, Biblical Research Press, 1968

Dawson, W. Bell
The Bible Confirmed by Science
London, Marshall, Morgan and Scott, n.d.

Deane, Wallace
The Development of the Supernatural in Human Experience
London, J. Clarke, 1938

De Broglie, Louis
The Revolution in Physics
New York, The Noonday Press, 1953

de Lubac, H.
The Discovery of God
New York, Kenedy, 1960

De Vries, John
Beyond the Atom: an Appraisal of our Christian Faith in this Age of Atomic Science
Grand Rapids, Eerdmans, 1948

Dibble, Charles Lemuel
A Grammar of Belief: a Revaluation of the Basis of Christian Belief in the Light of Modern Science and Philosophy
Milwaukee, Morehouse, 1922

Dillenberger, J.
Protestant Thought and Natural Science. A historical interpretation of the issues behind the 500-year old debate.
New York, Doubleday, 1960; London, Greenwood Press, 1977

Dingle, Reginald James
Faith and Modern Science
London, Burns, Oates and Washbourne, 1935

Dinsmore, Charles Allen
Religious Certitude in an Age of Science
Chapel Hill, University of North Carolina, University Press, 1924

Dobzhansky, Theodosius Grigorievich
The Biology of Ultimate Concern
New York, World, 1971

"Evolution as a Creative Process"
Proceedings of the Ninth International Congress of Genetics,
(Caryologie Suppl., 1954). pp. 435–48

Dolphin, Lambert
Lord of Time and Space
Westchester, Illinois, Good News Pub., 1974

Doorly, John Williams
God and Science
London, F. Muller, 1949

Drawbridge, Cyprian Leycester (ed.)
Religion of Scientists: being Recent Opinons Expressed by Two Hundred Fellows of the Royal Society on the Subject of Religion and Theology
London, Ernest Benn, 1932

Dubarle, D.
Scientific Humanism and Christian Thought
(Tr. Reginald F. Trevett)
London, Blackfriars, 1956

Dye, David L.
Faith and the Physical World: a Comprehensive View
Grand Rapids, Eerdmans, 1966; Exeter, Paternoster Press, 1967

du Noüy, Pierre Lecomte
Human Destiny
New York, Longmans Green & Co., 1947

Eccles, J. C.
Facing Reality. Philosophical Adventures of a Brain Scientist
Berlin, Heidelberg, and New York, Springer-Verlag, 1970

The Human Mystery. The Gifford Lectures, University of Edinburgh, 1977–78
Berlin, Heidelberg, New York. Springer International, 1979

Eccles, J. C., with Popper, Karl R.
The Self and its Brain. An Argument for Interactionism
Berlin, Heidelberg, and New York, Springer International, 1977

Eddington, Arthur Stanley
The Nature of the Physical World
Cambridge, University Press, 1928

Science and the Unseen
New York, Macmillan, 1930

Science and Religion
London, Friends Home Service Committee, 1931

The Philosophy of Physical Science
New York, Macmillan; Cambridge, University Press, 1939

Eddy, George Sherwood
New Challenges to Faith: What Shall I Believe in the Light of Psychology and the New Science
New York, George H. Doran, 1926

Esterer, Arnulf K.
Towards a Unified Faith
New York, Philosophical Library, 1963

Everest, F. Alton (ed.)
Modern Science and Christian Faith
Chicago, Van Kampen Press, 1950

Eyring, Henry
The Faith of a Scientist
Salt Lake City, Bookcraft, 1967

Faith, Science and the Future: Preparatory Readings for a World Conference Organised by the WCC at M.I.T. ed. Charles Birch et al.
Cambridge, Mass., July 12–24, 1979.
Geneva, WCC, 1978

Farmer, Herbert Henry
The World and God: a Study of Prayer, Providence and Miracle in Christian Experience
London, Nisbet, 1935

Farrer, Austin
Finite and Infinite
London, Dacre Press, 1948

The Freedom of the Will
London, A. and C. Black, 1958

Love Almighty and Ills Unlimited
London, Collins, 1962

A Science of God?
London, Geoffrey Bles, 1966

God is Not Dead
New York, Morehouse-Barlow, 1966

Faith and Speculation. An Essay in Philosophical Theology
London, A. and C. Black, 1967

Fechner, Gustav Theodor
Religion of a Scientist
New York, Pantheon Books, 1946

Feibleman, James
The Pious Scientist: Nature, God, and Man in Religion
New York, Bookman Associates, 1958

Ferris, A. J.
The Conflict of Science and Religion
Vancouver, Association of the Covenant People, 1969

Ferris, Theodore Parker
This Created World
New York, London, Harper and Brothers, 1944

Feynman, R. P.
"The Relation of Science and Religion," *Frontiers of Science,* ed. Edward
   Hutchings
New York, Basic Books, 1958

Finegan, Jack
Space, Atoms and God: Christian Faith and the Nuclear-Space Age
St. Louis, Bethany Press, 1959

Fisher, Ronald Aylmer
Creative Aspects of Natural Law
Fourth Arthur Stanley Eddington Memorial Lecture
Cambridge, University Press, 1950

Fisher, Stacey Stephen
Through Natural Laws to the First Great Cause
New York, Greenwich Book Publishers, 1958

Fiske, John
Through Nature to God
Boston and New York, Houghton, Mifflin, 1899

Fitti, Charles J.
Between God and Man
New York, Philosophical Library, 1978

Foster, Allyn King
The New Dimensions of Religion
New York, Macmillan, 1931

Foster, Michael B.
Mystery and Philosophy
London, SCM Press, 1957

Franciscan education conference
36th Rensselaer, N.Y., 1955
Nature, the Mirror of God
Washington, D.C., Franciscan educational conference, Capuchin College, 1956

Fruchtbaum, Harold
The Wisdom and the Works: Natural Theology and the Rise of Science
Ph.D. dissertation, Harvard University, 1964

Fulton, William
Nature and God: an Introduction to Theistic Studies, with Special Reference to the Relations of Science and Religion
Edinburgh, T. and T. Clark, 1927

Gager, Charles Stuart
The Relationship between Science and Theology: How to Think about It
Chicago and London, The Open Court Pub. Co., 1925

Gamow, G.
The Creation of the Universe
New York, Viking Press, 1952

Garrison, Webb B.
Wonders of Science: Mysteries that Point to God
New York, Sheed and Ward, 1956

> *Wonders of Man: Mysteries that Point to God*
> New York, Sheed and Ward, 1957

Gaskell, Augusta
Whence? Whither? Why? A New Philosophy Based on the Physical Sciences
New York, Putnam, 1939

Gelwick, Richard
The Way of Discovery. An Introduction to the Thought of Michael Polanyi
New York and Oxford, University Press, 1977

Gilkes, Anthony Newcombe
Faith for Modern Man
London, Faber and Faber, 1960

Gilkey, Langdon
Maker of Heaven and Earth
Garden City, N.Y., Doubleday, 1959

> *Religion and the Scientific Future: Reflections on Myth, Science and Theology*
> New York, Harper and Row, 1970

Gladden, Lee, and Gladden, Vivianne Cervantes
Heirs of the Gods: a Space Age Interpretation of the Bible
New York, Rawson Wade, 1978

Gopi, Krishna
The Biological Basis of Religion and Genius
New York, NC Press, 1971

Gosling, David L.
Science and Religion in India

Madras, Published for the Christian Institute for the Study of Religion and Society by Christian Lit. Soc., 1976

Grant, Frederick Clifton
Frontiers of Christian Thinking
Chicago, Willett, Clark, 1935

Gray, Bryan J. A.
Theology as Science. An Examination of the Theological Methodology of Thomas F. Torrance
Louvain, Catholic University of Louvain, 1975

Grene, Marjorie
The Knower and the Known
New York, Basic Books, 1966; London, University of California Press, 1974

Grene, Marjorie (ed.)
Interpretations of Life and Mind. Essays around the Problem of Reduction
New York, The Humanities Press, 1971; London, Routledge, Kegan Paul, 1977

Greenwood, William Osborne
Biology and Christian Belief
London, SCM Press, 1938

> *Christianity and the Mechanists*
> London, Eyre and Spottiswoode, 1941

Gregory, Richard Arman
Religion in Science and Civilisation
London, Macmillan, 1940

Guenther, Conrad
Nature and Revelation
Tr. Sigrid Munro
Ilfracombe, A. H. Stockwell, 1960

Haas, Ernst
The Creation
London, Joseph; New York, Viking Press, 1971

Habgood, John Stapylton
Truths in Tension: New Perspectives on Religion and Science
New York, Holt, Rinehart and Winston, 1965 (1964)

Haeckel, Ernst Heinrich Philipp August
The Confession of Faith of a Man of Science
Tr. J. Gilchrist
London, Black, 1903

> *The Riddle of the Universe*
> New York, Harper and Brothers, 1900

Haldane, John Burdon Sanderson
Possible Worlds and Other Papers
Freeport, N.Y., Books for Libraries Press, 1971 (1928)

Haldane, John Scott
Materialism
London, Hodder and Stoughton, 1932

Hand, James Edward (ed.)
Ideals of Science and Faith: Essays by Various Authors
New York, Longmans, 1904

Hardy, Alister Clavering
The Living Stream
London, Collins, 1965

> *The Divine Flame: An Essay Towards a Natural History of Religion*
> London, Collins, 1966

> *The Biology of God: A Scientist's Study of Man the Religious Animal*
> London, J. Cape, 1975

> *The Spiritual Nature of Man*
> Oxford, Oxford University Press, 1979

Harman, Nathaniel Bishop
Science and Religion
London, G. Allen and Unwin, 1935

Harold, Preston, and Babcok, Winifred
The Single Reality
Winston-Salem, N.C., Harold Institute (dist. by Dodd, Mead, New York), 1971

Hartshorne, Charles
A Natural Theology for our Time
La Salle, Illinois, Open Court, 1967

> *The Divine Relativity. A Social Conception of God*
> New Haven, Yale University Press, 1948

Hartshorne, Marion Holmes
The Promise of Science and the Power of Faith
Philadelphia, Westminster Press, 1958

Haselden, Kyle Emerson (ed.)
Changing Man: the Threat and the Promise; Five Scientists and Five Theologians on Christian Faith and Evolutionary Thought
Garden City, N.Y., Doubleday, 1968

Hayward, Alan
God's Truth: a Scientist Shows Why it Makes Sense to Believe the Bible
London, Marshall, Morgan and Scott, 1973

God Is: a Scientist Shows Why it Makes Sense to Believe in God
London, Marshall, Morgan and Scott, 1978

Heard, Gerald
Is God Evident? An Essay Toward a Natural Theology
New York, Harper, 1948

Heason, Herbert William
A Theology of Harmony: the Science of God
London, Regency Press, 1966

Hedley, George Percy
Religion and the Natural World
Seattle, Distributed by the University of Washington Press, 1962

Hefley, James C.
Adventurers with God: Scientists who are Christians
Grand Rapids, Zondervan, 1967

Hefner, Philip
The Promise of Teilhard. The Meaning of the Twentieth Century in Christian Perspective
Philadelphia, J. B. Lippincott, 1970

"The Future as Our Future, A Teilhardian Perspective," in Cousins, E. H. (ed.), *Hope and the Future of Man*
Philadelphia, Fortress Press, 1972

"Basic Assumptions about the Cosmos," in Yourgrau, W., and Breck, A. D., *Cosmology, History and Theology*
New York, Plenum Press, 1977

Heim, Karl
Christian Faith and Natural Science
London, SCM Press, 1953

The Transformation of the Scientific World View
London, SCM Press, 1953

Heinecken, Martin John
God in the Space Age
Philadelphia, J. C. Winston, 1959

Heisenberg, Werner
Across the Frontiers
New York, Harper Torchbooks, 1971

Physics and Beyond
London, George Allen and Unwin, 1971

Physics and Philosophy. The Revolution in Modern Science
St. Andrews Gifford Lectures, 1955–56
New York, Harper, 1958

Henderson, Lawrence Joseph
The Order of Nature: An Essay
Cambridge, Mass., Harvard University Press, 1925.

Hesse, Mary Brenda
Science and the Human Imagination: Aspects of the History and Logic of Physical Science
New York, Philosophical Library, 1955

Hick, John Harwood
Biology and the Soul. The twenty-fifth Arthur Stanley Eddington Memorial Lecture delivered at Cambridge, February 1, 1972.
Cambridge, University Press, 1972

Hill, Mabel (ed.)
Wise men worship; a Compilation of Excerpts from Scientists, Philosophers, and Professional Men concerning Science and Religion.
New York, E. P. Dutton, 1931

Hill, Owen Aloysius
Psychology and Natural Theology
New York, Macmillan, 1921

Himrod, David Kirk
"Cosmic Order and Divine Activity; a Study in the Relationship between Science and Religion, 1850–1950"
Ph.D. dissertation, University of California, Los Angeles, 1977

Hindmarsh, William Russell
Science and Faith
London, Epworth Press, 1968

Hiscox, Henry Orne
In the Beginning God stands Forth
New York, Revell, 1935

Hocking, William Ernest
Science and the Idea of God
Chapel Hill, University of North Carolina Press, 1944

Hodgson, Leonard
Theology in an Age of Science
(Inaugural Lecture, Oxford, November 3, 1944)
Oxford, Clarendon Press, 1944

Hodgson, P. E.
Is Science Christian?
London, Catholic Truth Society, 1978

Hofstadter, Douglas R.
Gödel, Escher, Bach: An Eternal Golden Braid
Brighton, Sussex, The Harvester Press, 1978

Hooykaas, Reijer
Philosophia Libera: Christian Faith and the Freedom of Science
Wheaton, Illinois, Tyndale Press, 1957

> *Religion and the Rise of Modern Science*
> Edinburgh, Scottish Academic Press, 1957

> *Natural Law and Divine Miracle: a Historical-Critical Study of the Principle of Uniformity in Geology, Biology and Theology*
> Leiden, E. J. Brill, 1959

> *The Christian Approach in Teaching Science*
> London, Published for the Research Scientists' Christian Fellowship by the Tyndale Press, 1960

Horton, Robert Forman
"Science as the Interpreter of Religion"
GREAT ISSUES 188–221. Great Issues.
London, T. F. Unwin, 1909

Horton, Walter Marshall
Theism and the Scientific Spirit
New York, Harper and Brothers, 1933

Hudson, A. O.
God of all Space
Hounslow, England, Bible Fellowship Union, 1971

Hulsbosch, Ansfridus
God's Creation: Creation, Sin and Redemption in an Evolving World
(Tr. Martin Versfeld)
London. New York, Sheed and Ward, 1965

Huntley, Herbert Edwin
The Faith of a Physicist
London, G. Bles, 1960

Huxley, Julian Sorell
Essays of a Biologist
New York, Knopf, 1923

> *Science, Religion and Human Nature*
> London, Watts, 1930

Hyman, Julius
The Riddle of the Individual and His Universe
Berkeley, California, Fundamental Research Press, 1970

Ikeda, Daisaku
Science and Religion
Tokyo, Sokagakkai, 1965

Ikin, Alice Graham
Wholeness is Living: Scientific Thinking and Religious Experience
London, G. Bles, 1970

Inge, William Ralph
Science and Ultimate Truth: Fison Memorial Lecture 1926
New York, London, Longmans, Green, 1926

> *God and the Astronomers*
> London, Longmans, Green, 1933

> *International Conference on the Unity of the Sciences,* 6th San Francisco, 1977.
> *The search for absolute values in a changing world: proceedings of the Sixth International Conference on the Unity of the Sciences,* November 25–27, 1977, San Francisco.
> New York, International Cultural Foundation Press, 1978

Irwin, James Benson
To Rule the Night: the Discovery Voyage of Astronaut Jim Irwin
Philadelphia, A. J. Holman, 1973

Isaacs, Alan
The Survival of God in the Scientific Age
Baltimore, Penguin Books, 1966

Jacobs, Thornwell
The New Science and the Old Religion
Oglethorpe University, California, University Press, 1927

Jaki, Stanley L.
The Relevance of Physics
Chicago, University of Chicago Press, 1966

> *Brain, Mind and Computers*
> New York, Herder and Herder, 1969

> *The Paradox of Olber's Paradox*
> New York, Herder and Herder, 1969

> *The Milky Way. An Elusive Road for Science*
> New York, David and Charles Neale Watson Academic Publications, 1972

> *Science and Creation: from Eternal Cycles to an Oscillating Universe*
> Edinburgh, Scottish Academic Press, 1974

> *Culture and Science: Two Lectures delivered at Assumption University, Windsor, Canada, on February 26 and 28, 1975*
> Windsor, Ontario, University of Windsor Press, 1975

> *Giordano Bruno. The Ash Wednesday Supper*
> Translated with an Introduction and Notes
> The Hague, Mouton, 1975

> *J. H. Lambert. Cosmological Letters On the Arrangement of the World-Edifice*
> Translated with an Introduction and Notes
> Edinburgh, Scottish Academic Press, 1976

The Origin of Science and the Science of its Origin
Edinburgh, Scottish Academic Press, 1978

Planets and Planetarians
Edinburgh, Scottish Academic Press, 1978

The Road of Science and the Ways to God
Edinburgh, Scottish Academic Press, 1978

Jammer, Max
Concepts of Space
Cambridge, Harvard University Press, 1954

Jauncey, James H.
Science Returns to God
Grand Rapids, Zondervan, 1961

Jeeves, Malcolm Alexander
The Scientific Enterprise and Christian Faith
Downers Grove, Illinois, Intervarsity Press, 1969

Joad, C. E. M.
God and Evil
London, The Religious Book Club, 1942

Johnson, Francis Howe
God in Evolution: a Pragmatic Study of Theology
New York, Longmans, Green, 1911

Johnson, Roger Alan et al.
Critical Issues in Modern Religion
Englewood Cliffs, N.J., Prentice-Hall, 1973

Jones, Bernard Ewart (ed.)
Earnest Enquirers after Truth: a Gifford Anthology
Excerpts from Gifford Lectures, 1888–1968
London, G. Allen and Unwin, 1970

Jordan, Pascual
Physics of the Twentieth Century
New York, Philosophical Library, 1944

Kaiser, Christopher B.
The Logic of Complementarity in Science and Theology
Ph.D. dissertation, University of Edinburgh, 1974

Kelly, Howard Atwood
A Scientific Man and the Bible
New York, Harper and Brothers, 1925

Keyser, Cassius J.
Science and Religion
New Haven, Yale University Press, 1914

Khan, Mohammed Yamin
God, Soul, and Universe in Science and Islam
Lahore, Sh. M. Ashraf, 1962

King-Farlow, John
Reason and Religion: Philosophy and Religion in a Scientific Age
London, Darton, Longman and Todd, 1969

Kingrey, David W.
Now is Tomorrow: Crucial Questions for Space-age Christians
Richmond, Indiana, Friends United Press, 1975

Kirk, Harris Elliott
Star, Atoms, and God
Chapel Hill, University of North Carolina Press, 1932

Klotz, John William
Modern Science in the Christian Life
St. Louis, Concordia, 1961

Knox, Ronald Arbuthnott
God and the Atom
New York, Sheed, 1945

Knutson, Evelyn Elizabeth
Reverence in a World of Science-based Technology
D. Min. dissertation, School of Theology at Claremont, 1978

Koestler, Arthur
The Sleepwalkers. A History of Man's Changing Vision of the Universe
New York, Macmillan, 1959; London, Hutchinson, 1968 and Penguin, 1970

Kolakowski, Leszek
The Alienation of Reason. A History of Positivist Thought
Garden City, New York, Doubleday, 1968

> *Main Currents of Marxism. Its Rise, Growth and Dissolution*
> Three volumes
> Oxford, Clarendon Press, 1978

Krimsky, Joseph Hayyim
A Doctor's Soliloquy
New York, Philosophical Library, 1953

Ladrière, J.
Language and Belief
Dublin, Gill and Macmillan, 1972

Laird, John
Theism and Cosmology: Being the first series of a course of Gifford Lectures on Metaphysics and Theism at the University of Glasgow in 1939

London, G. Allen, 1940
> *Mind and Deity: Being the second series of a course of Gifford Lectures on the general subject of Metaphysics and Theism given in the University of Glasgow in 1940*
> Hamden, Conn., Archon Books, 1970

Lammerts, Walter Edward (ed.)
Why not Creation? Selected Articles from the Creation Research Society Quarterly, Volume I–V (1964–1968)
Nutley, N.J., Presbyterian and Reformed Pub. Co., 1970
> *Scientific Studies in Special Creation*
> Nutley, N.J., Presbyterian and Reformed Pub. Co., 1971

Lanczos, Cornelius
Judaism and Science
Leeds, Leeds University Press, 1970

Langford, Jerome J.
Galileo, Science and the Church
New York, Desclee, 1966

Langmack, Holger Christian
God and the Universe: Unity of Science and Religion
New York, Philosophical Library, 1953
> *Science, Faith and Logic: Scientific Faith Substantiated by a Logical Science*
> New York, Philosophical Library, 1964

Larson, Muriel
God's Fantastic Creation
Chicago, Moody Press, 1975

Lattey, Cuthbert (ed.)
Religion and Science: Papers read at the Summer School of Catholic Studies, Cambridge, 1939
London, Burns Oates and Washbourne, 1940

Leaver, Jan
Where are we Headed? A Christian Perspective on Evolution
Grand Rapids, W. B. Eerdmans, 1970

Lecomte du Nouy, Pierre
Human Destiny
New York, Longmans, Green, 1947

Leete, Frederick De Land
Christianity in Science
New York, Cincinnati, Abingdon, 1928

Leighton, Gerald Rowley
Scientific Christianity: a Study in the Biology of Character
New York, Moffat, Yard, 1910

Lever, Jan
Where are we Headed? A Biologist Talks about Origins, Evolution, and the Future
(Tr. Walter Lagerway)
Grand Rapids, Eerdmans, 1970

Levitt, Zola
Creation: a Scientist's Choice
Wheaton, Illinois, Victor Books, 1976

Lewis, C. S.
The Problem of Pain
London, Geoffrey Bles, 1940, and Fount Paperbacks, 1977

    Miracles. A Preliminary Study
    London, Geoffrey Bles, 1947, and Fount Paperbacks, 1960

Lindsay, Alexander Dunlop
Religion, Science, and Society in the Modern World
New Haven, Yale; London, M. Milford, Oxford, 1943

Lodge, Oliver Joseph
The Substance of Faith Allied with Science: a Catechism for Parents and Teachers
New York and London, Harper, 1907

Lonergan, Bernard
Insight. A Study in Human Understanding
London, Longmans, Green, 1957

    Method in Theology
    London, Darton, Longman and Todd, 1971
    Philosophy of God and Theology
    London, Darton, Longman and Todd, 1974

Long, Edward Le Roy
Science and Christian Faith. A Study in Partnership
New York, Association Press, 1950

    Religious Beliefs of American Scientists
    Philadelphia, Westminster Press, 1952

Lonsdale, Kathleen Yardley
Science, Religion and the Student
London, Friends Home Service Committee, 1970

Lovell, Bernard
The Individual and the Universe. The 1958 Reith Lectures
Oxford, Oxford University Press, 1959

> *The Exploration of Outer Space*
> London, Oxford University Press, 1962

> *In the Center of Immensities*
> New York, Harper and Row, 1978; London, Hutchinson, 1979

Lucas, J. R.
The Freedom of the Will
Oxford, Oxford University Press, 1970

> *A Treatise on Time and Space*
> London, Methuen and Co., 1973

Lunn, Arnold Henry Moore
The Revolt against Reason
London, Eyre and Spottiswoode, 1950

Maatman, R. W.
The Bible, Natural Science, and Evolution
Grand Rapids, Reformed Fellowship Inc., 1970

McCallum, Martha, and Hamblin, Jane
God's Incredible Plan
Old Tappan, N.J., Revell, 1978

MacCormac, Earl R.
Metaphor and Myth in Science and Religion
Durham, North Carolina, Duke University Press, 1976

McCrady, Edward
Reason and Revelation: Argument for the Truth of Revealed Religion Based Solely upon the Evidence of Science and Philosophy
Grand Rapids, Eerdmans, 1936

Macdonald, Greville
The Religious Sense in its Scientific Aspect
London, Hodder and Stoughton, 1903

Macfie, Ronald Campbell
Science Rediscovers God; or, The Theodicy of Science
Edinburgh, T. and T. Clark, 1930

> *The Theology of Evolution*
> London, Unicorn, 1933

Mackay, Andrew C.
James Clerk Maxwell. Pathfinder of Modern Science
Dumfries, Community Council of Kirkpatrick Durham, 1979

MacKay, Donald MacCrimmon (ed.)
Christianity in a Mechanistic Universe
Chicago, Inter-varsity Press, 1965

MacKay, Donald MacCrimmon
Information, Mechanism and Meaning
Cambridge, Mass., M.I.T. Press, 1969

　　The Clock-work Image: a Christian Perspective on Science
　　Downers Grove, Illinois, Inter-varsity Press, 1974

　　Freedom of Action in a Mechanistic Universe
　　Eddington Lecture
　　London, Cambridge University Press, 1976

　　*Science, Chance and Providence: the Riddell Memorial Lectures delivered
　　at the University of Newcastle upon Tyne, March 1977*
　　New York, Oxford, 1978

　　Human Science and Human Dignity: London Lectures in Contemporary Christianity
　　London, Hodder and Stoughton, 1979

　　Brains, Machines and Persons
　　London, Collins, 1980; Grand Rapids, Eerdmans, 1980

McKinney, Richard W. A. (ed.)
Creation, Christ and Culture. Studies in Honour of T. F. Torrance
Edinburgh, T. and T. Clark, 1976

McKinnon, Alastair
Falsification and Belief
The Hague, Paris, Mouton, 1970

McLaughlin, Patrick J.
Modern Science and God
Dublin, Clonmore and Reynolds, 1952

　　The Church and Modern Science
　　New York, Philosophical Library, 1957

Macmurray, John
Freedom in the Modern World
London, Faber and Faber, 1932

　　Reason and Emotion
　　London, Faber and Faber, 1935

　　Interpreting the Universe
　　London, Faber and Faber, 1936

　　The Boundaries of Science
　　London, Faber and Faber, 1939

McNeur, Ronald W.
Space, Time and God
Philadelphia, Westminster Press, 1961

McPherson, Thomas
The Argument from Design
London, Macmillan; New York, St. Martin's Press, 1972

Macy, Christopher (ed.)
Science, Reason and Religion
Buffalo, N.Y., Prometheus Books, 1974

Maltby, Arthur
Religion and Science
London, Library Association, 1965

> *Man and His Nature: Broadcast talks in Religion and Philosophy*
> London, SCM Press, 1949

Mascall, Eric Lionel
Christian Theology and Natural Science: Some Questions of their Relations
London, Longmans, Green, 1956

> *The Secularisation of Christianity*
> London, Darton, Longman and Todd, 1965

> *The Openness of Being: Natural Theology Today*
> London, Darton, Longman and Todd, 1971

Mason, Mrs. Francis (Baker) (ed.)
The Great Design: Order and Progress in Nature
London, Duckworth Press, 1934

Mather, Kirtley Fletcher
Science in Search of God
New York, H. Holt, 1928

Mathews, Shailer
Contributions of Science to Religion
Freeport, N.Y., Books for Libraries Press, 1970

Matthews, Walter Robert
The Purpose of God: Alexander Robertson Lectures 1935
London, Nisbet, 1937

May, J. Lewis (ed.)
God and the Universe, the Christian Position: A Symposium, by S. C. Carpenter, M. C. D'Arcy, and Bertram Lee Woolf
New York, Dial Press, 1931

Merz, John Theodore
Religion and Science: a Philosophical Essay
Edinburgh and London, W. Blackwood, 1915

Meyers, Garth
Form and Nature of the Ultimate Power, as Seen through Science
Philadelphia, Dorrance, 1971

Miles, Thomas Richard
Religion and the Scientific Outlook
London, Allen and Unwin, 1959

Miller, Carl Wallace
A Scientist's Approach to Religion
New York, Macmillan, 1947

Millikan, Robert Andrews
Evolution in Science and Religion
New Haven, Yale; London, H. Milford, Oxford, 1927

Milne, Edward Arthur
Modern Cosmology and the Christian Idea of God
Oxford, Clarendon Press, 1952

Mohan, Robert Paul (ed.)
Technology and Christian Culture
Washington, D.C., Catholic University of America Press, 1960

Monsma, John Clover (ed.)
*The Evidence of God in an Expanding Universe: Forty American Scientists
    Declare their Affirmative Views on Religion*
New York, Putnam, 1958

    *Science and Religion: Twenty-three prominent Churchmen Express their
        Opinions*
    New York, Putnam, 1962

Moore, John N., and Slusher, Harold Schultz
Biology: a Search for Order in Complexity
Prepared by the Textbook Committee of the Creation Research Soci-
    ety
Grand Rapids, Zondervan, 1970

More, Louis Trenchard
The Limitations of Science
New York, H. Holt, 1915

Morris, Daniel Luzon
Possibilities Unlimited: a Scientist's Approach to Christianity
New York, Harper, 1952

Morris, Henry Madison (ed.)
Scientific Creationism, prepared by the technical staff and consultants of
    the Institute for Creation Research
San Diego, California, Creation-Life Publishers, 1974

Morris, Henry Madison et al. (eds.)
Creation: Acts, Facts, Impacts
San Diego, California, ICR Pub. Co., 1974

Morris, Henry Madison
Studies in the Bible and Science: or, Christ and Creation
Philadelphia, Presbyterian and Reformed Pub. Co., 1966

> *The Bible and Modern Science*
> Chicago, Moody Press, 1968

> *Biblical Cosmology and Modern Science*
> Grand Rapids, Baker Book House, 1970

> *The Remarkable Birth of Planet Earth*
> Minneapolis, Dimension Books, 1972

Morrison, Abraham Cressy
Man Does Not Stand Alone
New York, Revell, 1944

Morriss, Frank
The Forgotten Revelation: Essays on God and Nature
Chicago, Franciscan Herald Press, 1964

Morrison, James Horne
Christian Faith and the Science of Today
London, Hodder and Stoughton, 1936

Morton, John
Man, Science and God
London, Collins, 1972

Munitz, Melton K.
Space, Time and Creation
Glencoe, Illinois, Free Press, 1957

Murphy, William B. et al.
God and His Creation
Dubuque, Iowa, Priory Press, 1958

Murray-Rust, David Malcolm
God in the Universe: a Twentieth-Century Quaker Looks at Science and Theology
London, Published for Woodbrooke College by the Friends Home Service Committee, 1973

Murry, John Middleton
God, Being an Introduction to the Science of Metabiology
London, Jonathan Cape, 1929

Needham, Joseph
The Great Amphibium: Four Lectures on the Position of Religion in a World Dominated by Science
London, Student Christian Movement Press, 1931

Needham, Joseph (ed.)
Science, Religion and Reality
New York, G. Braziller, 1955

Neville, Robert Cummings
God the Creator: on the Transcendence and Presence of God
Chicago, University of Chicago Press, 1968

Newman, Barclay Moon
Science Rediscovers God
Princeton, Science Index Press, 1936

Noble, Edmund
Purposive Evolution: the Link between Science and Religion
New York, H. Holt, 1926

Northrop, Filmer S. C.
The Meeting of East and West
New York, Macmillan, 1946

> *The Logic of the Sciences and the Humanities*
> Cleveland and New York, The World Publishing Company, 1959
>
> *Man, Nature and God*
> New York, Trident Press, 1962

Noyes, Alfred
The Unknown God
New York, Sheed and Ward, 1934

Nygren, Anders
*Meaning and Method: Prolegomena to a Scientific Philosophy of Religion and
  a Scientific Theology*
Philadelphia, Fortress Press, 1972; London, Epworth Press, 1972

O'Brien, John Anthony
Religion in a Changing World: Christianity and Modern Thought
Huntington, Indiana, Our Sunday Visitor Press, 1939

Ostlin, Melvin T.
*Thinking Out Loud about the Space Age. Is the Christian Faith Adequate for a
  Space Age?*
Philadelphia, Dorrance, 1962

Otto, Rudolf
Naturalism and Religion
Tr. J. Arthur Thomson; ed. W. D. Morrison
New York, Putnam, 1907

Overman, R. H.
*Evolution and the Christian Doctrine of Creation:
A Whiteheadean Interpretation*
Philadelphia, Westminster Press, 1967

Overman, Ralph T.
Who Am I? The Faith of a Scientist
Waco, Texas, Word, 1971

Owen, Derwyn Randolph Grier
Scientism, Man, and Religion
Philadelphia, Westminster, 1952

Pack, Frederick J.
Science and Belief in God
Salt Lake City, Deseret News Press, 1924

Pannenberg W.
The Idea of God and Human Freedom
Philadelphia, Westminster Press, 1973

> *Theology and the Philosophy of Science*
> Tr. Francis McDonagh
> Philadelphia, Westminster Press, 1976

Parrott, Bob W.
Earth, Moon, and Beyond
Waco, Texas, Word, 1969

Patten, Donald W. (ed.)
Symposium on Creation I, II, and III
Grand Rapids, Baker Book House, 1968, 1970, 1971

Payne, Harriet Chaffey
Eternal Crucible:a New Cosmology
Hicksville, N.Y., Exposition, 1974

Peacocke, Arthur Robert
Science and the Christian Experiment
London, New York, Oxford, 1971

> *Creation and the World of Science*
> Oxford, Oxford University Press, 1979

> "Cosmos and Creation,
> in *Cosmology, History and Theology*, pp. 365–81,
> ed. W. Yourgrau and A. D. Breck
> New York, Plenum Press, 1977

> "The Nature and Evolution of Biological Hierarchies,"
> in *New Approaches to Genetics*, pp. 245–304,
> ed. P. W. Kent
> London, Oriel Press, Routledge and Kegan Paul, 1978

Perlman, Robert Odehyah
Science and Religion for Modern Man
Jerusalem, Jerusalem Institute for the Advancement of Philosophy, 1964

Peters, Eugene H.
The Creative Advance. An Introduction to Process Philosophy as a Context for Christian Faith
St. Louis, The Bethany Press, 1966

Peters, Karl Edward
The Concept of God and the Method of Science: An Exploration of the Possibility of Scientific Theology
PhD Dissertation, Columbia University, 1971

Phenix, Philip Henry
Infinitude: a Study of Science, Theology, and the Scientific Spirit with Special Reference to the "New Physics"
Ph.D. dissertation, Columbia University, 1950

Phin, John
The Evolution of the Atmosphere as a Proof of Design and Purpose in the Creation, and of the Existence of a Personal God: a Simple and Rigorously Scientific Reply to Modern Materialistic Atheism
New York, The Industrial Pub. Co., 1908

Pilkington, Roger
World without End
London, Macmillan; New York, St. Martin's Press, 1961

> *Heavens Alive: the Impact of Science on the Image of God*
> London, Macmillan, 1964

Pinkel, Benjamin
The Existential Adventure: the Roles of Science and Belief
Marina del Rey, California, DeVorss, 1976

Pirone, Frank John
Science and the Love of God
New York, Philosophical Library, 1957

Pius XII, Pope
Modern Science and God
Tr. P. J. McLaughlin
New York, Philosophical Library, 1954

Plotkin, Frederick
Faith and Reason. Essays in the Religious and Scientific Imagination
New York, Philosophical Library, 1970

Podeur, Lucien
Image Moderne du Monde et Foi chrétienne
Paris, Le Centurion, 1976

Polanyi, Michael
Science, Faith and Society
London, Oxford University Press, 1946

The Logic of Liberty
London, Routledge and Kegan Paul, 1951

Personal Knowledge: Towards a Post-Critical Philosophy
London, Routledge and Kegan Paul, 1958

The Study of Man
London, Routledge and Kegan Paul, 1959

The Tacit Dimension
London, Routledge and Kegan Paul, 1967

Knowing and Being
London, Routledge and Kegan Paul, 1969

Scientific Thought and Social Reality
Essays by Michael Polanyi, edited by Fred Schwarz, Psychological
    Issues Volume VIII/No. 4, Monograph 32
New York, International Universities Press, 1974

Polanyi, Michael, with Prosch, Harry
Meaning
Chicago, Chicago University Press, 1975

Pollard, William Grosvenor
The Cosmic Drama
New York, National Council of the Episcopal Church, 1955

*Chance and Providence: God's Action in a World Governed by Scientific
    Law*
New York, Scribner's, 1958

Physicist and Christian: a Dialogue between the Communities
Greenwich, Conn., Seabury Press, 1961

Science and Faith: Twin Mysteries
New York, T. Nelson, 1970

Powell, Arthur Edward
The Nature of Man: a Synthesis of Science and Religion
New York, Vantage Press, 1957

Price, George McCready
Modern Discoveries Which Help Us to Believe
New York, Revell, 1934

Price, H. H.
Some Aspects of the Conflict between Science and Religion
Cambridge, Cambridge University Press, 1953

Pupin, Michael Idvorsky
The new Reformation: from Physical to Spiritual Realities
New York, London, Scribner, 1927

Qadri, M. M.
Integration of Islam with Science
Lahore, Begum Humayun Trust, 1967

Queffélec, Henri
Technology and Religion
Translated from French by S. J. Tester
New York, Hawthorn, 1964

Quinton, Gertrude E.
Scientific and Religious Knowledge
London, SCM Press, 1950

Rabinovitch, Nachum L.
Probability and Statistical Inference in Ancient and Mediaeval Jewish Literature
Toronto, University of Toronto Press, 1973

Rabut, Olivier Andreas
God in an Evolving Universe
Tr. William Springer
New York, Herder and Herder, 1966

Rahn, Carl Leo
Science and the Religious Life: a Psycho-physiological Approach
New Haven, Yale; London, H. Milford, Oxford, 1928

Rahner, Karl
Theological Investigations, 14 volumes
London, Darton, Longman and Todd, 1963

Ramm, Bernard
The Christian View of Science and Scripture
Grand Rapids, Eerdmans, 1954

Ramsey, Ian Thomas
Religion and Science. Conflict and Synthesis: Some Philosophical Reflections
London, S.P.C.K., 1964

    Models and Mystery
    Oxford, Oxford University Press, 1964

    Christian Empiricism
    London, Sheldon Press, 1974

Ramsey, Ian Thomas (ed.)
Biology and Personality: Frontier Problems in Science, Philosophy and Religion
Oxford, Blackwell, 1965

Raven, Charles Earle
Evolution and the Christian Concept of God. Delivered before the University of

Durham at Armstrong College, Newcastle-upon-Tyne, November 1935
London, Oxford University Press, 1936

Science, Religion, and the Future
Cambridge, Cambridge University Press; New York, Macmillan, 1943

Science and the Christian Man
London, SCM Press, 1952

Natural Religion and Christian Theology
Cambridge, Cambridge University Press, 1953

Science and Religion
Cambridge, Cambridge University Press, 1953

Christianity and Science
New York, Association Press, 1955

Science, Medicine and Morals: a Survey and a Suggestion
London, Hodder and Stoughton, 1959

Ream, Robert J.
A Christian Approach to Science and Science Teaching
Nutley, N.J., Presbyterian and Reformed Pub. Co., 1972

Rehwinkel, Alfred Martin
The Wonders of Creation: an Exploration of the Origin and Splendors of the Universe
Minneapolis, Bethany Fell, 1974

Reichenbach, Bruce R.
The Cosmological Argument: a Reassessment
Springfield, Illinois, Thomas, 1972

Reid, James
Does Science Confront the Bible?
Grand Rapids, Zondervan, 1971

Reumann, John Henry Paul
Creation and New Creation: the Past, Present and Future of God's Creative Activity
Minneapolis, Augsburg Publishing House, 1973

Reuterdahl, Arvid
The God of Science
Minneapolis, The Arya Co., 1928

Rice, William North
Christian Faith in an Age of Science
London, Hodder and Stoughton, 1904

Science and Religion: Five So-called Conflicts
New York, Cincinnati, Abingdon, 1925

Richardson, Alan
Science, History and Faith
London, Oxford University Press, 1950

> *Science and Existence: Two Ways of Knowing*
> London, SCM Press, 1957

> *The Bible in an Age of Science*
> The Cadbury Lectures at the University of Birmingham, 1961
> London, SCM Press, 1968

Ridderbos, Nicolaas Herman
Is there a Conflict between Genesis 1 and Natural Science?
Grand Rapids, Eerdmans, 1957

Rimmer, Harry
Modern Science and the Genesis Record
Grand Rapids, Eerdmans, 1937

> *The Theory of Evolution and the Facts of Science*
> Grand Rapids, Eerdmans, 1946

> *Lot's Wife and the Science of Physics*
> Grand Rapids, Eerdmans, 1947

> *The Harmony of Science and Scripture*
> Grand Rapids, Eerdmans, 1949: 1936

Ritchie, Arthur David
Civilization, Science and Religion
London, Penguin Books, 1945

> *Essays in Philosophy and Other Pieces*
> London, Longmans, Green and Co., 1948

> *Studies in the History and Methods of the Sciences*
> Edinburgh, Edinburgh University Press, 1958

Ritland, Richard M.
A Search for Meaning in Nature: a New Look at Creation and Evolution
Mountain View, California, Pacific Press Pub. Assoc., 1970

Roth, Sol
Science and Religion
New York, Yeshiva University, Department of Special Pub. (Bloch
   Pub. Co.), 1967

Russell, Bertrand Russell
Religion and Science
London, Oxford, 1956

Russell, Colin Archibald (ed.)
Science and Religious Belief: a Selection of Recent Historical Studies
London, University of London, 1973

Russell, Henry Norris
Fate and Freedom
New Haven, Yale; London, H. Milford, Oxford, 1927

Rust, Eric Charles
Preaching in a Scientific Age: Being the Fifth Joseph Smith Memorial Lecture delivered in the Friends' Institute, Birmingham, October 13, 1951
Birmingham, Overdale College, Selly Oak, 1951

    Nature and Man in Biblical Thought
    London, Lutterworth Press, 1953

    Science and Faith. Towards a Theological Understanding of Nature
    New York, Oxford, 1967

    Evolutionary Philosophies and Contemporary Theology
    Philadelphia, Westminster Press, 1968

Sabine, Paul Earls
Atoms, Men and God
New York, Philosophical Library, 1953

Sajous, Charles Euchariste de Medicis
Strength of Religion as Shown by Science, Facilitating also Harmony within, and Unity among, various Faiths
Philadelphia, F. A. Davis, 1926

Salisbury, Frank Boyer
The Creation
Salt Lake City, Deseret Book Co., 1976

Sambursky, S.
The Physical World of Late Antiquity
London, Routledge and Kegan Paul, 1962

Sampooran Singh
Dynamic Interplay between Science and Religion
Jodhpur, Jainsons, 1978

Sanden, O. E
Does Science Support the Scriptures?
Grand Rapids, Zondervan, 1951

Sanford, Hugh Wheeler
Science and Faith; or, The Spiritual Side of Science
New York and London, G. P. Putnam's, 1930

Sardar, Ziauddin
Science, Technology and Development in the Muslim World
Humanities Press, 1977

Schaaffs, Werner
Theology, Physics and Miracles
Tr. Richard L. Renfield
Washington, Canon Press, 1974

Schilling, Harold Kistler
Science and Religion: An interpretation of two Communities
New York, Scribner, 1962

> *The New Consciousness in Science and Religion*
> Philadelphia, United Church Press, 1973

Schlesinger George
Religion and Scientific Method
Dordrecht, Holland and Boston, D. Reidel, 1977

Schmid, Rudolf von
The Scientific Creed of a Theologian
Tr. J. W. Stoughton
New York, Armstrong, 1906

Schnabel, A. O.
Has God Spoken?
San Diego, California, Creation-Life Publishers, 1974

Schoonenberg, Peter
God's World in the Making
Pittsburgh, Duquesne University Press, 1964

Schrödinger, Erwin
Mind and Matter
London, Cambridge University Press, 1958

> *What is Life?*
> New York, Doubleday Anchor, 1956

Schwarz, Hans
*On the Way to the Future. A Christian View of Eschatology in the Light of
Current Trends in Religion. Philosophy and Science*
Minneapolis, Augsburg Publishing House, 1972

> *Our Cosmic Journey. Christian Anthropology in the Light of Current
> Trends in the Sciences, Philosophy and Theology*
> Minneapolis, Augsburg Publishing House, 1977

> *Science and Religion, by Seven Men of Science: Speaks in Browning Hall
> during Science Week 1914*
> London, W. A. Hammond, 1915

> *Science and Your Faith in God: a selected compilation of writings and
> talks by prominent Latter-Day Saints scientist on the subjects of science
> and religion*
> Salt Lake City, Bookcraft, 1958

Science, Industry and Faith
Naturwissenschaft, Industrie und Glaube
Konstanz, F. Bahn Verlag, 1960

> *Science, Philosophy and Religion. Conference on Science, Philosophy and Religion in their Relation to the Democratic Way of Life,* 1941

Scott, William T.
"The Gentle Rain—A Search for Understanding," in Langford, T. A., and Poteat, W. H., *Intellect and Hope*
Dunham, North Carolina, Duke University Press, 1968

Sears, Jack Wood
Conflict and Harmony in Science and the Bible
Grand Rapids, Baker Book House, 1969

Shapley, Harlow (ed.)
Science Ponders Religion
New York, Appleton-Century-Crofts, 1960

Shafer, Robert
Christianity and Naturalism: essays in criticism, second series.
New Haven, Yale, 1926

Shastri, Vaidyanath
Sciences in the Vedas
New Delhi, Sarvadeshik Arya Pratinidhi Sabha, 1970

Shaw, Charles Gray
"Science and Theology,"
in Randall, J. H. and Smith, J. G., *The Unity of Religions*, pp. 303–19
New York, Thomas Y. Crowell, 1910

Shebbeare, Charles John
The Challenge of the Universe, a Popular Restatement of the Argument from Design
London, S.P.C.K.; New York, Macmillan, 1918

> *The Design Argument Reconsidered: a Discussion between the Rev. C. J. Shebbeare and Joseph McCabe*
> London, Watts and Co., 1923

Shepherd, John J.
Experience, Inference, and God
New York, Barnes and Noble, 1975; London, Macmillan, 1975

Shepherd, William C.
Man's Condition: God and the World Process
New York, Herder and Herder, 1969

Shideler, Emerson W.
Believing and Knowing: the Meaning of Truth in Biblical Religion and in Science
Ames, Iowa State University Press, 1966

Shields, Charles Woodruff
The Scientific Evidences of Revealed Religion
New York, Scribner, 1900

Short, Arthur Rendle
The Bible and Modern Research
London, Marshall, Morgan and Scott, 1931

Modern Discovery and the Bible
London, the Inter-varsity Fellowship of Evangelical Unions, 1945

Simmons, Daniel A.
The Science of Religion. Fundamental Faiths Expressed in Modern Terms
New York, Revell, 1916

Simpson, James Young
The Spiritual Interpretation of Nature
London, New York, Hodder and Stoughton, 1912

Landmarks in the Struggle between Science and Religion
London, Hodder and Stoughton, 1925

Nature: Cosmic, Human and Divine
New Haven, Yale; London, H. Milford, Oxford, 1929

The Garment of the Living God. Studies in the Relations of Science and Religion
London, Hodder and Stoughton, 1934

Singer, Charles
Religion and Science Considered in their Historical Relations
London, Ernest Benn, 1928

Sinnott, Edmund Ware
Two Roads to Truth. A Basis for Faith Under the Great Tradition
New York, Viking, 1953

The Biology of the Spirit
New York, Viking, 1957

Slosson, Edwin Emery
Sermons of a Chemist
New York, Harcourt, Brace, 1925

Smethurst, Arthur Frederick
Modern Science and Christian Beliefs
London, J. Nisbet, 1955

Smith, Francis Henry
Christ and Science: Jesus Christ Regarded as the Centre of Science
New York, Chicago, Revell, 1906

Smith, Norman Kemp
The Credibility of Divine Existence
London, Macmillan, 1967

Smith, Orlando Jay
The Agreement between Science and Religion
New York, C. P. Farrell, 1906

Smyth, Nathan Ayer
Through Science to God
New York, Macmillan, 1936

Spilman, John M.
My Universe and my Faith: a Catholic Layman's Views on Science and his Religion
New York, Exposition Press, 1959

Spring, David, and Spring, Eileen (eds.)
Ecology and Religion in History
New York, Harper Torchbooks, 1974

Stallaert, L. M.
Ethics, Science and Truth
Breukelen, Holland, Nijenrode, 1978

Stevens, Clifford J.
Astrotheology for the Cosmic Adventure
Techny, Illinois, Divine Word Publications, 1969

Stiernotte, Alfred P.
God and Space Time
New York, Philosophical Library, 1954

Stine, Charles M. A.
A Chemist and his Bible
Philadelphia, Sunday School Times, 1943

Story, Francis
Gods and the Universe in Buddhist Perspective: Essays on Buddhist Cosmology and Related Subjects
Kandy, Buddhist Publication Society, 1972

Streeter, Burnett Hillman
Reality. A New Correlation of Science and Religion
New York, Macmillan, 1926

Adventure. The Faith of Science and the Science of Faith
New York, Macmillan, 1928

Stuermann, Walter Earl
Logic and Faith. A Study of the Relations between Science and Religion
Philadelphia, Westminster Press, 1962

Sullivan, John William Navin
The Limitations of Science
New York, New American Library, 1933

Sweet, Louis Matthews
To Christ through Evolution
New York, Doran, 1925

   A Symposium on Creation, 3 volumes
   Volume 1, by Henry M. Morris et al.; Volume 2, edited by Donald
   W. Patten
   Grand Rapids, Baker Book House, 1968–1971

Tabrum, Arthur H.
*Religious Beliefs of Scientists, including one Hundred hitherto unpublished
   Letters on Science and Religion from Eminent Men of Science*
London, Hunter and Longhurst for the North London Christian Evi-
   dence League, 1913

Taylor, A. E.
Does God Exist?
New York, Macmillan, 1947

Taylor, Frank Sherwood
The Fourfold Vision. A Study of the Relations of Science and Religion
London, Chapman and Hall, 1945

Taylor, Robert Oswald Patrick
Does Science Leave Room for God?
London, Hodder and Stoughton, 1933

Teilhard de Chardin, Pierre
Activation of Energy
Tr. René Hague
London, Collins, 1965; New York, Harcourt Brace Jovanovich, 1971

   Science and Christ
   Tr. René Hague
   London, Collins, 1968

   Hymn of the Universe
   Tr. Gerald Vann
   London, Collins, 1965; New York, Harper and Row, 1969

   The Divine Milieu
   Gen. ed. Bernard Wall
   New York, Harper and Row, 1965

The Phenomenon of Man
Tr. Bernard Wall
New York, Harper and Row, 1959

Temperley, Harold Neville Vazeille
A Scientist who Believes in God
London, Hodder and Stoughton, 1961

Temple, William
Nature, Man, and God
London, Macmillan, 1934

Tennant, Frederick Robert
Philosophical Theology
Cambridge, Cambridge University Press, 1930

Thomas, Wendell Marshall
On the Resolution of Science and Faith
New York, Island Press, 1947

Thompson, Walter R.
Dialogue on Science, Psychology and God
New York, Philosophical Library, 1967

Thomson, Alexander
The Concept of Tradition and Authority in Science and in Theology with Special Reference to the Thought of Michael Polanyi
M. Phil. dissertation, University of Edinburgh, 1979

Thomson, John Arthur
Science and Religion
New York, Scribner, 1925

Thornton, William Mundell
The Scientific Background of the Christian Creeds, delivered before the University of Durham at Armstrong College, Newcastle-upon-Tyne, November 21 and 28, 1929
Newcastle-upon-Tyne, A. Reid, 1930

Thorpe, William H.
Biology and the Nature of Man
Oxford, Oxford University Press, 1962

Animal Nature and Human Nature
New York, Doubleday, Anchor Book, 1974; London, Methuen, 1975

Thurston, H.
The Physical Phenomena of Mysticism
London, Burns and Oates, 1952

Tiller, Paul David
Reflections on the Relationships of Science and Christianity
Ph.D. dissertation, University of Northern Colorado, 1978

Tinkle, William John
Heredity. A Study in Science and the Bible
Grand Rapids, Zondervan, 1970

Torrance, Thomas Forsyth
Theology in Reconstruction
London, SCM Press, 1965

> *Space, Time and Incarnation*
> London, Oxford University Press, 1969
>
> *Theological Science*
> Based on the Hewett Lectures for 1959
> London, Oxford University Press, 1969
>
> *God and Rationality*
> London, Oxford University Press, 1971
>
> *Space, Time and Resurrection*
> Edinburgh, Handsel Press and Grand Rapids, Eerdmans, 1976
>
> "The Integration of Form in Natural and in Theological Science,"
> in *Science, Medicine and Man*, Volume 1.3, pp. 143–172
> Oxford, Pergamon Press, 1973
>
> "Christian Theology in the Context of Scientific Revolution,"
> in *Pluralisme et Oecuménisme en Recherches Théologiques*, pp. 295–311
> Paris, Editions Duculot, 1976
>
> *The Ground and Grammar of Theology*
> Charlottesville, University of Virginia Press, 1980
>
> *Divine and Contingent Order*
> Oxford and New York, Oxford University Press, 1980

Torrance, Thomas Forsyth (ed. & Introduction, Chapter 1 and Notes)
*Belief in Science and the Christian Life: The Relevance of Michael Polanyi's
   Thought for Christian Faith and Life*
Edinburgh, Handsel Press, 1980

> 'The Framework of Belief'
> in *Belief in Science and the Christian Life*, Chapter 1

Towers, Bernard
Concerning Teilhard, and other writings on Science and Religion
London, Collins, 1969

Trinklein, Frederick E.
*The God of Science: Personal Interviews with 38 leading American and Euro-
   pean Scientists on the Nature of Truth, the Existence of God, and the Role of
   the Church*
Grand Rapids, Eerdmans, 1971

Tuan, I-fu
Hydrologic Cycle and the Wisdom of God: a Theme in Geoteleology
Toronto, University of Toronto Press, 1968

Turner, Dean
Commitment to Care. An Integrated Philosophy of Science, Education, and Religion
Old Greenwich, Conn., Devin-Adair, 1978

Twining, R. H.
Science and Religion: Convergence or Collision
Lakemont, Ga., CSA Press, 1972

Tyndall, Charles Herbert
Through Science to God. Nature a Medium in the Revelation of Spiritual Truth
New York, Chicago, Revell, 1926

Unwin, Ernest Ewart
Religion and Biology
New York, Doran; London, Swarthmore, 1922

Utt, Richard H. (ed.)
Creation: Nature's Designs and Designer
Mountain View, California, Pacific Press Pub. Assoc., 1971

Van der Ziel, Aldert
The Natural Science and the Christian Message
Minneapolis, T. S. Denison, 1960

> *Genesis and Scientific Inquiry*
> Minneapolis, T. S. Denison, 1965

Van Melsen, Andrew J.
Science and Technology
Pittsburgh, Pennsylvania, Duquesne University Press, 1961

Van Nuys, Kelvin
Science and Cosmic Purpose
New York, Harper, 1949

Vick, Edward William Harry
Quest: an Exploration of some Problems in Science and Religion
London, Epworth Press, 1975

von Balthasar, Hans Urs
Science, Religion and Christianity
London, Burns and Oates, 1958

Vogel, Heinrich
Consider Your Calling
Edinburgh, Oliver and Boyd, 1962

von Weizsäcker, C. F.
The History of Nature
Chicago, University of Chicago Press, 1949

> *The Relevance of Science: Creation and Cosmogony*
> London, Collins, 1964

Vrooman, Hiram
Science and Theology: their Co-ordination and Differences
Chicago, Swedenborg Philosophical Centre, 1947

> *Science and Theology Coordinated: one of Swedenborg's major Contributions to Theology*
> Chicago, Swedenborg Philosophical Centre, n.d.

Wadud, Abdul
Phenomena of Nature and the Quran
Lahore, Sayed Khalid Wadud, 1971

Wagar, Walter Warren (ed.)
Science, Faith, and Man: European Thought since 1914
London, Macmillan, 1968

Waggett, Philip Napier
Religion and Science: Some Suggestions for the Study of the Relations between Them
London, New York, Longmans, Green, 1904

> *The Scientific Temper in Religion, and other Addresses*
> London, New York, Longmans, Green, 1905

Waldo, Howard Lansing
God is Writing a Book
Philadelphia, Dorrance, 1925

Walker, Paul L.
Understanding the Bible and Science
Cleveland, Tennessee, Pathway Press, 1976

Wallace, W. A.
"Science and Religion"
College Outlines of Sacred Doctrine.
Dubuque, Priory Press, 1962

Wallace, William Kay
The Scientific World View
New York, Macmillan, 1928

Walsh, James Joseph
Catholic Churchmen in Science: Sketches of the Lives of Catholic Ecclesiastics who were among the Great Founders of Science
Freeport, N.Y., Books for Libraries Press, 1966

Waltemyer, William Claude
The Quest of a Personal God in an Age of Physical Science
Ph.D. dissertation, The American University, 1929

Walter, R. Kenneth
Science, Saints, and Sense
Salt Lake City, Bookcraft, 1973

Walters, Gerald (ed.)
Religion in a Technological Society
Bath, Bath University Press, 1968

   Science and Religion: the Re-opening Dialogue
   Bath, Bath University Press, 1970

Ward, Leo Richard
God and World Order. A Study of Ends in Nature
St. Louis, Herder, 1961

Waters, F. William
The Way In and the Way Out: Science and Religion Reconciled
Toronto, Oxford University Press, 1967

Watson, John M.
Science as Revelation
New York, Macmillan, 1925

Watts, Alan Wilson
The Supreme Identity. An Essay on Oriental Metaphysics and the Christian Religion
New York, The Noonday Press, 1957

Weinberg, Steven
The First Three Minutes: A Modern View of the Origin of the Universe
London, André Deutsch, 1977

Wells, Albert Norman
The Christian Message in a Scientific Age
Richmond, John Knox Press, 1962

Westaway, Frederic William
Science and Theology. Their Common Aims and Methods
London, Blackie, 1920

Wettimuny, R. G. de S.
Buddhism and its Relation to Religion and Science
Colombo, M. D. Gunasena, 1962

Weyl, Hermann
The Open World. Three Lectures on the Metaphysical Implications of Science
New Haven, Yale; London, H. Milford, Oxford, 1932

Whaling, Thornton
Science and Religion Today
Chapel Hill, University of North Carolina, 1929

Whately, A. R.
The Focus of Belief
Cambridge, Cambridge University Press, 1937

White, Edward Arthur
Science and Religion in American Thought: the impact of Naturalism
Stanford, Stanford University Press, 1952

White, George LeRoy, Sr.
The Growing Accord between Science and Religion
Ph.D. dissertation, The University of North Dakota, 1934

White, Hugh C. (ed.)
Christians in a Technological Era
New York, Seabury Press, 1964

White, Joseph L.
The Creation of a God. The Struggle of Life for Perfection in a Spiritual World of Science
Madison, Tennessee, White Pub., 1975

Whitehead, Alfred North
The Concept of Nature. Tarner Lectures delivered at Trinity College, November 1919
Cambridge, Cambridge University Press, 1926

  Religion in the Making
  New York, Macmillan, 1926

  Science and the Modern World
  Cambridge, Cambridge University Press, 1927

  Process and Reality. An Essay in Cosmology
  Cambridge, Cambridge University Press; New York, Macmillan, 1929

  Adventures of Ideas
  Cambridge, Cambridge University Press, 1933

  Modes of Thought
  Cambridge, Cambridge University Press, 1938

Whitehouse, Walter Alexander
Christian Faith and the Scientific Attitude
Edinburgh, Oliver and Boyd, 1952

  Order, Goodness, Glory
  London, New York, Oxford, 1960

Whittaker, Edmund Taylor
Space and Spirit: Theories of the Universe and the Arguments for the Existence of God
London, T. Nelson, 1946

Wieman, Henry Nelson
Religious Experience and Scientific Method
Westport, Conn., Greenwood Press, 1970

> *Seeking a Faith for a New Age. Essays on the Interdependence of Religion, Science and Philosophy*
> Ed. Cedric L. Hepler
> Metuchen, N.J., Scarecrow Press, 1975

Wier, Frank E.
The Christian Views Science
Nashville, Published for the Cooperative Publication Association by Abingdon Press, 1969

Wilkes, Keith
Religion and the Sciences
Oxford, Religious Education Press, 1969

> *Religion and Technology*
> Oxford, Religious Education Press, 1972

Williams, John Gordon
Christian Faith and the Space Age
Cleveland, World Pub. Co., 1968

Williston, Arthur Lyman
Beyond the Horizon of Science
Boston, W. A. Wilde, 1944

Wilson, J. M.
Six Lectures on Pastoral Theology, with an Appendix on the Influence of Scientific Training on the Reception of Religious Truth
London, Macmillan, 1903

Wilson, Robert Whipple
Kinship of Religion and Science
Tampa, Florida, The Author, 1974

Wolthuis, Enno
Science, God and You
Grand Rapids, Baker Book House, 1963

Wood, William Hamilton
The Religion of Science
New York, Macmillan, 1922

Woodburne, Angus Stewart
The Relationship between Religion and Science: a Biological Approach
Chicago, University of Chicago Press, 1920

Woods, Francis Henry
For Faith and Science
London and New York, Longmans, Green, 1906

Wren-Lewis, John
Religion in the Scientific Age
11th Vaughan Memorial Lecture
Doncaster, Gazelle Press, 1963

Wynn, Walter
Man and the Universe
London, Rider, 1931

Yarnold, Greville Dennis
Christianity and Physical Science
London, A. R. Mowbray, 1950

> *The Spiritual Crisis of the Scientific Age*
> New York, Macmillan, 1959

> *The Moving Image. Science and Religion, Time and Eternity*
> London, Allen and Unwin, 1966

Yinger, J. Milton
The Scientific Study of Religion
New York, Macmillan, 1970

Young, Norman James
Creator, Creation, and Faith
London, Collins, 1976

Zimmerman, Paul Albert (ed.)
Creation, Evolution, and God's Word
St. Louis, Concordia, 1972

Scientific Periodicals

Anderson, V. E.
"Christian Commitment and the Scientist"
Journal of American Scientific Affiliation 16 (March 1964):8–9

Austin, William Harvey
Waves, Particles and Paradoxes
Houston, Texas, Rice University Studies, vol. 53, No. 2, September 1967

Ballhaussen, Louise E.
"Astronomy and Religion"
Popular Astronomy 48, (October 1940):418–26

Barber, Bernard
"Resistance by Scientists to Scientific Discovery"
Science 134, (September 1, 1961): 596–602

Barnes, Ernest William
"Christian Revelation and Modern Science"
Nature 106, (September 2, 1920):10–12

> "Influence of Science on Christianity"
> *Nature* 112, (September 29, 1923):477–78

> "Science, Religion and Moral Judgments"
> *Nature* 166, (September 16, 1950):455–7

Bube, R. H.
"Christian Responsibilities in Science"
Journal of American Scientific Affiliation 21, (March 1969):2–8

Burrill, D. R.
"Science, Theology and the Interpretation of Evidence"
Journal of American Scientific Affiliation 16, (Sptember 1964):68–72

Capra, Fritjof
"Bootstrap and Buddhism"
American Journal of Physics 42/1, (January 1974):15–19

Compton, Karl Taylor
"Religion in a Scientific Era"
Scientific Monthly 50, (January 1940):73–77

David, William Morris
"Faith of Reverent Science"
Scientific Monthly 38, (May 1934):395–421

Dingle, Herbert
"Physics and God"
Hibbert Journal 27, (October 1928):35–46

> "Religion and Science" (Abstract)
> *Nature* 156, (August 25, 1945):232

Dubarle, D.
"Future of the Relationship between Science and Religion"
Bulletin of Atomic Scientists 12, (December 1956):365–69
Reply: J. Calingaert, (May 1957):184

Duffy, J. F.
"Catholic Church and Science"
St. Bonaventure Science Studies 8, (June 1940):13–14

Duncan, George Stewart
"Bible and Science"
Scientific Monthly 23, (September 1926):201–5

Einstein, Albert
"Science and Religion"
Science News Letter, (September 2, 1940):182

"Science and Religion"
Nature 146, (November 9, 1940):605–7

"Science and Religion; Excerpts from *Out of My Later Years*"
Fortnightly 174, ns 168, (August 1950):69–75

Field, Richard M.
"Religious Responsibilities of Scientists"
Science Counselor 12, (December 1949):119–20

Glutz, M.
"Scientific Method and Religion"
Albertus Magnus Guild Bulletin 10, (May 1963):1

Gregory, R.
"Religion in Science"
Nature 143, (January 14, 1939):68–70

"Contacts of Religion and Science" Abstract
Nature 144, (September 16, 1939):522–3

"Religion in Science"
Scientific Monthly 48, (February 1939):99–108

Haldene, J. S.
"Biology and Religion"
Nature 114, (September 27, 1924):468–71

Haskell, Edward F.
"Religious Force of Unified Science"
Scientific Monthly 54, (June 1942):545–51

Heddendorf, R.
"Religious Beliefs of Scientists"
Journal of American Scientific Affiliation 23, (March 1971):10–11

Howerth, Ira. Woods
"Science and Religion"
Scientific Monthly 25, (August 1927):151–61

Johnson, R. W.
"Science and Religion in Space Exploration"
Journal of American Scientific Affiliation 19, (June 1967):35–9

Joint Statement upon the Relations of Science and Religion, by Religious Leaders and Scientists.
Science n.s. 75, (June 1, 1923):630–31

Keener, C. S.
"Religion and the Limits of Science"
Journal of American Scientific Affiliation 15, (December 1963):104–7

LaForest, P.
"Religion and Science; Complementary or Contradictory"
St. Bonaventure Science Studies 12, (June 16, 1944):13

Leo, Br.
"Religion and Science Again"
Science Counselor 18, (September 1955):103–5

Lindsey, Arthur Ward
"Faith of Science"
Scientific Monthly 66, (May 1948):395–98

McLaren, Robert Bruce
"Science and Contemporary Theology"
Bulletin of Atomic Scientists 22, (March 1966):25–26

Moraczewski, Albert
"Contribution of Science to Religion"
Bulletin of the Atomic Scientists 13, (January 1957):27–31

Neidhart, W.
"Science and the Cultural Meta System"
Journal of American Scientific Affiliation 30/2, (June 1978):94–96

"Personal Knowledge: an Epistemology of Discovery"
Journal of American Scientific Affiliation, (September 1977):118–23

Nogar, Raymond J.
"Toward an Improved Dialogue between Science and Theology"
Albertus Magnus Guild Bulletin 7, (February 1960):1–3

Pearson, R.
"Give-and-take between Science and Religion"
Journal of American Scientific Affiliation 15, (March 1963):4–6

Rasmusson, H. Richard
"Pastor Talks to the Man of Science: discussion"
Scientific Monthly 80, (June 1955):392–94

"Religion and Zoology"
Science n.s. 7, (February 17, 1928): sup. 14

Russell, R. H.
"Christian Looks at Science"
Journal of American Scientific Affiliation 10, (December 1958):7–8

"Science and Religion"
Bulletin, California Institute of Technology, (March 1922)

"Science and Religion"
Nature 111, (June 2, 1923):729–30

"Science and Religion"
Nature 114, (September 13, 1924):373–75

"Science and Religion"
Nature 118, (October 23, 1926):577–78

Simpson, George Gaylord
"Letter on Science and Religion"
Natural History 55, (September 1946):342

Skutch, Alexander Frank
"Naturalist's Dilemma. Search for Proof of the Spiritual Element in
the Universe"
Scientific Monthly 61, (November 1945):361–71

Slosson, E. E.
"Religion and Science"
Scientific Monthly 17, (July 1923):88–91

"Truth and Doctrine in Science and Religion"
Nature 116, (July 11, 1925):83–84

"Unity of Science and Religion"
Nature 106, (September 2, 1920):1–2

Visscher, Maurice B.
"Duty to Doubt and the Will to Believe"
Bulletin of the Atomic Scientists 12, (December 1956):356–59

Wallace, W. A.
"Science, Technology and God"
Albertus Magnus Guild Bulletin 9, (November 1961):1

Watts, W. W.
"Natural Science and Christian Faith as Elements in a Cultural Con-
tinuum"
Journal of American Scientific Affiliation 25, (September 1973):91–6

Webster, Arthur Gordon
"Scientific Faith and Works"
Popular Science Monthly 76, (February 1910):105–23

Wiebe, Robert H.
"Science and Religion: Compatible"
Journal of the American Scientific Affiliation 30, (December 1978):4

Wiilson, Jim
"Science and the Church"
Nature 104, (November 6, 1919):201–2

Religious and Theological Periodicals

Agar, William M.
"Religion and Science" *Commonweal* 25 (March 19, 1937–March 26, 1937):569–71, 599–600, 662–64, 689–92; (April 9, 1937–April 16, 1937)

"Religion and Science Today" *Commonweal* 27 (January 28, 1938–February 4, 1938):371–73, 399–401

Agassi, Joseph
"Can Religion Go Beyond Reason?" *Zygon* 4 (June 1969):128–68

al Faruqi, Isma'il R.
"Science and Traditional Values in Islamic Society"
Zygon 2 (September 1967):231–46

Ames, Edward Scribner
"Christianity and Scientific Thinking"
Journal of Religion 14 (January 1934):

"Apollo 11 Astronauts: Recognition of Religion?"
Christianity Today 13 (July 18, 1969):31–32

Aquinas, Sr.
"Correlating Science with Religion"
National Catholic Educational Association Bulletin 51 (August 1954):503–7

"Are Science and Religion Enemies?"
Catholic Messenger 80 (July 12, 1962):8

Ashley, Benedict
"Integration of Sacred Doctrine and natural science"
Society of Catholic Teachers of Sacred Doctrine–Proceedings 3 (1957):24–28

Aveling, Francis
"Catholic Church and Science"
Catholic World 111, (June 1920):330–42

"Faith and Science"
Catholic World 85, (July 1907):470–81

Bagnell, Robert
"Science and Theology"
Methodist Review 108, (July 1925):561–69

Bahner, Carl Tabb
"Science and God's Creation"
Review and Expositor 51, (July 1954):324–8

Baillie, J.
"Faith and the Scientific Impulse"
Theology Today 9, (October 1952):304–5

Barbour, Ian Graeme
"Are there Religious Perspectives in the Physical Sciences?"
Religion in Life 26, (Fall 1957):513–25

    "Commentary on Theological Resources from the Physical Sciences"
    Zygon 1, (March 1966):27–30

Barnes, E. W.
"Science is Making Religion New!"
Christian Century 40, (October 11, 1923):1290–91

Battista, O. A.
"God, Science and You"
Mary 19, (October 1958):76–82

    "Science Finds God Alive"
    Columbia 46, (July 1966):20–22

    "Science Reveals Mechanisms of God"
    America 66 (March 28, 1942):681–82

Bedau, Hugo Adam
"Complementarity and the Relation between Science and Religion"
Zygon 9, (September 1974):202–24

Bennett, H. Stanley
"The Scope and Limitations of Science"
Zygon 3, (September 1968):343–53

Berkhof, Hendrikus
"God in Nature and History"
Study document prepared for the Division of Studies of the World Council of Churches, 1965

Birch, L. C.
"What does God do in the World?"
Union Seminary Quarterly Review 30, (Winter–Summer 1975):76–84

Bonner, Gerald
"Christianity and the Modern World View"
Eastern Churches Review 5, (Spring 1973):1–15

Breig, Joseph Anthony
"Science and Theology"
Ave Maria 81, (June 18, 1955):7

Boojamra, John L.
"On Science and Theology"
St. Vladimir's Theological Quarterly 13, no 3, (1969):131–48

Boutroux, E.
"Science and Religion"
Monist 29, (July 1919):406–31

Bright, Laurence
"Christian Theology and Natural Science"
Blackfriars 38, (February 1957):50–56

   "Science and Religion: Areas of Contact between the Contents of
      Scientific and Theological Knowledge"
   Blackfrairs 44, (June 1963):244–51

Bro, Harmon H.
"Philosophers and Scientists Meet"
Christian Century 74, (January 9, 1957):62–63

Brown, Elmer E.
"Science's Service to Religious Unity"
Christian Century 48, (January 21, 1931):110–11

Brown, Ronald A.
"Science and Religion: a Meeting of Minds"
Modern Churchman 16, (January 1973):137–46

Brown, Sanborn C.
"Can physics Contribute to Theology?"
Zygon 1, (March 1966):14–21

Brownhill, Robert J.
"Michael Polanyi and the Problem of Personal Knowledge"
Journal of Religion 48, (1968): 115–123

   "Polanyi on Method in the Natural Sciences and the Study of His-
      tory and his Development of the Concept of Interpretative
      Framework"
   Convivium 8, (Summer 1979):14–33

Buerger, Martin J.
"Scientists and God"
Christianity Today 8 (August 28, 1964):6–8

Burhoe, Ralph Wendell
"The Concepts of God and Soul in a Scientific View of Human Pur-
   pose"
Zygon 8, (December 1973):412–42

   "Potentials for Religion from the Sciences"
   Zygon 5, (June 1970):110–29

"Natural Selection and God"
Zygon 7, (March 1972):30–63

"What Does Determine Human Destiny?—Science Applied to Interpret Religion"
Zygon 12, (December 1977):336–89

Burnell, Acton
"Science and Religion"
Westminster Review 154, (October 1900):440–45

Butcher, Harold
"Scientists Seek Religion; 11th Conference of the Institute on Religion in an Age of Science, Star Island"
Albertus Magnus Guild Bulletin 12, (December 1964):1–5

Butler, Basil Christopher
"Belief in Science and Reason in Religion"
Downside Review 84, (January 1966):1–14

Caldin, E. F.
"Scientist's Approach to Faith"
Life of the Spirit 9, (February 1955):363–71

Carus, Paul
"Minister and Scientific Advance"
Religious Education 7, (October 1912):429–37

"Science, Theology, and the Church"
Open Court 33, (September 1919):574–83

Carvin, Walter P.
"Faith and Cosmology"
Foundations (Baptist) 13, (October–December 1970):355–59

Castro, Emilio (ed.)
"The Gospel and the Scientific World"
International Review of Mission 66, (April 1977):107–45

Cauthen, Kenneth
"Science and Theology: from Orthodoxy to Neo-Orthodoxy"
Zygon 1, (September 1966):256–74

Chapman, Edward Mortimer
"Science and the Unseen World"
Based on Nature of the Physical World, by A. S. Eddington.
Homiletic Review 98, (December 1929):439–41

Chenu, M.-D.
"Churchmen and Scientists Discuss Mutual Problems; Meeting of the Churchmen's Union for the Advancement of Liberal Religious Thought"

Christian Century 41, (September 25, 1924):1244

"Christianity and Scientific Concerns"
Christianity Today 17, (May 25, 1973):8–14

Cherbonnier, E. L.
"Biblical Contributions to the Development of Scientific Method"
MCM 17, (1973):24–39

Clark, J. R.
"Scientific and Theological Approaches"
HIS 19, (June 1959):11–15

"The Great Living System; the World as the Body of God"
Zygon 9, (March 1974):57–93

Clarke, A. H. T.
"Old Testament in the Light of Science"
English Review 57, (July 1933):72–79

Clarke, W. Norris
"Christians Confront Technology"
America 101, (September 26, 1959):761

Clément, Olivier
"Science and Faith"
(reprint, translated by D. Black)
St. Vladimir's Seminary Quarterly 10, No. 3, (1966):120–27

Cobb, John Boswell
"Can Natural Theology be Christian?"
Theology Today 23, (April 1966):140–42

Collingwood, R. G.
"Religion, Science and Philosophy"
Truth and Freedom II.7, 1926

Connell, Francis J.
"God the Creator"
Holiletic and Pastoral Review 37, (November 1936):206–10

"Church and Science"
Ecclesiastical Review 112, (February 1945):127–28

Cooper, William H.
"Place of Scientific Method in Theology"
Lutheran Church Quarterly 12, (April 1939):150–67

Costa de Beauregard, Professor
"The Scientist and Problems of Faith"
Albertus Magnus Guild Bulletin 6, (November 1959):6

Coulson, C. A.
"Christian Religion and Contemporary Science"
Modern Churchman 40, (September 1950):205–15

"Some Recent Developments in Science and their Implications to
   Theology"
London Quarterly and Holborn Review 184, (July 1959):176–88

"Changing Relationships of Science and Religion"
London Quarterly and Holborn Review 184, (October 1959):280–83

Coulter, John Merle
"Making of Religious Citizens through Biology"
Religious Education 8, (December 1913):420–24

"Witness of Nature to Religion"
Biblical World 45, (June 1915):346–53

"Science and Religion"
Biblical World 54, (January–November 1920):339–47, 458–65,
   561–67

"Religion and Science"
Religious Education 18, (August 1923):223–29

Crolly, Dennis F.
"Scientific Theology"
Truth 35, (July 1931):14–15

Cross, F. L.
"God and Modern Physics"
Church Quarterly Review 112, (April 1931):1–19
D'Arcy, Eric
"The Scientist as Christian"
Tablet 221, (April 1, 1967):343–44; (April 8, 1967):378–79; (April 15,
   1967):401–2

David Mary, Bro.
"Science and Faith"
Lasallian Digest 4, (September 1962):72–78

Dawson, W. B.
"Science and Divine Revelation"
Biblical Review 16, (January 1931):77–96

DeGuglielmo, Antonine
"Bible and the Knowability of God from Purely Natural Revelation"
Franciscan Studies 24, (December 1943):339–63

Dillenberger, J.
"Nature versus Biblical Literalism"
Christian Century 76, (May 20, 1959):609–11

"Science and Theology Today"
Christian Century 76, (June 17, 1959):722–25

Ditmanson, Harold H.
"Call for a Theology of Creation"
Dialog 3, (Autumn 1964):264–73

Dockx, S.
"Man's Eschatological Condition"
pp. 20–34, *Scottish Journal of Theology*, Volume 27, 1974
Cambridge, University Press, 1974

Doeschner, W. O.
"Natural Science and Christian Theology"
Theology Today 9, (October 1952):306–18

Duchrow, W.
"The Spiritual Dimensions of the Scientific World"
Gospel in Context 1/4, (October 1978):4–23

Dumas, Andre
"Creation—God's Glory in His World"
Reformed World 34, (September–December 1977):311–15

Dwight, T.
"Science and Religion"
Catholic World 121, (May 1925):248–49

Dyson, Anthony Oakley
"Status of Theology in a Scientific World-View"
Modern Churchman No. 7, (October 1963): 41–49

East, Edward Murray
"Religion in Science"
Forum 81, (February 1929): sup. 44

Easton, W. Burnet
"Christianity and the Man on Mars"
Christian Century, (June 20, 1956)

Einstein, A., Murphy, J., and Sullivan, J. W. N.
"Science and God: a German Dialogue"
Forum and Century 83, (June 1930):373–79

Einstein, A.
"Einstein Discourses on Religion"
Christian Century 47, (November 26, 1930):1437–38

Elliott, Harrison
"Science in Religion"
Religious Education 22, (April 1927):422–25

Etkin, William
"Religious Meaning of Contemporary Science"
Judaism 12, (Spring 1963):179–89

Emerson, Alfred E., et al.
"Commentary on Theological Resources from the Biological Sciences"
Zygon 1, (March 1966):49–59

Evans, C. Stephen
"Christian Perspectives on the Sciences of Man"
Christian Scholar's Review 6, nos. 2–3, (1976):97–113

Everett, Charles Carroll
"Faith of Science and the Science of Faith"
Immortality 141–69. Immortality and other essays.
Boston, American Unitarian Association, 1902

Fairchild, Henry Pratt
"Science in the Trinity"
Forum 79, (May 1928):772–75

"Faith and the Scientific Mind"
Biblical World 38, (July 1911):3–7

Feigl, Herbert
"Is Science relevant to Theology?"
Zygon 1, (June 1966):191–99

Felix, John
"Catholic and scientific"
Bibliotheca Sacra 75, (July 1918):436–50

Fischer, Irene Kaminka
"A Layman's Search for Understanding the Message of Judaism in Modern Terms"
Judaism 21, (September 1972):134–50

Fiske, A. Longfellow
"Honest Science Begets True Faith"
America 56, (February 6, 1937):415–16

Foley, Leo P.
"God, the Cause of all Things"
Journal of Religious Instruction 5, (September 1934):72–77

Foster, Michael B.
"The Christian Doctrine of Creation and the Rise of Modern Natural Science"

Mind, vol. xliii, no. 171, 1934, pp. 446–468; vol. xliv, no. 176, 1935, pp. 439–466; vol. xlv, no. 177, 1936, pp. 1–27.

Friend, J. A.
"From Raven to Peacocke: Some Thoughts on Science and Religion"
Reformed Theological Review 37, (January–April 1978):1–9

Gardner, Frank Nelson
"Christian Thought and the Thought of Modern Science; the Critical Necessity for a Dynamic Encounter"
Encounter 20, (Winter 1959):14–25

Gastonguay, Paul R.
"Church and Future Science"
Catholic World 208, (January 1969):164–68

   "Scientists and their Religious Beliefs"
   America 130, (June 22, 1974):503

Gelnick, R.
"Discovery and Theology"
Scottish Journal of Theology, Volume 28, (1975):301–21

Gerdes, Egon W.
"Theology and Science in Theological Perspective"
Zygon 3, (March 1968):92–104

Gilby, Thomas
"Three Sisters: Science, Philosophy and Faith"
Blackfriars 32, (May 1951):211–14

Gilkey, Lansdon
"Religious Dimensions of Scientific Inquiry"
Journal of Religion 50, (July 1970):245–67

   "Religion and the Technological Future"
   Criterion 13, (Spring 1974):9–14

Gilson, Etienne
"Science, Philosophy and Religious Wisdom"
American Catholic Philosophical Association—Proceedings 26, (1952):5–13

Glanville, W. E.
"Christianity and Physical Science"
Homiletic Review 90, (July 1925):17–18

Goatley, James L., and Graham, W. Fred
"Natural Theology and the Natural Sciences"
Religion in Life 47, (Spring 1978):23–32

   "God and Science"
   Ava Maria 74, (December 22, 1951):770

Godbey, John C.
"Brief Remarks on the Need for a Scientific Theology"
Zygon 4, (June 1969):125–27

"Further Remarks on the Need for a Scientific Theology"
Zygon 5, (1970):194–215

Graham, Robert Andrew
"Church and Science"
America 98, (March 22, 1958):718

Green, F. O.
"Science and Faith: they Agree"
Christian Life 22, (April 1961):18–20

Griffin, Norman J.
"Catholics and Science"
Catholic School Journal 51, (January 1951):13–15

Gruner, Rolf
"Science, Nature and Christianity"
The Journal of Theological Studies 26, (April 1975):55–81

Gunton, Colin
"The Theologian and the Biologist"
Theology 77, (October 1974):526–28

Gusdorf, Georges
Science et Foi: un Débat de Conscience de l'Occidental Moderne
Paris, *La Revue de l'Évangelisation*, 1956:336–411. Offprint from *La Revue*, no. 65, September–October 1956

Gustafson, James M.
"Theology Confronts Technology and the Life Sciences"
Commonweal 105, (June 16, 1978):386–92

Haldane, J. S.
"Biology and Religion"
The Modern Churchman 14, (1924):269–82

Hammond, Thomas Chatterton
"Bible and Science"
Christianity Today 2, (November 25, 1957):14–15

Harrington, Donald Szantho
"Science and the Search for a Rational Religious Faith"
Zygon 1, (March 1966):97–107

"Science, Theology, and Human Values"
Zygon 6, (December 1971):271–84

Harris, Peter F.
"Natural Theology and the Historicity of Faith"
New Blackfriars 54, (January 1973):12–19

Hart, Charles Aloysius, and Donovan, Sr. A.
"God as Creator and Law Giver in the Light of Reason"
American Catholic Philosophical Association—Proceedings 28,
    (1954):250–53

Hartzler, H. H.
"How the Study of Science Has Increased My Faith"
Journal of American Scientific Affiliation 9, (December 1959):7–11

Hartshorne, C.
"The Theistic Proofs"
Union Seminary Quarterly Review 20, (January 1965):115–29

Haselden, K. E.
"Science and Religion"
Christian Century 79, (June 20, 1962):771–72

Hastings, Cecily
"Religion and the Scientist"
Commonweal 56, (June 18, 1952):368–69

    "Science and the Trinity"
    Blackfriars 33, (June 1952):254–61

Hatfield, C.
"Science and Christianity"
Christianity Today 12, (August 16, 1968):14–19; 12 (August 20,
    1968):6–9

Hawk, Ernest M.
"It Takes Two for Dialogue; Interpretation and Dialogue Between the
    Science-Technology Community and the Church"
Christian Century 88, (December 1, 1971):1418–20

Hawkins, D. J. B.
"Inference in Natural Theology"
Church Quarterly Review 150, (1950):254–57

Hayward, John Frank
"Natural Theology and the Question of the Trinity"
Encounter 33, (Spring 1972):141–58

Heathcote, A. W.
"Science and Religion Today"
London Quarterly and Holborn Review 184, (October 1959):284–88

Hefley, J. C.
"Astronauts: Space Shaped Our Faith"
Christian Life 31, (February 1970):48–51

Hefner, P.
"To What Extent Can Science Replace Metaphysics? Reflecting with
   Ralph Wendell Burhoe on the 'Lord of History' "
Zygon 12, (March 1977):88–104

Heisenberg, W.
"Scientific Truth and Religious Truth"
Cross Currents 24, (Winter 1975):463–73

Henry, C. F. H.
"What Some Scientists Say about God and the Supernatural"
Christianity Today 9, (August 27, 1965):5–13

Herzfeld, Charles M.
"Science and the Church"
Commonweal 70, (May 22, 1959):198–201

Herzfeld, Karl Ferdinand
"Scientific Research and Religion"
Commonweal 9, (March 20, 1929):560–62

   "Science and Religion"
   Commonweal 17, (February 15, 1933):432–34

Hess, Earl H.
"Reflections of a Brethren Scientist; the striking compatability of his
   profession with his religious heritage"
Brethren Life 19, (Autumn 1974):197–203

Hesse, Mary
"Criteria of Truth in Science and Theology"
Religious Studies 11, (December 1975):385–400

Hindmarsh, W. R.
"Faith of a Physicist"
Expository Times 82, (December 1970):68–70

   "Science and Christianity"
   Expository Times 85, (March 1974):180–83

Hitchcock, Charles Henry
"Bible and Recent Science"
Bibliotheca Sacra 64, (April 1907):299–313

Hodgson, P. E.
"Science and Religion: Common Factors"
Tablet 223, (October 18, 1969):1018–19

"The Judaeo-Christian Origin of Science."
The Ampleforth Journal, Autumn 1974, vol. lxxix, part iii, pp. 39–44

Holmes, Arthur
"Faith of the Scientist"
Biblical World 48, (July 1916):3–7

Holmes, John Haynes
"Is Science Vindicating Religion?" A sermon.
Homiletic Review 108, (October 1934):282–90

Horgan, John
"Our Knowledge of God"
Irish Ecclesiastical Record 5ser 58, (August–September 1941):229–52

Hosinski, Thomas E.
"Science, Religion, and the Self-understanding of Man"
Religion in Life 42, (Summer 1973):179–93

Hough, Lynn Harold
"Science and Religion"
Christian Century 41, (April 10, 1924):462–63

Howe, Charles A.
"A Minister-Scientist Looks at Science Teaching in Relation to the Separation of Religion from Science"
Zygon 7, (December 1972):244–49

Howe, Günter
"Physics and the Christian World-View"
Ecumenical Review 6, (October 1953):103–6

Hubbard, Gertrude L.
"Science and Faith"
Franciscan Studies 10, (March 1950):1–8

Huffman, James L.
"Science for Clergymen; Religion for Scientists?"
Christianity Today 13, (August 22, 1969):40–41

Hutchinson, George Evelyn
"Methodology and Value in the Natural Sciences in Relation to Certain Religious Concepts"
Journal of Religion 32, (July 1952):175–87

Jalei, S. L.
"The Role of Faith in Physics"
Zygon 2, (June 1967):187–202

James, Fr.
"Masking the Truth; the Creator"
Sponsa Regis 27, (July 1956):281–84

John XXIII, Pope
"To the UN Conference on New Sources of Energy; Scientists' Recognition of the Immensity of the Creator"
Catholic Messenger 80, (March 22, 1962):5

Johnson, George
"Religion of the Scientifically Minded"
Princeton Theological Review 27, (January 1929):60–82

Johnston, L.
"Religion of Scientists"
Truth 36, (November 1932):7–9

Josey, Charles C.
"Contribution of Science to Modern Religion"
Journal of Religion 16, (October 1936):463–75

Kaiser, C. R.
"Some Recent Developments in the Sciences and their Relevance for Christian Theology"
Reformed Review 29, (Spring 1976):148–155

Kaiser, Charles Hillis
"Religion and Modern Physics"
Journal of Religion 28, (April 1948):92–8

Kanter, Shamai
"Where is the War? A Rapprochement of Science and Religion"
Conservative Judaism 20, (Fall 1965):36–43

Kaplan, L.
"Fundamental Assumptions for Discussions of Religion and Science"
Tradition 10, (Summer 1968):87–99

Kaplan, Mordecai Menahem
"The Interdependence of Science and Religion"
Reconstructionist 43, (February 1977):7–11

Keeton, William T.
"Scientist's Question: Is Theology Based on Evidence?"
Dialog 4, (Spring 1965):98–111

Kitchin, William P. H.
"Scientific Attainment and Christian Faith"
Truth 37, (August 1933):15–18

Klotz, J. W.
"Science and Religion"
United Evangelical Action 17, (June 15, 1958):185–6

Ladrière, J.
"Integration of Scientific Research within Christian Life"
Lumen Vitae 15, (September 1960):433–50

Langenauer, Arthur
"Viable Religion in an Age of Science"
Reconstructionist 36, (March 27, 1970):7–11

Langford, Thomas
"Michael Polanyi and the Task of Theology"
Journal of Religion 46, (January 1966):45–55

Lansing, John W.
"Similarities and Differences between Scientific and Theological Thought"
Zygon 7, (June 1972):110–24

Leach, K. A.
"Clergy-Scientist Dialogue"
Christian Century 83, (February 23, 1966):244

Le Buffe, Francis P.
"Can Science Discover God?"
America 47, (July 30, 1932):398–99

Lechner, Robert F.
"Doors to the Sacred in the Contemporary World"
Catholic Messenger 79, (June 22, 1961):5

Lecomte du Nouy, P.
"Science Is Not All"
Catholic World 165, (April 1947):76

"Science Proves That God Exists"
Catholic Digest 11, (April 1947):1–7

Leith, T. H.
"Why I Believe There Is a God; a Scientist's Personal Statement"
Gordon Review 4, (Summer 1958):85–8

Leprince-Ringuet, Louis
"The Scientist and the Believer"
Commonweal 74, (July 14, 1961):391–94

Leuba, J. H. and Brown, W. A.
"Basic Assumptions of Religion in their Bearing upon Science"
Religious Education 23, (April 1928):297–303

Liénart, Achille
"Science and the Bible"
Commonweal 50, (June 17–24, 1949):241–43, 265–67

Locher, Gottfried W.
"Can Technology Exist without Belief?"
Theology Digest 21, (Fall 1973):221–23

Lodge, O. G.
"Christianity and Science"
Living Age 249, (May 12, 1906):331–39; 250, (July 21, 1906):171–81

"Religion and Science"
Homiletic Review 99, (March 1930):175–78

Macarthur, John Stewart
"Church and Science"
Scottish Journal of Theology 10, (March 1957):35–44

Maccabee, Ben
"Science and Judaism"
Jewish Information 3, (Spring 1964):12–17; 4, (Summer 1964):12–20;
(Fall 1963):49–54; 4, (Winter 1964):99–101

McConnell, Francis John
"Science and Religion: Reconciliation through Cooperation"
Homiletic Review 87, (April 1924):268–71

McCrady, E.
"Religious Perspectives in Biology"
Theology Today 9, (October 1952):319–32

McDonnell, Kilian
"All Things Praise the Lord"
Sign 36, (November 1956):37

McGinley, A. A.
"Testimony of Science to Religion"
Catholic World 72, (November 1900):235–40

McGinley, Laurence J.
"Religion and the Scientist"
Thought 31, (Winter 1956):487–94

"Religion and the Scientist"
Catholic Mind 55, (August 1957):298–304

McIntyre John A.
"Appeal of Christianity to a Scientist"
Christianity Today 12, (March 15, 1968):6–8

"Science and Religion; Has the Situation Changed?"
Expository Times 70, (October–November 1958):15–18, 36–39

"Physicist Believes"
His 21, (June 1961):9–10

"Faith of a Physicist"
Evangelical Christian, (February 1962):10–11

MacKay, D. Mac C.
"Complementarity in Scientific and Theological Thinking"
Zygon 9, (1974):225–44

Mackinnon, Edward
"Science: Towards a Synthesis of Science and Theology"
Furrow 13, (May 1962):280–87

"'Double Faith' Necessary to Harmonize Religion and Science"
excerpts
Catholic Messenger 82, (August 13, 1964):2

"Theism and Scientific Explanation"
Continuum 5, (September 1967):70–88

Maclaughlin, P. J.
"Science, Philosophy and Religion"
Irish Ecclesiastical Record 5, ser 63, (January 1944):1–6

McMullin, Ernan
"Natural Science and Christian Thought"
Irish Theological Quarterly 26, (January 1959):1–22

"Science and the Catholic Tradition"
America 102, (December 12, 1959):346–50

"Faith in the Space Age"
Lamp 59, (July 1961):5–7

MacMurray, John
"Science and Religion"
Expository Times 61, (1959):72–73

Maher, Ethna
"Faith and Technology; Can They Build the World Together?"
Living Light 10, (Spring 1973):34–43

Majella, Sr. M. Gerard
"From Nature up to Nature's God"
Journal of Religious Instruction 17, (September 1946):31–34

"Religion Must Inspire Science"
Catholic Educator 18, (May 1948):455–57

Manno, Brunno V.
"Michael Polanyi on the Problem of Science and Religion"
Zygon 9, (March 1974):44–56

Marker, David G.
"Science and Theology; Opponents or Partners?"
Reformed Review 22, (March 1969):18–20

Markson, Francis
"Belief in God"
Ave Maria 68, (December 25, 1948):824

Mascail, E. L.
"Doctrine of Analogy"
Cross Currents 1, (Summer 1951):38–57

Meland, Bernard E.
"For the Modern Liberal: Is Theology Possible? Can Science Replace It?"
Zygon 2, (June 1967):166–86

Melsen, Andrew G. van
"Science and Christianity as Universals of Culture"
Thomist 31, (April 1967):137–58

Mercier, Charles
"Science and Revelation"
Catholic World 125, (July 1927):493–98

Meserve, Harry C.
"Encounter between Science and Religion" editorial
Journal of Religion and Health 4, (October 1964):3–6

Metz, Johannes
The Evolving World and Theology, vol. 26, *Concilium. Theology in an Age of Renewal*
New York, Paulist Press, 1967

Michalson, Carl
"Between Nature and God"
Journal of Religion 35, (October 1955):229–41

Middleton, Austin Ralph
"Creator's Plan of the Universe"
Methodist Quarterly Review 72, (April 1923):258–87

Mie, Gustav A. F. W. L.
"Natural Science and Faith in God" Tr. J. C. Mattes
Lutheran Church Quarterly 11, (October 1938):405–13

Milavec, Aaron
"Modern Exegesis, Doctrinal Innovations, and the Dynamics of Discipleship"
Anglican Theological Review, (January 1978)

Miller, John Franklin
"Science and Religion; Their Logical Similarity"
Religious Studies 5, (October 1969):49–68
Reply: N. C. Siefferman, 6, (September 1970):281–89

Miller, L. G.
"Are Scientists Irreligious?"
Liguorian 47, (March 1959):30–31

Miller, Samuel Howard
"Church and the Scientists"
Ecumenical Review 9, (July 1957):380–94

Millikan, R. A.
"Scientist Confesses His Faith"
Christian Century 40, (June 21, 1923):778–83

Monro, C. C. A.
"Science in Relation to Religion"
Tablet 174, (August 12, 1939):210–11

Montefiore, Hugh
"Man and Nature; a Theological Assessment"
Zygon 12, (September 1977):199–211

Montgomery, John Warwick
"How Scientific is Science?"—American Scientific Affiliation
Christianity Today 16, (September 29, 1972):52–3

Moore, Edward Caldwell
"Christian Doctrine of Nature"
Journal of Religion 3, (January 1923):1–21

Morehouse, D. W.
"Basic Assumptions of Science in their Bearing upon Religion"
Religious Education 23, (April 1928):289–92

Morris, H. M.
"Bible is a Textbook of Science"
Bibliotheca Sacra 121, (October–December 1964):341–50

Morrison, Charles Clayton
"Protestantism and Science"
Christian Century 63, (April 24, 1946):524–27

Morrissey, Robert A.
"Science and Religion"
Catholic Mind 50, (March 1952):129–34

Myers, Edith
"What Science Explains"
Friar 19, (June 1963):54–58

Nachtergaele, Jean
"Scientific Method and Spiritual Experience"
Lumen Vitae 13, (December 1958):650–54

Nagurney, M. J.
"Science and Religion, No Conflict"
Catholic School Journal 47, (April 1947):127

"Newer Science and its Challenge to the Churches"
Religion in Life 30, (Summer 1961):334–73

Nichols, Edward Leamington
"Physical Science and Religious Citizenship"
Religious Education 8, (December 1913):424–25

Nietmann, William D.
"Science and Religion"
Journal of Religious Thought 18, no. 2, (1961–1962):93–102

Northrup, F.S.C.
"The Methods and Grounds of Religious Knowledge"
Zygon 12, (December 1977):273–88

O'Brien, Ignatius
"The World and the Word of God"
Irish Theological Quarterly 25, (July 1958):247–61

O'Brien, J. A.
"Search for God"
Homiletic and Pastoral Review 42, (July 1942):889–98

O'Connor, T.
"The Scientist and Doctrine"
Doctrine and Life 10, (May 1960):108–10

O'Conor, John S.
"Scientific Approach to Religion"
Catholic Mind 38, (November 22, 1940):457–65

O'Hear, Anthony
"Analysis and New Approaches to Natural Theology"
Heythrop Journal 15, (April 1974):183–88

O'Shea, John Joseph
"Science and Religion": Exit Tyndall, Enter Lodge"
American Catholic Quarterly Review 38, (October 1913):561–72

O'Toole, George Barry
"Closing of the Rift between Science and Religion"
Catholic Educational Review 36, (March 1938):129–46

    "Science and Religion"
    Catholic Digest 2, (May 1938):7–10

Pannenberg, W.
"The Doctrine of the Spirit and the Task of a Theology of Nature"
in *Theology*, Volume LXXV, No. 619, pp. 8–21
London, SPCK, January 1972

Patten, Arthur Hardwell
"Science and Religion"
Christian Century 48, (June 24, 1931):843

Payne, J. B.
"No Conflict between *these* Scientists and Theologians"
United Evangelical Action 18, (August 1959):182–83

Peacocke, A. R.
"Christian Faith in a Scientific Culture"
Modern Churchman n.s. 4, (October 1960):21–33

    "The nature and purpose of man in science and Christian theology"
    Zygon 8, (1973):373–94

    "Reductionism; a review of the epistemological issues and their relevance to biology and the problem of consciousness"
    Zygon 11, (1996):306–34

    "Christian Faith in a Scientific Age"
    Religious Education 58, (July–August 1963):372–76

Pearce-Higgins, John Denis
"Bible in an Age of Science"
Modern Churchman n.s. 7, (October 1963):72–83

Penner, Hans H., and Yonan, E. D.
"Is a Science of Religion Possible?"
Journal of Religion 52, (1972):107–133

Percival, A. S.
"Religion and Science"
Westminster Review 176, (October 1911):436–46

Phillips, H. B.
"Creation"
Zygon 1, (December 1966):401

Pieper, Sr. Mary Benita
"Catholic Educators and Science"
America 90, (October 3, 1953):14–16

Pius XII, Pope
"Natural Laws and the Divine Government of the World"
Catholic Doctrine 1, (Epiphany 1950):3–10

    "To the Pontifical Academy of Science: Proofs for the Existence of God; Characteristics of the Cosmos"
    Catholic Doctrine 6, (February 1952):17–27

Pleasants, Julian
"Catholics and Science"
Commonweal 58 (August 28, 1953):509–14

"Religion and Science"
Commonweal 73 (October 7, 1960):31–34

"Science and Religion: Examination of the Prevalent Christian Stance"
Commonweal 78, (April 19, 1963):91–92

"Pope and the Scientists"
Address to the Pontifical Academy of Science, November 22.
America 86, (December 8, 1951):274–75

Posner, Harry
"Science versus Religion in the 20th Century"
Reconstructionist 35, (May 23, 1969):23–35

Pratt, James Bissett
"Buddhism and Scientific Thinking"
Journal of Religion 14, (January 1934):13–24

    "Prayer and the Laboratory"
    Commonweal 15, (March 16, 1932):537–38

Price, Charles P.
"Revealed Religion in an Age of Science"
Zygon 2, (March 1967):23–33

Pritchett, Henry Smith
"Faith of Science"
Outlook 100, (February 3, 1912):283–85

    "Psychology, Biology and Religion"
    Commonweal 15, (February 10, 1932):396–97

Purdy, William A.
"Science and Religion"
The British Association at Nottingham
Tablet 220, (September 10, 1966):1010–12

Quin, James
"God and Science"
Christian Order, (March 1964–August 1964)

Rabinovitch, N. L.
"Torah and Science; Conflict or Complement"
Jewish Life 3, (September–October 1965):43–48

Ramsey, I. T.
"Religion and Science, a Philosopher's Approach"
Church Quarterly Review 162, (January–March 1961):77–91

Raven, C. E.
"Christianity and Biology"
Modern Churchman 4, (October 1960):74–83

    "Religion in an Age of Science": sermon
    Modern Churchman 7, (October 1963):3–8

Reardon, B. M. G.
"Christian Dogma and Scientific Method"
Congregational Quarterly 33, (July 1955):204–15

Rehwaldt, August C.
"Christian World-View and the New Era in Science"
Concordia Theological Monthly 40, (January 1969):13–23

Reid, J. W.
"Space: God Is There"
Christian Life 27, (January 1966):30–1

Reid, William Stanford
"Christian and the Scientific Method"
Westminster Theological Journal 24, (November 1961):1–28

Reiland, Karl
"Science and Religion: a sermon"
Homiletic Review 94, (October 1927):315–19

   "Religion-Science Question"
   Commonweal 54, (September 21, 1951):574

   "Religion Speaks to America's Men of Science"
   Christianity Today 3, (January 19, 1959):27

   "Religious Value of the Scientific Spirit"
   Biblical World 32, (August 1908):83–86

Revell, William F.
"The Religion of Science"
Westminster Review 177, (January 1912):84–99

Reyniers, James A.
"Harmony between Science and Religion"
Catholic Mind 48, (May 1950):285–91

Roberts, Louis
"Intellectual Quest of the Modern Scientist"
America, (July 16, 1956):387–89

Robinson, Charles K.
"Biblical Theism and Modern Science"
Journal of Religion 43, (April 1963):118–38

Rohrbach, H.
"Modern Science and Christian Faith"
His 18, (October 1957):33–8

Ronflette, P.
"Biological Finality and God's Existence"
Theology Digest 4, (Winter 1955):13–17

Roth, Nathan
"Dichotomy of Man: Religion versus Science"
Journal of Religion and Health 15, (July 1976):151–58

St. John-Stevas, Norman
"Science and Faith"
Wiseman Review 238. (Summer 1964):138–46
Reply: *Catholic Mind* 62, (December 1964):16–22

Schall, James V.
"Science and the Scriptural View of the Universe"
Catholic World 202, (January 1966):233–37

Schaub, Frederick
"Kinship of Science and Religion"
Methodist Review 113, (January 1930):73–78

Schilling, H. K.
"Toward the Confluence of the Scientific and Christian Faiths"
Zygon 4, (June 1969):113–24

Schilpp, Paul Arthur
"Science, Theology, and Ethical Religion"
Zygon 1, (June 1966):186–90

Schlesinger, G.
"Confirmation of Scientific and Theistic Hypotheses"
Religious Studies 13, (March 1977):17–28

Schmitz, Kenneth L.
"The Redemptive Role of the Knowledge of Nature"
Franciscan Studies 24, (1964):223–60

    "Science Aids Religion"
    Ave Maria 74, (December 22, 1951):772

    "Science and Christianity"
    Sign 43, (June 1964):34

    "Science and Creative Purpose"
    Living Age 238, (July 11, 1903):117–20

    "Science and Faith"
    Outlook 97, (February 25, 1911):387–89

    "Science and Religion"
    America 92, (December 18, 1954):311

    "Science and Religion"
    Catholic Mind 39, (June 22, 1941):32

    "Science and Religion"
    Commonweal 25, (January 29, 1937):386

    "Science and Religion"
    Dialogue: a journal of Mormon thought 8, nos. 3–4, (1973):21–143

    "Science and Religion"
    Review and Expositor 59, (April 1962):136–99

"Science and the Church"
Catholic Mind 39, (June 18, 1941):30

"Science and the Church"
Catholic Mind 42, (October 1944):638–39

"Science and Theology"
Ave Maria 86, (August 3, 1957):5

"Science, Faith Compatible?"
Ave Maria 80, (July 24, 1954):4

"Science Reaches Back to God"
Catholic Educator 22, (February 1952):297

"Science, Religion and Reality"
Church Quarterly Review 102, (July 1926):334–40

"Scientific Outlooks and Religious Conceptions. A Composite Study"
Religious Education 23, (February 1928):154–63

Scott, W. T.
"A Bridge from Science to Religion, Based on Polanyi's Theory of Knowledge"
Zygon 5, (March 1970):41–62

"Seeing God through Science; F. D. Rossini"
Sign, (September 1962):25

Sheerin, John Basil
"Faith of Scientists"
Homiletic and Pastoral Review 52, (October 1951):11–15

"Union of Laboratory and Altar"
Homiletic and Pastoral Review 56, (August 1956):899–903

Shideler, E. W.
"Can Science and Theology Converse?"
Christian Century 77, (February 24, 1960):215–17

"Theological Study of Science"
Dialog 4, (Spring 1965):90–7

Sider, Roger
"New Biology in Search of a Soul"
Christianity Today 22, (March 24, 1978):28–29

Sider, Ronald J.
"The Historian, the Miraculous and Post-Newtonian Man"
Scottish Journal of Theology 25, (August 1972):309–19

Sinnott, E. W.
"Scientist as a Christian Layman"
Religion in Life 31, (Winter 1961–62):78–84

Smith, B. L.
"Biology and the Christian Faith"
Christianity Today 13, (April 11 and 25, 1969):11–14

Smith, Gerald Birney
"Preacher and the Scientist"
Christian Century 40, (February 1, 1923):137–40

Smith, G. B., and Aubrey, E. E.
"Nature of Science and of Religion and their Interrelation"
Religious Education 23, (April 1928):304–14

Smith, Harmon L.
"Open Windows; Southern Exposure; Scientists and Theologians Discussing Science, Religion and Man's Future"
Christian Century 84, (October 18, 1967):1311–13

Smith, J. Macdonald
"Can Science Prove that God Exists?"
Heythrop Journal 3, (April 1962):126–38

Smith, Rembert G.
"Religion and Science"
Homiletic Review 98, (September 1929):185–87

Smith, Thomas Vernor
"Religion and the Scientific Mind"
Christian Century 48, (May 20, 1931):679–83

Spanner, D. C.
"Can a Scientist Believe?"
HIS 17, (October 1956):10–12

Spero, Samuel W.
"Science and our Sages"
Jewish Life 33, (July–August 1966):21–30

Sperry, William Learoyd
"Religion in an Age of Science"
Journal of Religion 15, (July 1935):253–71

Spradley, Joseph L.
"Christian Roots of Science"
Christianity Today 14, (March 13, 1970):7–8

Stafford, B. J.
"Scientific Infallibility"
Bibliotheca Sacra 80, (October 1923):495–504

Standen, Anthony
"Are Scientists Getting Religion?"
Sign 34, (August 1954):9–11

Stewart, David M.
"God's Existence: Can Science Prove it?"
Religion in Life 44, (Summer 1975):166–177

Strom, Carl Walther
"Faith, Materialism and Science"
Christian Century 78, (February 1, 1961):139–42
Reply: I. G. Barbour, (March 29, 1961):383–84

> "Studying Religion Scientifically"
> Society for the Scientific Study of Religion.
> *Christian Century* 79, (October 17, 1962):1249

Sullivan, J. M.
"Pulpit and Science"
Methodist Quarterly Review 75, (October 1926):567–77

Sutherland, Malcolm R., Jnr.
"Introductory Remarks to the Convocation: a Theological School Looks to the Sciences"
Zygon 1, (March 1966):108–10

Taylor, F. S.
"Church and Science"
Month 180, (March 1944):89–102
(Same: *Catholic Mind* 42, (September 1944):513–26)

> "Science and Religion"
> *Commonweal* 52, (May 26, 1950):174

Tennant, F. R.
"Theism and Laws of Nature"
Harvard Theological Review 17, (October 1924):375–91

Teske, Myron M.
"Christianity and Science—Out of Step?"
Lutheran Quarterly 21, (August 1969):242–50

> "On Recycling Symbols in Dialogue between Theologians and Scientists"
> *Lutheran Quarterly* 23, (November 1971):317–28

Thomas, David Edward
"Religion and the Science Mind"
Christian Century 47, (October 22, 1930):1276–78

Thomson, J. A.
"Science and Religion"
Homiletic Review, (December 1923), Funk and Wagnalls Co.

Thorson, Walter R.
"The Concept of Truth in the Natural Sciences"

Themelios, (1968), vol. 5, no. 2, pp. 27–39
Lausanne, International Fellowship of Evangelical Students, 1968

Titius, A.
"Natural Science and the Christian Faith"
Journal of Religion 11, (January 1931):20–29

Tobias, Robert
"Ecumenics beyond Ecclesiology. Can Science and Theology Make Common Cause?"
Encounter 25, (Spring 1964):202–23

Toombs, Lawrence E.
"Christianity and the New Physics"
Religion in Life 24, (Fall 1955):245–55

Torrance, T. F.
"Newton, Einstein and Scientific Theology"
Religious Studies 8, (September 1972):233–50

"The Church in an Era of Scientific Change"
Month 6, (April 1973):136–42, 176–80

"Determinism and Free Creation According to the Theologians"
Abba Salama, Athens, (1977):9–29

"The Open Universe and the Free Society"
in *Convivium,* No. 7, (Spring 1979):6–21 and in *Ethics in Science and Medicine,* vol. 6, pp. 145–53
Oxford, Pergamon Press, 1979

'God and the Contingent World'
Zygon, (March, 1980)

Townes, Charles H.
"The Convergence of Science and Religion"
Zygon 1, (September 1966):301–11

Treanor, P. J.
"Dialogue with Scientists"
Month 33, (May 1965):289–301

Trevor, George Henry
"Old Gospel and the New Science"
Methodist Review 110, (September–November 1927):703–12, 921–32

Underwood, Richard A.
"An Essay on Religion in an Age of Science: Reflections upon the Words 'salvation', 'fulfillment', and 'success' "
Zygon 2, (December 1967):331–64

Vander Kolk, Justin
"Meaning of Faith in the World of Science"
Reformed Review 22, (March 1969):2–11

Van Wylen, G.
"Scientist's Approach to Jesus Christ"
HIS 17, (February 1957):8

Wald, George
"The Search for Common Ground"
Zygon 1, (March 1966):43–49

Wallace, W. A.
"Science and Religion in the Twentieth Century"
Homiletic and Pastoral Review 63 (October 1962):23–31

"Catholics and the Science Explosion"
Catholic World 200, (November 1964):109–15

Walsh, James Joseph
"Scientists and Faith"
American Catholic Quarterly 35, (April 1910):216–38

"Science and Religion Then and Now"
Catholic World 99, (September 1914):779–90

"Scientist and his Faith"
America 51, (October 6, 1934):606–7

Waltemyer, W. C.
"Quest of a Personal God in an Age of Science"
Lutheran Church Quarterly 2, (July 1929):289–302

Weaver, W.
"Science and Faith"
Christian Century 72, (January 5, 1955):10–13

Weaver, W.
"Why a Scientist Must Believe"
Eternity 10, (July 1959):17–20

Westgate, Lewis Gardner
"Modern Science and Christian Faith"
Methodist Review 113, (May 1930):414–24

Whillans, J. W.
"Spirituality of Science"
Christian Century 42, (January 8, 1925):51–52

White, Robert M.
"An Astronaut's View of God"
Interview by C. Stevens
Catholic Layman 77, (June 1963):4–11

Whitehouse, W. A.
"Towards a Theology of Nature"
Scottish Journal of Theology 17, (June 1964):129–45

Whitley, D. Gath
"Scientific Foundations of Belief in God"
Bibliotheca Sacra 66, (October 1909):606–38

Wittaker, E. T.
"Science Seeks Almighty God"
Catholic Digest 13, (November 1948):48–55

Wieman, H. N.
"Religion and the Physical Sciences"
World Tomorrow 13, (February 1930):56–59

    "Science and a New Religious Reformation"
    Zygon 1, (June 1966):125–39

    "Co-operative Functions of Science and Religion"
    Zygon 3, (March 1968):32–58

Wilburn, Ralph Glenn
"What Science Contributes to Theology"
Lexington Theological Quarterly 2, (January 1967):13–24

    "What Theology Contributes to Science"
    Lexington Theological Quarterly 2, (April 1967):47–58

Williams, Charles Garrett
"Scientist Looks at Religion"
Modern Churchman n.s. 11, (January 1968):85–99

Williams, Samuel Robinson
"Laws of God. A Physicist's Faith"
Christian Century 70, (February 25, 1953):223–25

Wilmer, Cary Brekinridge
"Science and Religion"
John Calvin McNair Lectures, 1925
Sewanee Review 34, (April 1926):223–27

Windle, Bertram Coghill Alan
"Voice of Science, the Voice of God?"
Catholic World 116, (February 1923):647–54

Wishart, John Elliott
"Idea of God in the Light of Modern Science"
Bibliotheca Sacra 87, (April 1930):166–81

Wolf, Hans Heinrich
"Old Problem: Science and the Christian Faith"
Ecumenical Review 9, (July 1957):357–66

Wood, Herbert George
"Science and Religion"
Congregational Quarterly 31, (July 1953):206–11

"Contemporary Religious Trends; Science and Religion"
Expository Times 67, (June 1956):283–86

Woods, C. S.
"Christian Attitude toward Science"
His 17, (December 1956):17–18

Wright, George Frederick
"Present Aspects of the Relations between Science and Revelation"
Bibliotheca Sacra 71, (October 1914):513–33

Wyman, Henry H.
"Modern Science and the Catholic Faith"
Catholic World 71, (April 1900):1–9

Yancey, P. H.
"American Catholics and Science"
Thomist 24, (October 1961):639–56

Yu, Carver T.
"Stratification of the Meaning of Time" in *Scottish Journal of Theology*,
   32.6, 1979.
Edinburgh, Scottish Academic Press, 1979

Zerbe, A. S.
"Scientific, Philosophical, and Theological Faith"
Reformed Church Review 4, (January–April 1925): 55–72, 175–87

General and Popular
Periodicals

Allport, Floyd Henry
"Religion of a Scientist"
Harper's Magazine 160 (February 1930):352–66

Baker, Kenneth W.
"Faith and Science" Address: February 5, 1963
Vital Speeches 29, (May 1, 1963):437–39

Barker, Joseph Warren
"Faith in an Atomic Age"
Vital Speeches 19, (July 15, 1953):585–88

Barth, Karl
"Basing Religion on Science"
Literary Digest 89, (June 19, 1926):27–28

Beaman, Frank Clement Offley
"Church and Science"
Nineteenth Century and After 89, (March 1921):467–74

Beck, Stanley D.
"Science and Christian Understanding"
Dialog 2, (Autumn 1963):314–17

"Behind Every Door: God"
Time 58, (December 3, 1951):75–77

Bell, Arthur Ernest
"Science Teacher Looks at Divinity; Discussion of the Norwood Report"
Hibbert Journal 44, (October, 1945):59–62

Belloc, Hillaire
"Science and Religion"
American Review 2, (February 1934):405–10

Bemporad, Jack
"Stumbling Blocks to Faith; a Symposium: Judaism and Scientific Thought"
Dimensions 1, (Summer 1967):21–28

Best, Edward E.
"Can a Scientist Be a Christian?"
Interracial Review 6, (July 1933):127–28

Bing, Edward J.
"Modern Science Discovers God"
American Mercury 52, (June 1941):722–29

Blakemore, William Barnett
"Science and Religion: a Cultural Encounter"
Encounter 25, (Spring 1964):185–201

Blanshard, Paul
"Roman Catholic Science"
Nation 166, (May 15–22, 1948):521–24, 574–76

Boardman, Norman
"Science, Philosophy, and Religion"
Open Court 40, (August 1926):469–83

Burroughs, J.
"Scientific Faith"
Outlook 97, (February 25, 1911):461–64

Caillard, Emma Marie
"Christianity and Subjective Science"
Contemporary Review 96, (September 1909):317–26

Cairns, David Smith
"Science and Providence"
Contemporary Review 77, (March 1900):358–65

"Science and Providence"
Contemporary Review 142, (October 1932):430–37

Callister, Frank
"Common Sense, Science and Religion"
London Quarterly and Holborn Review 181, (July 1956):218–22

Capra, F.
"Modern Physics and Eastern Philosophy"
Human Dimensions Volume 3, No. 2, (Summer 1974):3–8
Buffalo, New York, 1974

Clark, Robert Edward David
"Newton's God and Ours"
Hibbert Journal 37, (April 1939):425–34

Conklin, Edwin G.
"Biology and Religion"
Princeton Alumni Weekly, (March 1925)

Cook, S.
"Religion of Science and the Science of Religion"
Hibbert Journal 41, (January 1943):131–36

Croly, Herbert
"Naturalism and Christianity"
New Republic 34, (February 28, 1923):9–11

Crowther, Samuel
"Scientist's God," Interview with R. A. Millikan
Collier's 76, (October 24, 1925):5–6

D'Alviella, E. Goblet
"Religion of Biology: its Truth and its Superstitions"
Open Court 27, (May 1913):257–73

D'Arcy, Martin Cyril
"Science and Theology"
American Review 3, (May–June 1934):129–47, 370–84

Demaree, Ralph G.
"Religion and Research"
Social Forces 4, (December 1925):365–70

Dinsmore, C. A.
"Influence of Science on Modern Religious Thought"
Journal of Social Forces 2 (January 1924):239–44

Doepfner, Julius
"Church and Science in the World View of the Council"
Review of Politics 29, (January 1967):3–12

Du Bois, Augustus Jay
"Religion of a Civil Engineer"
Yale Review 2, (July 1913):729–45

"Faith and the Scientist"
Time 79, (June 29, 1962):53–54

Ferre, Luis A.
Address: December 18, 1963 "Science and Religion"
Vital Speeches 30, (February 15, 1964):277–79

"Finding God through the Telescope"
Literary Digest 107, (October 25, 1930):22

Forbes, Alexander
"Science and Religion"
Harvard Graduates' Association Magazine 33, (June 1925):555–64

Fosdick, H. E.
"Science and Religion"
Harper's Monthly Magazine 152, (February 1926):296–300

"Religion's Debt to Science"
Good Housekeeping 86, (March 1928):21

Gibbs, J. T.
"Science and Religion"
Open Court 45, (January 1931):48–55

Gibson, William Ralph Boyce
"From Science to Religion"
Hibbert Journal 17, (October 1918):90–98

Gill, Henry Vincent
"Science Gets Religion!"
Month 157, (April 1931):310–19

Gittelsohn, Roland B.
"Where Religion and Science Meet"
Saturday Review 46, (March 23, 1963):23–24

"God and Science: New Allies in the Search for Values"
Symposium.
Saturday Review 5, (December 10, 1977):13–23

"God and Scientists"
Social Justice Review 59, (October 1966):208

"God in Nature"
Times Literary Supplement 2768, (February 18, 1955):105

"God of a Scientist"
Literary Digest 85, (June 27, 1925):31–32

"God's Finger-prints in the Universe"
Literary Digest 108, (January 24, 1931):27–28

Haldane, John Scott
"Natural Science and Religion"
Hibbert Journal 21, (April 1923):417–35

Hall, Alfred Daniel
"Faith of a Man of Science"
Nineteenth Century and After 110, (December 1931):717–22

Hoffer, Eric
"God and the Machine Age"
The Reporter 14, (February 23, 1956):36

    "How Can a Scientist Be a Christian?"
    Current Literature 39, (November 1905):520–21

Huxley, J. S.
"Religion Meets Science"
Atlantic Monthly 147, (March 1931):373–83

Ibbotson, Ernest
"Science and Revelation"
World Today 56, (September 1930):320–27

    "Ideals of Science and Faith"
    Current Literature 38, (February 1905):114–16

Jastrow, R.
"Have Astronomers Found God? The Big Bang Theory"
NY Times Magazine, (June 25, 1978):18–20

Johnson, Harry Miles
"Can Religion Blend with Modern Science?"
Virginia Quarterly Review 6, (July 1930):321–34

Jordan, H. E.
"Call of Science to the Church"
Open Court 27, (May 1913):274–88

Julian, Frederick Bennet
"Influence of Religion on the Progress of Medicine"
Hibbert Journal 51, (April 1953):254–61

Keller, A. G.
"Religion and Science"
Outlook 152, (August 14, 1929):619

Knox, H. H.
"Present Relation of Science and Religion"
Personalist 23, (October 1942):369–78

Langdon-Davies, John
"Science and God"
Spectator 146, (January 31, 1931):137–38

Laws, John W.
"Toward a Theology of Nature"
Intellect 103, (May 1975):533–35

Leuba, J. H.
"Religious Beliefs of American Scientists"
Harper's Magazine 169, (August 1934):291–300

Levy, Hyman
"Scientists and Pietists"
New Republic 83, (June 12, 1935):123–5

Lidgett, J. S.
"Idea of God"
Contemporary Review 142, (November 1932):561–67

    "Science, Philosophy, and Religion"
    Contemporary Review 136, (November 1929):593–604

McDougall, William
"Religion and the Sciences of Life"
South Atlantic Quarterly 31, (January 1932):15–30

MacKay, D. Mac C.
"Science in Christian Perspective"
New Humanist 88, No. 6, (1972):227–28

Maclaurin, Richard Cockburn
"Science and Religion: the End of the Battle"
Outlook 99, (September 9, 1911):71–74

MacPherson, H. G.
"What Would a Scientific Religion Be Like?"
Saturday Review 52, (August 2, 1969):44–47
Discussion: September 6, 1969:60

Magnus, Laurie
"Science and Religion; the New Phase"
Cornhill Magazine 70, (January 1931):117–26

Mallock, William Hurrell
"Religion and Science at the Dawn of the Twentieth Century"
Fortnightly Review 76:395–414, 812–31; 77, 277–96; 78, 134–52, 684–703. S., N. 1901; F., Jl., O. 1902

Martin, Louis Claude
"Science Is Not Enough"
Fortnightly Review 176, n.s. 166, (October 1949):266–71

Martin, Malachi B.
"Sons and Daughters, not Orphans; Space Exploration and Christianity"
National Review 27, (July 18, 1975):776

Mather, K. F.
"God of Science"
Forum 81, (January 1929):47–49

Mead, Margaret
"Is the Church Powerless in a Scientific World?"
Redbook 129, (July 1967):44

    "Religious System with Science at its Core"
    Excerpt from *Twentieth Century Faith*
    Saturday Evening Post 245, (November 1973):16–17

    "Men of Science Also Men of Faith"
    Literary Digest 78, (July 14, 1923):30–31

Mesthene, Emmanuel G.
"What Modern Science Offers the Church"
Saturday Review 49, (November 19, 1966):29–31

Morrison, A. C.
"Seven Reasons Why a Scientist Believes in God"
Reader's Digest 44, (December 1946):11

Murphey, Murray G.
"On the Relationship between Science and Religion"
American Quarterly 20, pt. 2, (Summer 1968):275–95

Murray, Thomas Edward
"Opening Doors; Remarriage of Religion and Science"
Vital Speeches 19, (July 1, 1953):559–62

Nance, John
"Scientific Bases for Belief"
Hibbert Journal 45, (July 1947):342–9

Needham, J.
"Limitations of Optick Glasses: Some Observations on Science and
    Religion"
Hibbert Journal 24, (April 1926):463–80

    "Religion in a Scientific Age"
    Nineteenth Century and After 110, (November 1931):580–93

    "Common Ground of Science and Religion"
    Rice Institute Pamphlets 24, (October 1937):282–92

Oursler, Fulton
"God's Newest Witness, a Biologist"
Reader's Digest 50, (March 1947):39–44

Oxnam, G. B.
"Religion and Science in Accord"
Annals of the American Academy of Political and Social Science, (March
    1948):141–47

Polanyi, M.
"Science and Religion: Separate Dimensions or Common Ground?"
Philosophy Today 7, (September 1963):4–14

Poteat, William Louis
"Religion in Science"
South Atlantic Quarterly 6, (April 1907):147–64

"Present Relations between Science and Religion: a Symposium"
Hibbert Journal 54, (October 1955):1–69

"Reconciling Science and Religion"
New Republic 44, (September 9, 1925):57–59

Rees, Phoebe
"Faith for the Space Age"
Drama Survey 79, (Winter 1965):38–9

Reinheimer, Hermann
"Science and Religion"
London Quarterly Review 146, (October 1926):239–43

   "Religion and Science: Working Together to Close the Gaps"
   U.S. News 78, (March 17, 1975):47–49

Ritter, William Emerson
"Religion of a Naturalist"
Open Court 37, (January 1923):30–36

Routh, Dennis Alan
"Churches and Science"
Hibbert Journal 52, (October 1953):56–64

Rowland, John
"Science and Religion"
Hibbert Journal 60, (October 1961):1–9

Rust, E. C.
"Christian Faith and Scientific Knowledge"
Philosophy Today 9, (Winter 1965):278–93

Savage, Thomas Edmund
"Science and the Bible"
Open Court 38, (March 1924):129–41

Scheltens, D. F.
"Reflections on Natural Theology"
International Philosophical Quarterly 11, (March 1971):75–86

Schiller, Ferdinand Canning Scott
"Science and Life"
Hibbert Journal 19, (October 1920):101–11

"Science and Religion"
Discovery 14, (November 1933–April 1934):336–38, 368–71; 15:3–4, 31–34, 78–80, 101–2

"Science and Religion" A Symposium
Discovery 15, (May–July 1943):132–36, 164–66, 187–89

"Science and Religion"
An Address delivered at St. John's University, Brooklyn, N.Y., November 19, 1939.
Vital Speeches 6, (December 15, 1939)

"Science and Religion: an Editorial"
Outlook 151, (January 16, 1929):102

"Science and the Knowledge of God"
Outlook 134, (June 6, 1923):115–16

"Science Finding God"
Literary Digest 111, (November 21, 1931):21–22

"Science no Refutation of Religion"
Literary Digest 75, (November 25, 1922):32–33

"Science, Religion and Sacraments"
Outlook (London) 58, (August 14, 1926):156

"Scientific View of the Relation between Nature and Religion"
Current Opinion 59, (September 1915):186–87

"Scientist-Minister Begins Dual Career"
Today's Health 41, (December 1963):85

Scott, W. T.
"Tacit Knowing and the Concept of Mind"
The Philosophical Quarterly, (January 1971):22–35

Sen, Boshi
"Science and Religion"
Forum 94, (December 1935):379–83

Singer, Kurt (ed.)
"Nine Scientists Look at Religion"
Reader's Digest 82, (January 1963):92

Steinmetz, Charles Proteus
"Science and Religion"
Harper's Monthly Magazine 144, (February 1922):296–302

Tawney, Guy Allen
"Religion and Experimentation"
International Journal of Ethics 36, (July 1926):337–56

Taylor, Hugh Stott
"Science and Religion: There Can Be No Conflict"
Vital Speeches 6, (December 15, 1939):145–46

  "Science and Religion; towards Unity"
  Perspectives 5, (June 1960):4–10

Tennant, F. R.
"Present Relations of Science and Theology"
Constructive Quarterly 9, (December 1921):578–95; 10, (June 1922):274–90

Tester, S. J.
"Science and Christian Belief"
Hibbert Journal 56, (October 1957):20–30

Tute, Richard Clifford
"Space-time, a Link between Religion and Science"
Hibbert Journal 38, (January 1940):261–70

  "Two Cultures Harmonized under God"
  Life, (April 20, 1962):4

Vaughan, Ted R. et al.
"Religious Orientations of American Scientists"
Social Forces 44, (June 1966):519–26

von Braun, W.
"Why I Believe"
Moody Monthly 66, (June 1966):45

Watts, Harvey Maitland
"As a Naturalist Sees It"
Open Court 40, (October 1926):624–31

Weaver, W.
"Can a Scientist Believe in God?"
Look 19, (April 5, 1955):27–31

  "Scientist Ponders Faith"
  Saturday Review 42, (January 3, 1959):8–10

  "Science and the Goodness of God"
  Excerpt from *Science and the Imagination.*
  Redbook 130, (December 1967):47

Whitehead, A. N.
"Religion and Science"
Atlantic Monthly 36, (August 1925):200–7

Whitman, Howard
"What Scientists Believe"
Colliers 128, (August 11, 1951):26–27

Wiggam, A. E.
"Religion of the Scientist"
World's Work 50, (August 1925):391–99

"Science and Religion"
World Today 46, (September 1925):851–58

"Science is Leading us Closer to God"
Interview with M. Pupin
American Magazine 104, (September 1927):24–25

Wilson, J. M.
"Scientific Training and Religious Truth"
Contemporary Review 83, (March 1903):320–36

Wren-Lewis, J.
"Liberal Religion and the Scientist"
Hibbert Journal 58, (April 1960):223–30

"Science, Religion and the Unity of Mankind"
London Quarterly and Holborn Review 189, (October 1964):319–25

"Science and Religion"
Twentieth Century 177, No. 1036, (1968):54–8

Wright, Charles James
"God and the Unfathomed Universe"
London Quarterly and Holborn Review 155, (April 1931):145–58

Wright, Jonathan
"Religious Factors of Science"
Open Court 41, (December 1927):705–14

Yarros, Victor S.
"From Modern Physics to Religion"
Based on *The Nature of the Physical World* by A. S. Eddington, and
Religion by E. S. Ames.
Open Court 44, (January 1930):37–47

"Science and Religion. Another Attempt at Reconciliation"
Open Court 45, (May 1931):309–14

Foreign Language Publications

Aichelin, Helmut, and Liedke, Gerhard (eds.)
Naturwissenschaft und Theologie; Texte u. Kommentäre
Neukirchen-Vluyn, Neukirchener Verlag, 1975

Altner, Günter
Charles Darwin und Ernst Haeckel. Ein Vergleich nach theologischen Aspekten mit einem Gleichwort von Wulf Emmo Ankel

Theologische Studien 85
Zurich, Theologisher Verlag Zurich, 1966

> *Grammatik der Schöpfung; theologische Inhalte der Biologie*
> Stuttgart, Kreuz-Verlag, c. 1971

> *Schöpfung am Abgrund. Die Theologie vor der Umweltfrage*
> Neukirchan-Vluyn, Neukirchener Verlag, 1978

> *Zwischen Natur und Menschengeschichte; anthropologische, biologische,*
> *ethische Perspektiven für eine neue Schöpfungstheologie*
> Munich, Kaiser, 1975

> "Biologie und Schöpfung. Die Erfahrung des Lebendigen durch
> die moderne Biologie"
> *Schopfung und Erfahrung,* 31, 1975

Altner, Günter (ed)
Kreatur Mensch
Munich, Deutscher Taschenbuch Verlag GmbH & Co., 1969

> *Zur Theologie der Natur,*
> Themaheft, *Evangelische Theologie,* 1, 1977

Altner, G. and Hofer, H.
Die Sonderstellung des Menschen
Stuttgart, Gustaf Fisher Verlag GmbH & Co., 1972

Auzou, Georges
Au Commencement Dieu créa le monde; L'histoire et la foi
Paris, Editions du Cerf, 1973

Babel, Henri
La Religion à l'Aube d'une ère nouvelle
Neuchatel, La Baconniere, 1970

Beck, Horst Waldemar
Weltformel contra Schöpfungsglaube, Theologie und empirische Wissenschaft
von einer neuen Wirklichkeitsdeutung
Zurich, Theologischer Verlag, 1972

Auer, Johann
Die Welt—Gottes Schöpfung
Regensburg, F. Pustet, 1975

Beck, H. W.
"Denken und Entscheiden im kybernetische Modell—Eine kritische
Stellungname zum thema 'Theologie und Empirie' "
Zeitschrift f. Evangelische Ethik, 18/4, July 1974, pp. 225–245

> *Biologie und Weltanschauung—Gott der Schöpfer und Vollender und die*
> *Evolutionskonzepte des Menschen,* Band 1, *Wort und Wissen,* ed. by
> H. W. Beck
> Neuhausen-Stuttgart, Hänssler Verlag, 1979

Schritte über Grenzen zwischen Technik und Theologie
Part I *Der Mensch im System. Perspektiven einer kybernetischen Kultur*

Part 2 *Schöpfung und Vollendung. Perspektiven einer Theologie der Natur*

Band 6 *Wort und Wissen,* ed. by H. W. Beck
Neuhausen-Stuttgart, Hänssler Verlag, 1980

Die Welt as Formel. Gegen den Mythos vom geschlossenen Weltbild
Wuppertal, 1971

Beinert, Wolfgang
Christus und der Kosmos; Perspektiven zu einer Theologie der Schöpfung
Freiburg, Herder, 1974

Ben-Chorin, Schalom
Judentum und Christentum im technologischen Zeitalter (33 essays)
Meitingen, Freising, Kyrios-Verlag; Linz, Wien, Passau, Veritas-Verlag, 1972

Boll, Marcel
"La Science et la Foi"
Mercure de France 256, (November 15, 1934):77–91

Bonifazi, C.
Eine Theologie der Dinge. Der Mensch in seiner natürlichen Welt
Stuttgart, Klett-Cotta/SVK 1977

Bresch, Carsten
Zwischenstufe Leben. Evolution ohne Ziel?
Zurich, Munich, R. Piper Verlag, 1977

Brugarola, Martin
Sociologia y teologia de la técnica
Madrid, Editorial Catolica, 1967

Brunner, Peter
"Gott, das Nichts und die Kreatur" in *Kerygma und Dogma,* 6, 1960, pp. 172 ff
Göttingen, Vandenhoeck und Ruprecht, 1968

Brunner, Rudolf
Christus im All. Weltraumfahrt aus dem Glauben
Feldmeilen-Zürich, Grundstein-Verlag, 1963

Bucaille, Maurice
La Bible, le Coran et la Science: les Ecritures saintes examinées a la lumière des connaissances modernes
Paris, Seghers, 1976

Bucher, Zeno
Das Schöpferische der Natur als fortdauernde Schöpfung
Salzburg, Munich, Pustet, 1973

Bukovics, Erich
Glaube und Naturwissenschaft
Vienna, Evangelischer Pressverband in Österreich, 1968

Bundscherer, Norbert
Moderne naturwissenschaft und christlicher Glaube
Munich, J. Pfeiffer, 1961

Cammerer, Josef Sebastian
Die gläserne Wand: Essays über den Zwiespalt von Naturwissenschaften und Theologie
Munich, Verlag J. Pfeiffer, 1969

Chapey, Fernand
Science et Foi: affrontement de deux langages
Paris, Le Centurion, 1974

Chenu, Marie-Dominique
Théologie de la Matière: Civilisation Technique et Spiritualité Chrétienne
Paris, Editions du Cerf, 1967

"Christianity, Science and the religion of humanity"
Political Quarterly 13, (July 1942):280–93

"Colloque sur la refléxion et la recherche interdisciplinaires comme modalité du dialogue Église-monde"
Louvain, 1967

Recherche interdisciplinaire et théologie, Sous la direction de Francois Houtart.
Paris, Editions du Cerf, 1970

Daecke, S. M.
"Soll die Theologie an der Universität bleiben? Zur Auseinandersetzung um eine Begründung der Theologie als Wissenschaft"
in Pannenberg, W., et al. Grundlagen der Theologie, pp. 7–28.
Stuttgart, Kohlhammer Verlag, 1974

"Neue Beiträge zu einer Theologie der Natur und der Umwelt"
Anstösse, Hofgeismar, 5/1976

"Schöpfungsglaube als Gotteserkenntnis, Selbstverständnis, Weltverantwortung, Naturerfahrung und Umweltbewusstsein. Uberlegungen einer Theologie der Natur und der Umwelt in der Schöpfungslehre"
Wissenschaft und Praxis in Kirche und Gesellschaft, 9/1978, 12/1979

"Auf dem Weg zu einer Practischen Theologie der Natur"
in Meyer-Abich, K. M. (ed.), *Frieden mit der Natur,*
Freiburg, Herder, 1979

"Naturwissenschaft und Theologie. Ein Ueberblick über das Gesprach zwischen den beiden Wissenschaften und über die Literatur"
Der Evangelische Erzieher, 1977, pp. 242–268

Déchet, Ferruccio
L'ottavo giorno della creazione
Milan, Marzorati, 1969

Delleman, Th.
Wording van mens en wereld
Franeker, Wever, 1971

Dembowski, H.
"Ansatz und Umrisse einer Theologie der Natur," in *Zur Theologie der Natur,* ed. G. Altner
Göttingen, 1977

Dennert, Eberhard
Bibel und Naturwissenschaft: Gedanken und Bekenntnisse eines Naturforschers
Stuttgart, M. Kielmann, 1904

Dessauer, Friedrich
Die Teleologie in der Natur
Basel, E. Reinhardt, 1949

Dilschneider, Otto
Das christliche Weltbild
Gütersloh, Gerd Mohn, 1951

Dockx, S. (ed.)
Archives de l'Institut International des Sciences Théoriques
Brussels, Office International de Librairie S.A., Volumes 1–23

Dockx, S.
"Vers und Synthese moderne du Savoir"
Volume 7, *Archives de l'Institut International des Sciences Théoriques,* Brussels, Office International de Librairie, 1950

Dockx, S. (ed.)
Science, Philosophie, Foi
Archives de l'Institut des Sciences Theoriques, vol. 19
Brussels, 1974

De la Méthode. Méthodologies Particulières et Méthodologie Genérale
Archives de l'Institut des Sciences Théoriques, vol. 18
Brussels, 1973

Dockx, S.
La Connaissance Scientifique

XIX Congrès International de Philosophie des Sciences, 1949
Paris, Hermann, 1951

La Théorie fondamentale du système périodiques des éléments
Brussels, Office International de Librairie, 1959

"Ciencia Y Filosophia"
Mexico, National University of Mexico, 1960

La structure organique du corps vivant, condition de l'exercise de la liberté humaine
Brussels, Office International de Librairie, 1963

La structure matricielle du système périodiques des éléments
Brussels, Office International de Librairie, 1970

Dolch, Heimo
Kausalität im Verständnis des Theologen und der Begründer der neuzeitlichen Physik
Freiburg, 1954

Döring, Heinz
Umwelt-Verantwortlichkeit; die Schöpfung einer geordneten Natur und ihre fortschreitende Zerstörung . . .
Kassel, Verlag Evangelischer Presseverband Kurhessen-Waldeck, 1975

Dubarle, Dominique
Approaches d'une théologie de la science
Paris, Editions du Cerf, 1967

"Univers de la Science et Foi chrétienne"
Vie Spirituelle Supplement No. 45, (1958):175–87

Duhem, P.
Essai sur la Notion de Théorie Physique de Platon a Galilée
Paris, Hermann, 1908

Le Système du Monde, 5 volumes
Paris, Hermann, 1913–1917

Emeis, Dieter
Wegzeichen des Glaubens: über die Aufgabe der Katechese angesichts einer von Science und Technick geprägten, Mentalität
Freiburg, Herder, 1972

Ewald, Günter
Naturgesetz und Schöpfung. Zum Verhältnis von Naturwissenschaft und Theologie
Wuppertal, 1966

Fogazzaro, Antonio
Ascensioni Umane: Teoria dell' Evoluzione e Filosofia Christiana
Milan, Longanesi, 1977

Föhr, Ernst
Naturwissenschaftliche Weltsicht und christlicher Glaube; das moderne Weltbild
Freiburg, Basel, Vienna, Herder, 1974

"Wissenschaft and Religion"
Deutsche Rundschau 75, (April 1949):319–30

Francke, Joh.
Het Vooroordeel in de Wetenschap
Groningen, De Vuurbaak, 1971

Frauenknecht, Hans
Urknall, Urzeugung und Schöpfung; ein Informationsbuch zum Dialog zwischen Naturwissenschaft und Glauben
Wiesbaden, Brockhaus, 1976

Friedman, Georges
La Puissance et la Sagesse
Paris, Gallimard, 1970

Ganoczy, Alexandre
Der schöpferische Mensch und die Schöpfung Gottes
Mainz, Matthias-Grünewald-Verlag, 1976

Ganzevoort, B. W.
De Bijbel in het Geding
Kampen, J. H. Kok, 1968

Garrido, Jules
Cathéchisme pour Scientifiques et Techniciens Religieusement Sous-développés
Paris, Editions du Cèdre, 1970

Gemelli, Agostino
Religione e Scienza
Milan, Società editrice "Vita e pensiero", 1922

Gerdes, Hayo
"Die christliche Theologie als Wissenschaft"
Neue Zeitschrift für Systematische Theologie und Religions-Philosophie 6, No. 1, (1964):1–13

Geyer, Hans Georg, Esser, Hans Helmut, Horn, Herrman, and Schulze, Hans
Beilage zu Naturwissenschaft und Theologie Grenzgespräche Band 6
Neukirchen-Vluyn, Neukirchener Verlag, 1974

Giret, A.
L'Astronomie Actuelle et la Notion de Dieu
Paris, Paillard, 1956

L'Astronomie et le Sentiment Religieux
Paris, Librairie Paillard, 1964

Glöckner, Martin
Unsere Welt, Zufall oder Schöpfung?
Hamburg, Saatkorn-Verlag, 1969

Goez, Wilhelm
Naturwissenschaft und Evangelium
Heidelberg, Quelle and Meyer, 1954

Goldziher, Ignacz
Stellung der alten islamischen Orthodoxie zu den antiken Wissenschaften
Berlin, Verlag der Königl. Akademie der Wissenschaften, 1916

Grabner-Haider, Anton
Theorie der Theologie als Wissenschaft
Munich, Kosel, 1974

Grape, Johannes
Urmensch-Pardies-Ebenbild Gottes. Eine apologetische Studie
Halle (Saale), R. Mühlmann Verlagsbuchhandlung, 1913

Günter, E.
Der Mensch als Geschöpf und kybernetische Machine
Wuppertal, 1971

Haag, Herbert
Biblisches und naturwissenschaftliches Weltbild
Graz, Vienna, Cologne, Styria, 1971

Haeckel, E. H. P. A.
Der Kampf um den Entwicklungsgedanken. Ausgewählte kleinere Schriften und Reden
Leipzig, Reclam, 1967

Heine, Walter
Glauben und Wissenschaft; Geschichte eines Bewusstseins
Dortmund, Ruhfus, 1974

Heisenberg, W.
Der Teil und das Ganze. Gespräche im Umkreis der Atomphysik
Munich, 1969

Heitler, Walter
Die Natur und das Göttliche
Zug, Switzerland, Klett und Balmer, 1976
   "On the Complementarity of Living and Lifeless Matter"
   Det Kongelige Norske Videnskabers Selskab Skrifter, No 1, (1978):1–12
   Oslo, Universitetsforlaget, 1978

Hemleben, Johannes
Biologie und Christentum
Stuttgart, Verlag Urachhaus, 1971

Hendricks, J. A.
Van Oertijd Tot Eindtijd
Amsterdam, H. J. Paris, 1965

Henneman, Gerhard
Naturwissenschaft und Religion
Berlin, Duncker und Humblot, 1963

Hirsch, Eike Christian
Das Ende aller Gottesbeweise? Naturwissenschaftler antworten auf die religiöse Frage
Hamburg, Furche-Verlag, 1975

Hollweg, Arnd
Theologie und Empirie. Ein Beitrag zum Gespräch zwischen Theologie und Sozialwissenschaften in den USA und Deutschland
Stuttgart, Evangelisches Verlag, 3rd edition, 1974

Howe, Günter
Gespräch zwischen Theologie und Physik
Gladbeck, Freizeiten-Verlag, 1950

   Mensch und Physik
   Witten/Berlin, Eckhardt- und Luther-Verlag, 1963

   Gott und die Technik
   Hamburg, Furche-Verlag, 1971

   "Zu den Aeusserungen von Niels Bohr über religiöse Fragen"
   KuD, (1957):20–46

   Die Christenheit im Atomzeitalter
   Stuttgart, 1970

Howe, Günter, and Tödt, Eduard
Frieden im wissenschaftlich-technischen Zeitalter Oekumenische Theologie und Zivilisation
Stuttgart/Berlin, Ernst Klett-Verlag, 1966

Hübner, Jürgen
Theologie und biologische Entwicklungslehre. Ein Beitrag zum Gespräch zwischen Theologie und Naturwissenschaft
Munich, Beck, 1966

Huntemann, Georg Hermann
Provozierte Theologie in Technischer Welt
Wuppertal, R. Brockhaus Verlag, 1968

Illies, Joachim
Der Mensch in der Schöpfung; ein Naturwissenschaftler liest die Bibel
Zurich, Edition Interfrom, 1977

Für eine menschenwürdige Zukunft. Die gemeinsame Verantwortung von Biologie und Theologie
Freiburg, Herder, 1972

Jenseits der Erkenntnis; Fragen statt Antworten hrsg. von Leonhard Reinisch
1. Aufl. Frankfurt am Main, Suhrkamp, 1977

Jordan, Pascual
Der Naturwissenschaftler vor der religiösen Frage; Abbruch einer Mauer
Oldenburg and Hamburg, Gerhard Stalling, 1964

Wie frei sind wir? Naturgesetz und Zufall
Osnabrück, 1971

Der Naturwissenschaftler vor der religiösen Frage. Abbruch einer Mauer
Oldenburg/Hamburg, 1963

Schöpfung und Geheimnis
Oldenburg/Hamburg, 1970

Kahane, Ernest
La Science et la Religion
Paris, Cercle Ernest-Renan, 1975

Kalsbeek, L.
Schepping en Wording
Baarn, Bosch & Keuning, 1968

Köberle, Adolf
Christentum und modernes Naturerleben; drei Vorlesungen
Gütersloh, C. Bertelsmann, 1932

Koch, Ernst
La Science et la Religion sur une Base Unique et Idéale
Paris, H. et H. Durville, 1916

Konrad, Alois
Das Weltbild in der Bibel
Graz, Verlagsbuchhandlung "Styria," 1917

Kornet, A. G.
Het Boek van Gods Lach
Kampen, Kok, 1973

Krebs, Engelbert Gustav Hans
Theologie und Wissenschaft nach der Lehre der Hochscholastik
Münster in W., Aschendorff, 1912

Ladrière, J.
L'articulation du Sens; Discours Scientifique et Parole de la Foi
Paris, Aubier Montaigne, 1970

> *La Science, le Monde and la Foi*
> Tournai, Casterman, 1972

Laloup, Jean
"Ainsi la Science Aide Dieu"
Revue Nouvelle 34, (November 1961):384–94

> "Signification Chrétienne de la science"
> *Revue Nouvelle* 32, (September 1960):164–77

Lannes, Serge
"Sciences de l'Homme et Science de Dieu"
Études Théologiques et Religieuses 53, No. 1, (1978):59–71

Läuchli, A.
Wandlungen des naturwissenschaftlichen Weltbildes und christlicher Glaube
Zurich, Zwingli-Verlag, 1956

Lay, Rupert
Der neue Glaube an die Schöpfung
Olten, Walter-Verlag, 1971

Lejeune, Erwin
"Der Christ in der Spannung zwischen Naturwissenschaft und Glauben"
Reformatio 15, (July 1966):365–79

Leese, Kurt
Recht und Grenze der natürlichen Religion
Zurich, Morgarten Verlag, 1954

Lehmann, Richard
Naturwissenschaft und biblische Wunderfrage
Kaiserlautern, Verlag des Evang. Vereins für die Pfalz, 1930

> *Neutestamentliche Wunderberichte und Naturwissenschaft*
> Berlin, E. Runge Verlag, 1925

Lévi, Robert
Refléxions sur la Science et l'Existence de Dieu
Paris, Desforges (dist.), 1971

Liebig, Rudolf
Die andere Offenbarung; christlicher Glaube im Gespräch mit der modernen Wissenschaft
Augsburg, Verlag Winfried-Werk, 1969

Liedke, G. et al.
Baustelle Gottesdienst. Das gottesdienstliche Mahl in der wissenschaftlich-technischen Welt
Heidelberg, Studiengemeinschaft, 1968

Link, Christian
Die Welt als Gleichnis. Studien zum Problem der natürlichen Theologie
Munich, *Beiträge zur Evangelische Theologie*, 73, 1976
"Zum Gesprach zwischen Theologie und Naturwissenshaft"
Schöpfung und Erfahrung, 1975, no. 31

Lixfeld, Hannjost
Gott und Teufel als Weltschöpfer; eine Untersuchung über die dualistische Tiererschaffung in der europäischen und aussereuropäischen Volksüberlieferung
Munich, W. Fink, 1971

Löbsack, Theo
Wunder, Wahn und Wirklichkeit: Naturwissenschaft und Glaube
Munich, Bertelsmann, 1976

Lodge, O. J.
"La Science et le Monde Invisible" Tr. L. Baillon de Wailly
Revue Politique et Litteraire 71, (April 15, 1933):225–26

Lodovici, E. S.
Tra Cosmologia e Metafisica. Note sul Concetto di Cosmo
Reprint from *Il Demoniaco nella Musica*
Turin, G. Giappichelli, n.d.

Loyer, Pierre
Du Cosmos à Dieu
Paris, Nouvelles Editions latines, 1971

Luyten, Norbert A.
Führt ein Weg zu Gott?
Freiburg, K. Alber, 1972

Mackay, D. MacC.
"Signale vom Gehirn"
Bild der Wissenschaft 7, (1970):52–68

Mairlot, Édouard
Science et Foi Chrétienne: Dimensions Religieuses de l'Activité Scientifique
Brussels, La Pensée catholique, 1968

Marquette, Jacques de
Le créativisme. Essai sur l'Immortalisation de l'Âme
Geneva, Perret-Gentil, 1969

Martinez, Sebastián
Dios y el universo
Tegucigalpa, 1970

Martinez de Castro, Manuel
El Milagro del Amor Divino
México, 1969

Martinez de Galinsoga de Vega, Carlos
Hacia una Teologia de la Técnica
Madrid, S. M., 1972

Masi, Roberto, and Allessandri, Michelangelo
Religione, Scienza e Filosofia
Brescia, Morcelliana, 1958

Mercier, André
Mystik und Wissenschaftlichkeit
Bern and Frankfurt, Herbert Lang, 1972

Meschkowski, Herbert
Das Christentum im Jahrhundert der Naturwissenschaften
Munich, E. Reinhardt, 1961

Metz, Johann Bapt, and Rendtorff, Trutz
Die Theologie in der interdisziplinären Forschung
Düsseldorf, Bertelsmann Universitätsverlag, 1971

Meurers, Joseph
Die Frage nach Gott und die Naturwissenschaft
Munich, A. Pustet, 1962

Meyer-Abich, Klaus M.
"Zum Begriff Einer Praktischen Theologie Der Natur"
Evangelische Theologie 37, (January–February 1977):3–20

Mierlo, S. van
La science, la Raison et la Foi
Paris, Presses Universitaires due France, 1948

Minozzi, Bruno
Le interpretazioni naturalistische della religione
Bologna, Il mulino, 1968

Misch, Manfred
*Apis est animal, apis est ecclesia; ein Beitrag zum Verhältnis von Naturkunde
und Theologie in spätantiker und mittelalterlicher Literatur*
Bern, Herbet Lang; Frankfurt, Peter Lang, 1974

Mohr, H.
"Wissenschaft wider die ligitimierte Korruption,"
in *Evangelische Kommentare*, pp. 671ff.
Neukirchen-Vluyn, Neukirchener Verlag, 1972

Mondrone, D.
"Vertigini scientifiche e Realtà Cristiane"
Civiltà Cattolica 109 (2), (May 1958):254–68

Monod, Victor
Dieu dans l'Univers; Essai sur l'Action exercée sur la Pensée chrétienne par les grands Systèmes cosmologiques depuis Aristote jusqu' à nos jours
Paris, Fischbacher, 1933

Moock, Wilhelm
Natur und Gottesgeist
Frankfurt am Main, J. Knecht, 1948

Morcillo González, Casimiro
El Hombre Cristiano ante la Técnica
Madrid, Euramérica, 1962

Morel, Bernard
Cybernétique et Transcendance
Paris, La Colombe, 1964

Mulder, Dirk Cornelius
Iman dan ilmu pengetahuan
Djakarta, Badan Penerbit Kristen, 1965

Müller, A. M. Klaus
Erwägungen zu einer Theologie der Natur
Gütersloher Verlagshaus, G. Mohn, 1970
> *Die präparierte Zeit: der Mensch in der Krise seiner eigenen Zielsetzungen*
> Stuttgart, Radius-Verlag, 1972

Müller, A. M. Klaus (ed.)
Zukunftsperspektiven. Zu einem integrierten Verständnis der Lebenswelt
Stuttgart, 1976

Müller, A. M. Klaus, with Pannenberg, Wolfhart
Erwägungen zu einer Theologie der Natur
Gütersloh, Gerd Mohn, 1970

Müller, Armin
Bios und Christentum: Wege zu einer "natürlichen" Offenbarung
Stuttgart, E. Klett, 1958

Müller, Wilhelm Alfred
Die Wiederkehr des Zufalls; Kontingenz und Naturerfahrung bei Naturwissenschaftlern, Philosophen und Theologen
Gütersloh, Gütersloher Verlagshaus, G. Mohn, 1977

Müller-Markus, Siegfried
Physik, Glaube, Gott. Entwurf einer Theologie des Schöpferischen
Einsiedeln, Johannes Verlag, 1970

> *Wo die Welt nochmal beginnt. Moderne Physik und die Möglichkeit des Glaubens*
> Olten, Walter-Verlags, 1970

Müller-Schwefe, Hans Rudolf
Technik und Glaube: eine per anente Herausforderung
Göttingen, Vandenhoeck und Ruprecht, 1971

Muschalek, Hubert
Gottbekenntnisse moderner Naturforscher
Berlin, Morus-Verlag, 1960

Musso, Bruno
E Dio gettò i dadi e disse. Scienza e rivelazione, oggi
Torino, P. Gribaudi, 1972

> "Naturwissenschaft und christlicher Glaube"
> *Reformatio* 16, (March 1967):145–220

Neidhart, Walter
Krone der Schöpfung? Humanwissenschaften und Theologie
Stuttgart, Kreuz-Verlag, 1977

Nordström, Stefan
Naturvetenskap och kristen tro
Stockholm, EFS-förlaget, 1970

Noto, Vincenzo
Creazione e Lavoro
Rome, Coines, 1972

Otter, W. den
Harmonie tussen Bijbel en Natuur
Goes, Oosterbaan & Le Cointre, 1976

Pannenberg, Wolfhart
Erwägungen zu einer Theologie der Natur II. *Kontingenz und Naturgesetz*
Gütersloh, Gerd Mohn, 1970

Panteghini, Gabriele
Il Mondo Materiale nel Piano della Salvezza
Rome, Edizioni paoline, 1968

Pegand, Georges
Ascèse et Science
Paris, La Colombe, Editions du Vieux Colombier, 1963

Peschek, Alois
Die Schöpfungsfrage—eine gelöste Frage
Hartberg, Selbstverl des Verf., 1971

Peursen, Cornelis Anthonie van
Het kennen van de toekomst
Driebergen, Kerk en Wereld, 1967

Pfister, Friedrich
*Religion und Wissenschaft: ihr Verhältnis von den Anfängen bis zur Gegen-
    wart*
Bern, Francke Verlag, 1972

Phaure, Jean
*Le Cycle de l'Humanité adamique: Introduction à L'étude de la Cyclologie
    traditionnelle et de la Fin des Temps*
Paris, Dervy-Livres, 1973

Philberth, Bernhard
Der Dreieine: Angang und Sein. Die Struktur der Schöpfung
Aschaffenburg, Pattloch, 1971

Picht, G.
"Die geschichtliche Natur des Menschen, S. Leben und Tod"
Mensch und Technik, 23, 1976

Portmann, A.
Biologie und Geist
Zurich, 1956

    Aufbruch der Lebensforschung
    Zurich, 1965

    Entlässt die Natur den Menschen?
    Munich, 1970

    Vom Lebendigen. Versuche zu einer Wissenschaft vom Menschen
    Frankfurt, 1973

    An den Grenzen des Wissens. Vom Beitrag der Biologie zu einen Weltbild
    Vienna/Dusseldorf, 1974. Frankfurt, 1976

    Der Pfeil des Humanen. Ueber Teilhard de Chardin
    Freiburg/Munich, 1960

Rad, Michael von, et al.
Anthropologie als Thema von psychosomatischer Medizin und Theologie
Stuttgart, etc., Kohlhammer, 1974

Rapp, Hans Reinhard
Mensch, Gott und Zahl. Kybernetik im Horizont der Theologie
Hamburg, Furche-Verlag, 1967

Reis, Manuel Augusto da Encarnação
O Cristão no Mundo hoje
Lisbon, Livraria Morais Editora, 1965

Rohrbach, Hans
Naturwissenschaft, Weltbild, Glaube
Wuppertal, R. Brockhaus, 1967

Roqueplo, Philippe
La Foi d'un Mal-croyant; ou, Mentalité scientifique et Vie de Foi
Paris, Les Editions du Cerf, 1969

> *L'Energie de la Foi: Science, Foi, Politique*
> Paris, Les Editions du Cerf, 1973

Rougier, Louis
"Les Rapports de la Science et de la Religion"
Mercure de France 217, (January 15, 1930):257–76

Russo, Francois et al.
Science et Theologie: Methode et Langage
Paris, Desclee de Brouwer, 1969

Sandberg, Max
Theokosmos: die Schöpfung, das Göttliche, der Mensch
Zurich, Origo, 1960

Sauter, Gerhard
Theologie als Wissenschaft. Aufsätze und Thesen
Munich, Ch. Kaiser Verlag, 1971

> *Wissenschaftstheoretische Kritik der Theologie; die Theologie und die neuere wissenschaftstheoretische Diskussion. Materialien, Analysen, Entwürfe*
> Munich, Ch. Kaiser, 1973

> "Der Wissenschaft der Theologie"
> *Evangelische Theologie* 35, (1975):283–309

Schapnitz, Eberhard
Ingenieur und Theologe. Grundlagen für einen Dialog übder die geistige Existenz in der technischen Welt
Würzburg, Werkbund-Verlag, 1968

Scheffczyk, Leo
Die Welt als Schöpfung Gottes
Aschaffenburg, Pattloch, 1968

Schiffers, Norbert
Fragen der Physik an die Theologie: die Säkularisierung der Wissenschaft und das Heilsverlangen nach Freiheit
Düsseldorf, Patmos-Verlag, 1968

Schilt, Heinz
"Die Frage nach Gott vom Standpunkt eines Naturwissenschaftlers"
Reformatio 16, (December 1967):738–40

Schmitt, Alois
Bibel und Naturwissenschaft
Münster in Westf., Aschendorff, 1912

Schnellmann, Guido
Theologie und Technik: 40 Jahre Diskussion um die Technik, zugleich ein Beitrag zu einer Theologie der Technik
Cologne, Hanstein, 1974

Schnitker, Werner
"Theologie und Naturwissenschaft in ihrer beziehung zum Lebensgefühl der Zeit"
Neue Zeitschrift für Systematische Theologie und Religionsphilosophie 7 no 1, (1965):15–48

   Wissenschaft und Lebensgefühl: Grundlagen der klassischen Elektrodynamik und der Leben-Jesu Forschung in ihrer Entwicklung
   Weiden, Hans Reykers, 1968

Scholz, Heinrich
Mathesis Universalis. Abhandlungen zur Philosophie als strenger Wissenschaft
Basel/Stuttgart, Benno Schwabe, 1961

   "Der Gottesgedanke in der Mathematik"
   Blatter für Deutsche Philosophie 8, (1934–5)

   "Was ist under einer theologischen Aussage zu Verstehen?"
   Theologische Aufsätze, Karl Barth Zum 50 Geburtstag, pp. 25–37, Munich, 1936

   "Ein theologisches Paradozon nach Arnauld von Ch. Hartshorne, mitgeteilt von Heinrich Scholz"
   Philosophisches Jahrbuch der Görres-Gesellschaft 59, 1949, 249–251

   "Warum ich mich zu Karl Barth bekenne. Ein Beitrag zu einer Studie über Treue gegen Linientreue"
   Antwort, Festschrift zum 70 Geburtstag von Karl Barth, pp. 865–896, Zurich, 1956

Schoneveld, A. J.
Van waterstof tot wederkomst: ein intuitiefempiristische benadering van de Godsvraag
The Hague, Boekencentrum, 1976

Schrey, Heinz-Horst
Weltbild und Glaube im 20. Jahrhundert
Göttingen, 1955

Schüepp, Otto
Gott sprach—es ward. Natur und Schöpfung als Werden und Werk
Bern, Munich, Francke, 1970

Schulz, Paul
Ist Gott eine mathematische Formel? Ein Pastor in Glaubensprozess seiner Kirche
Reinbeck/Hamburg, 1977

> *Science et Théologie: Méthode et Langage*
> Paris, Desclée de Brouwer, 1970

> *Science, Philosophie, Foi. Colloque de l'Académie internationale de Philosophie des Sciences*
> Paris, Beauchesne, 1974

Seeberger, Kurt
Ich sehe keinen Gott: ein Dialog zwischen Naturwissenschaft und Theologie
Munich, Sudwest Verlag, 1971

Sendy, Jean
Ces dieux qui firent le Ciel et la Terre, le Roman de la Bible
Paris, R. Laffont, 1969

Sesti, Luigi
La Divinità e il Mondo
Rome, L: Lucarini, 1977

Siegmund, Georg
Naturordnung als Quelle der Gotteserkenntnis: Neubegründung des teleologischen Gottesbeweises
Freiburg, Verlag Herder, 1950

Spülbeck, Otto
Zur Begegnung von Naturwissenschaft und Theologie
Einsiedeln, Benziger Verlag, 1969

> *Grenzfragen zwischen Naturwissenschaft und Glaube*
> Munich, Verlag Ars Sacra, 1970

Staudinger, Hugo
Die Glaubwürdigkeit Gottes in unserer modernen Welt

in *IBW-Journal* No. 12, (December 1978), reprint
Paderborn, Deutsche Institut für Bildung und Wissen e.V., 1978

Staudinger, Hugo and Behler, Wolfgang
Chance and Risiko der Gegenwart
Paderborn, Ferdinand Schöningh, 1976

Süssman, Georg (ed.)
Glaube und Naturwissenschaft
Göttingen, Quellenstücke, 1973

Syro Giraldo, Samuel
Religion, Ciencia y Paz (Ensayos)
Medellin, Universidad Pontificia Bolivariana, 1971

Thielicke, Helmut
Weltanschauung und Glaube
Stuttgart, Deutsche Verlags-Anstalt, 1946

Thill, Georges
La fête scientifique. D'une Praxéologie scientifique à une Analyse de la Décision chrétienne
Paris, Aubier-Montaigne, 1973

Timm, H.
Glaube und Naturwissenschaft in der Theologie Karl Heims
Witten, Eckhardt- und Luther-Verlag, 1968

Timm, H. (ed.)
Gott und die Technik
Hamburg/Zurich, 1971

Titius, Arthur
Natur und Gott
Göttingen, Vandenhoecke und Ruprecht, 1926

Torelli, Matteo
Il Riscatto degli Uomini
Nuova Cliternia, Arca 7, 1970

Torrance, T. F.
Determinismus und freie Schöpfung aus der Sicht der Theologie
IBW-Journal. Sonderlage, December 1979
Paderborn, Deutsches Institut für Bildung und Wissen

Torres Torres, Salvador
Nuevos Conceptos Sobre Animal, Hombre y Cosmos
México, B. Costa-Amic, 1970

Track, Joachim
"Naturwissenschaften und Theologie: Erwägungen zu einem Interdisziplinären Dialog"
Kerygma und Dogma 21, (April–June 1975):99–119

Tresmontant, Claude
Comment se pose aujourd'hui le Problème de l'Existence de Dieu
Paris, Éditions du Seuil, 1966

Trutwin, Werner (ed.)
Religion, Wissenschaft, Weltbild
Düsseldorf, Patmos-Verlag, 1970

Ullmann, Manfred
Die Natur- und Geheimwissenschaften im Islam
Leiden, E. J. Brill, 1972

Van Steenberghen, Fernand
"Sciences Positives et Existence de Dieu"
Revue Philosophique de Louvain 57, (August 1959):397–414

Viganò, Mario
Il mancato Dialogo tra Galileo e i Teologi
Rome, La civiltà cattolica, 1969

Villacèque, Fernand
Grandeur, Erreurs et Lacunes de la Pensée chrétienne
Paris, Union rationaliste, 1971

von Walert, Gerd
Der Mensch biologisch und biblisch
Stuttgart, 1968

von Weizsächer, C. F.
"Das Problem der Zeit als philosophisches Problem,"
in *Erkenntnis und Glaube,* Schriften der Evangelischen Forschungsaka-
demie Ilsenburg, Band 28
Berlin, Wichern-Verlag, n.d.

> "Der zweite Hauptsatz und der Unterschied von Vergangenheit
> und Zukunft"
> in *Die Einheit der Natur,*
> Munich, 1971
>
> 'Die Unendlichkeit der Welt'
> *Zum Weltbild der Physik*
> Stuttgart, 1958
>
> 'Säkularisierung und Naturwissenschaft'
> *Zum Weltbild der Physik*
> Stuttgart, 1958

von Weizsácker, C. F. (ed.)
Offene Systeme I
Stuttgart, Ernst Klett-Verlag, 1974

von Weizsäker, Viktor
Am Anfang Schuf Gott, Himmel und Erde. Grundfragen der Naturphilosophie
Göttingen, Vandenhoeck und Ruprecht, 1956

Walschap, Gerard
Muziek voor twee stemmen: of. Wereld en geloof: een ontwerp van stilz-
wijgende overeenkomst tussen wetenschap en religie
Antwerp, S. M. Ontwikkeling, 1963

Weber, Hans-Ruedi (ed.)
Experimente am Menschen
Studies of the World Council of Churches no. 5, Geneva, 1969

Weidlich, Wolfgang
"Fragen der Naturwissenschaft an den christlichen Glauben"
Zeitschrift für Theologie und Kirche 64, no. 2, (1967):241–57

"Zum Begriff Gottes im Felde zwischen Theologie, Philosophie
und Naturwissenschaft"
Zeitschrift für Theologie und Kirche 68, no. 3, (1971):381–94

Weischedel, W.
Der Gott der Philosophen
Darmstadt, 1971

Wildiers, Norbert Max
Weltbild und Theologie vom Mittelalter bis heute
Zurich, Benziger Verlag, 1974

Wereldbeeld en teologie. Van de middeleeuwen tot vandaag
Antwerp, Standard Wetenschappelijke Uitg., 1974

Wissenschaft und Glaube; Voträge von Emil Brunner, Andreas Spei-
ser, Marc de Munnynck, Otto Veraguth, Deitrich Schindler und
Fritz Medicus.
Erlenbach-Zürich, Eugen Rentsch, 1944